Palestinian Refugee Women from Syria to Jordan

Palestinian Refugee Women from Syria to Jordan

Decolonizing the Geopolitics of Displacement

Afaf Jabiri

I.B. TAURIS

LONDON • NEW YORK • OXFORD • NEW DELHI • SYDNEY

I.B. TAURIS

Bloomsbury Publishing Plc, 50 Bedford Square, London, WC1B 3DP, UK
Bloomsbury Publishing Inc, 1385 Broadway, New York, NY 10018, USA
Bloomsbury Publishing Ireland, 29 Earlsfort Terrace, Dublin 2, D02 AY28, Ireland

BLOOMSBURY, I.B. TAURIS and the I.B. Tauris logo
are trademarks of Bloomsbury Publishing Plc

First published in Great Britain 2024
This paperback edition published in 2025

Series design by Adriana Brioso
Cover image © Louai Beshara/AFP/Getty Images

A catalogue record for this book is available from the British Library.

Library of Congress Cataloging-in-Publication Data
Names: Jabiri, Afaf, author.
Title: Palestinian refugee women from Syria to Jordan : hidden violence / Afaf Jabiri.
Description: New York, NY : I.B. Tauris, an imprint of Bloomsbury
Publishing, [2024] | Includes bibliographical references and index.
Identifiers: LCCN 2023020469 (print) | LCCN 2023020470 (ebook) |
ISBN 9780755644803 (hardback) | ISBN 9780755644841 (paperback) |
ISBN 9780755644810 (pdf) | ISBN 9780755644827 (epub) | ISBN 9780755644834
Subjects: LCSH: Women refugees–Jordan–Social conditions. | Women refugees–Syria–
Social conditions. | Women, Palestinian Arab–Violence against–Jordan. | Women's rights.
Classification: LCC HV640.5.S97 J33 2024 (print) | LCC HV640.5.S97 (ebook) |
DDC 338/.04086914095695–dc23/eng/20230814
LC record available at https://lccn.loc.gov/2023020469
LC ebook record available at https://lccn.loc.gov/2023020470

ISBN: HB: 978-0-7556-4480-3
PB: 978-0-7556-4484-1
ePDF: 978-0-7556-4481-0
eBook: 978-0-7556-4482-7

Typeset by Integra Software Services Pvt. Ltd.

For product safety related questions contact productsafety@bloomsbury.com.

To find out more about our authors and books visit www.bloomsbury.com
and sign up for our newsletters.

To my mother
Rashida Hassan Fdilat
1936 Iraq Al-Mansheya/Palestine–2021 Baqa'a
Camp Jordan

Contents

Acknowledgements

Alas, I cannot overtly acknowledge those whose contribution was most valuable to this book: Palestinian refugee women from Syria whom I met, discussed, and spent endless hours listening to their journeys and stories of displacement. Their names, sadly, must be anonymized as many continue to live 'illegally' in Jordan. To these women, I am greatly indebted for your insight, trust, and generosity in sharing your thoughts and journeys with me. This book is a testament to you and the Palestinian struggle for liberation.

Frontline workers in UNRWA refugee camps in Syria, Lebanon and Jordan – doctors, nurses and social workers, especially those I met during UNRWA workshops in 2014 – initiated the idea for this book and influenced its theoretical grounding. When telling me of their humanitarian experiences with Palestinian refugees from Syria, they offered their own analysis and judgement of the situation, not only stories. 'Because they are Palestinian' was a common response to the question 'Why are Palestinian refugees from Syria not welcome in Jordan, Lebanon, or elsewhere?' This statement, 'because they are Palestinian', was also a reminder of what refugees in Palestinian camps usually attribute to their conditions, with Nakba-1948 being a defining element of their lives.

'You cannot cover the sun with a sieve' was how my grandmother ended almost any talk of Palestine. In so many ways, remembering my grandmother's voice whilst hearing 'because they are Palestinian' repeated by frontline workers made me think of the sieve in various literature on Palestine, which tends to obscure what for Palestinian refugees is a straightforward case of justice; indeed, believing in the just nature of their case is what informs Palestinian refugees' endurance of the everyday cruelty of life in the camps. My discussions with frontline workers inevitably centred my analysis around the question of categories and centrality of Palestinianism, and the need for conjunctural analysis through the articulation of intersecting forces – borrowed from Stuart Hall – first emerged from these discussions. Thus, to those frontline workers, wherever they are today, I am forever grateful.

I am indebted to many Jordanian and Palestinian activists in Palestinian camps and their surrounding areas who helped me to reach and arrange meetings with Palestinian refugee women. My first gratitude is to Jamal Al-Milahi, who both arranged several trips to the Cyber City Detention Centre in northern Jordan in 2015 and introduced me to small charities working in Palestinian camps in the same area. I am also very grateful to the Jordanian Women's Union (JWU) and its staff, particularly Rasha Alkhazallah, Kifah Jaberi, Asmahan Sarhan, Ikram Salameh, and Myasser Ismail, who introduced me and arranged several meetings with women. My great appreciation goes to JWU's General Director, Nadia Shamrokh, for facilitating the support of JWU centres in the Palestinian camps. I am also thankful to many other humanitarian and charity workers who preferred to remain anonymous but whose support was invaluable in either helping me arrange discussions with women or sharing their experiences of supporting Palestinian refugees from Syria in Jordan with me.

I am grateful to friends and colleagues in London and the UK who read draft chapters of this book and offered thoughts. I would especially like to thank Maja Korac, Azrini Wahidin and Ruba Salih. And I so greatly appreciate the time, energy and incredible insights of my friend Victoria Brittain, who read the final draft. To the peer-reviewers of both the book proposal and final manuscript, your comments and suggestions were extremely useful.

I wish to also thank the editors at Bloomsbury/I B Tauris, Sofie Rudland, Yasmin Garcha and Nayiri Kendir, for their outstanding engagement and support. Shaina Greiff's work, professionalism, patience and dedication are also immensely appreciated.

To my husband Jihad and sons Sham, Ward and Aram, your love and unwavering support are my pillars.

Introduction: Anti-Palestinianism: Epistemic violence of settler colonialism

'Nowadays, nothing's worse than the conditions of Palestinian refugees from Syria', Mansour, a Palestinian humanitarian aid worker told me. I had met Mansour and other Palestinian aid workers in a workshop I facilitated for the United Nations Relief and Works Agency for Palestine Refugees (UNRWA) in Jordan in November 2014, which was organized to discuss UNRWA's response to sexual and gender-based violence in emergency settings. There were seven aid workers from Syria in attendance, alongside four from Lebanon and seven from Jordan. During workshop breaks and in the evenings, I had informal conversations with the participants, trying to understand the context of their work. While the aid workers from Syria and Lebanon were well aware of the situation of both Palestinian refugees from Syria in Lebanon and those internally displaced in Syria, the aid workers from Jordan had very little knowledge of Palestinian refugees from Syria's situation in Jordan. 'We are only working with those who entered Jordan legally before 2013', Hadeel, an aid worker from Jordan explained, 'but there are many who are not yet registered with UNRWA. If they are not registered, then we do not know about their situation and if they are illegal, they will be afraid to register with UNRWA'. Prior to 2013, Palestinian refugees from Syria were dealt with on a case-by-case basis in Jordan; since 2013, however, Jordan has implemented a strict no-entry policy for Palestinians. Hadeel explained further: 'those who entered Jordan after 2013 are either returned to Syria or detained in the Cyber City Camp'.

Hadeel's comments prompted a discussion among the aid workers about where Palestinian refugees from Syria faced the worst situation: in Lebanon, Jordan or displaced in Syria? The aid workers from Syria shared stories of friends and relatives denied entry to Jordan, and Rima – a former co-worker of the aid workers from Syria, who had been smuggled into Jordan and was living 'illegally' in the country – also visited the group one evening and joined our conversation. Rima, a Palestinian woman married to a Syrian man, told her story of being smuggled into Jordan (analysed in detail in Chapter 3) and shared the stories of other women she met on the journey from Damascus to Amman. In one especially painful story, Rima spoke of a young mother who was bitten by a snake while sleeping in the desert near the Jordanian border, with her two small children nearby:

> She started screaming and asking us for help. Luckily, there was a man who knew what to do, I do not know if he was a doctor or nurse, but he managed to save her. Whilst we were trying to help her, she was begging us to take care of her kids and gave us the address of her relatives in Jordan. I will never forget the fear in her eyes and her kids' eyes, it will haunt me forever.

After Rima finished, everybody fell silent for a while, until Ahmed, a doctor at UNRWA's medical practice in Yarmouk Camp, broke the silence: 'there are even crueller stories. As Mansour said, now, there is nothing worse than being a Palestinian from Syria'. 'But why?', Dima, a nurse from Syria, implored. While this was perhaps a simple question, how can one make sense of why Palestinian refugees from Syria have to go through such horrific journeys in order to escape death? Why are they not allowed, like Syrian refugees, to enter Jordan? These were some of the questions asked by the group, but they only found Mansour's answer somewhat satisfactory: 'because they are Palestinian'. Everybody, including myself, nodded in agreement.

Mansour's answer to Dima's question, 'because they are Palestinian', is one of those self-evident answers Palestinians commonly use to explain many aspects of their lives and what they go through, and often refers to the 1948 Nakba. 'Appeals to the past', as Said posits, 'are among the commonest of strategies in interpretation of the present. What animates such appeals is not only disagreement about what happened in the past and what the past was, but uncertainty about whether the past really is past, over and concluded, or whether it continues, albeit in different forms, perhaps' (Said, 1993, p. 7).

This book engages with both the 'but why' question and Mansour's answer 'because they are Palestinian' by investigating the ways in which the epistemic violence of settler colonialism has created an anti-Palestinianism that continues to shape Palestinian refugee women's experiences of new displacements. The book argues for the centrality of anti-Palestinianism in the examination of the experience of Palestinian refugee women displaced from Syria to Jordan. Anti-Palestinianism and the oppression Palestinians endure, as this book suggests, are related first and foremost to them being Palestinians before being women or refugees. In line with Stuart Hall's model of conjunctural analysis, the book aims to centre the dominant episteme of the powerful force of settler colonialism as a fixed element in relation to women's lived experience of displacement whilst other categories of differentiation of gender, ethnicity, refugee-ness and nationality are more floating.

Anti-Palestinianism is defined as key to settler colonial techniques of epistemic violence, as it aims to normalize Palestinian displacement, deny their right to return home and effect a continuous, invisible Nakba through silencing their voices. In the context of this research, settler colonial techniques of anti-Palestinianism are exemplified by the Jordanian State's no-entry and detention policies, international humanitarian organizations' denial of asylum and humanitarian assistance to Palestinian refugees from Syria, and Palestinian refugee women from Syria's marginalization in literature addressing gender and the displacement of Syrian refugees.

Anti-Palestinianism, as a dominant episteme of settler colonialism, is central to the understanding of the violence and discrimination that Palestinian refugee women from Syria have been experienced, which is profoundly related to them being Palestinians before being women or refugees. This book proposes that the epistemic violence of settler colonialism in Palestine extends both beyond Palestine's territorial boundaries and beyond the practices of the settler colonial project in Palestine. As such, it looks at the intersection of the forces of settler colonialism, nationalism, and global asylum and refugee governance with gender regimes and identity formation, connecting these forces to examine processes of differentiation between refugees through the invention of new categories. This is one method of what Hall proposes for conjunctural analysis through which an examination of how forces operate in relation to one another, particularly how national forces speak to or can be linked to international forces and how present relations can be explained vis-à-vis colonial history and the continuity of power. As Quijano described, categorization is 'the deepest and most enduring expression of colonial domination' (Quijano, 2000, p. 1). Therefore, by understanding the particularity of Palestinian refugees' experience of displacement within the wider context of Syrian displacement, the aim is to interrupt, deconstruct and destabilize Western knowledge of displacement experiences as linear, direct consequences of one system or another.

Thus, the central aim of this book is to expose the history and geopolitics of oppressive systems that work through and upon gendered bodies of Palestinian refugee women in humanitarian settings. There is still a need to challenge the theorization of displacement experiences dominated by hegemonic discourses and power relations, as well as counter the universality of the displacement experience within the Syrian refugee crisis. Feminist geopolitical analyses that attempt to go beyond Western, colonialist and orientalist ideas of nationalism and state discourses of refugee inclusion and exclusion are challenged here, as – discussed throughout the book – such literature still fails to apply its own analytical base to the situation of Palestinian refugees from Syria. Through narrating the experiences of Palestinian women from Syria, I argue for a feminist analysis of the epistemic violence of settler colonialism that created the conditions and atmosphere for anti-Palestinianism – where Palestinianism has become an excluded category – and the impact this has on the lives of Palestinian refugee women, particularly the effects-severity of categorizing them as 'illegal' refugees, 'UNRWA's refugees', a 'complex problem'.

Making such connections will also allow understanding of how othering works within new colonial technologies of power. Correspondingly, the methodological foundation of this undertaking begins with exploring ideas in relation to the category of Palestinianism; relationships between the past and present suggested here as the functions that inform Palestinian refugees from Syria's displacement experience in Jordan. Before gendering the lived experience of Palestinian refugee women from Syria in Jordan, however, Chapters 1 and 2 first look at connections, continuities and discontinuities between past and contemporary oppressive systems in relation to Palestinian refugees' first and second displacements and ask: Is there a direct connection between past and present oppressive systems? What are the formal/informal relationships that created the arrangements for this displacement experience? Through these questions, I show the historical continuities of settler colonialism, discontinuities that have developed, and the emergence of new regimes of power that work in alliance with Zionism to maintain settler colonialism in Palestine and its material effects on Palestinian refugees from Syria.

Palestinian refugees from Syria and Syrian refugee 'crisis'

Since the onset of the crisis in Syria, Palestinians, unlike their Syrian refugee counterparts, have not enjoyed access to Jordan. As Hadeel noted above, Palestinians entering Jordan were dealt with on an individual basis until 2013, after which Jordan implemented a strict no-entry policy for Palestinians (White, 2013, p. 70). Furthermore, in the unlikely case that entry is granted, Palestinians are then imprisoned in the Cyber City Camp for refugees in North Jordan, where they experience restricted freedom, are denied access to services and can only see visitors with official permits. Before the crisis began in 2012, there were 526,744 registered Palestinian refugees displaced across nine camps in Syria. Yarmouk, the largest such camp, hosted over 160,000 registered refugees, most of whom were forced to flee to the Syrian Arab Republic in 1948. While Palestinians, particularly who were displaced as a result of Nakba 1948, in Syria have enjoyed the same civil rights as Syrians, they were not given Syrian citizenship; a decision justified as preserving their Palestinian identity (Al-Hardan, 2012, 2016).

According to UNRWA (2021), there are around 18,000 Palestinian refugees from Syria in Jordan. The question here is why Jordan would reject this small number when it already hosts a large population of Palestinian refugees; indeed, Palestinian refugees constitute about 60 per cent of the population. Further, Jordan has accepted nearly 700,000 Syrian refugees, so why is this small number of Palestinians their target? This is not to say that Jordan has implemented an adequate policy with regard to Syrian refugees, as there are many discriminatory and well-documented practices at play (Cohen, 2013; Achilli, 2015; Lenner and Turner, 2018; Beaujouan and Rasheed, 2019; El Arab and Sagbakken, 2019), but again only a limited number of studies examine the case of Palestinian refugees within the context of the conflict in Syria. Largely, studies that consider Palestinian refugees do so through the lens of the availability of health and education services, the burden on services provided for refugees (particularly in the context of Lebanon) and the relationship with the host community (Charles, 2013; Strong et al., 2015; Alameddine et al., 2019). Fewer studies have looked at the particularity of Palestinian refugees, their different treatment and particular situation, arguing that Palestinian refugees' ability to return to their homes in Syria is uncertain, thus rendering them more vulnerable than Syrian refugees, who may eventually return (Morrison, 2014).

In her examination of Syrian and Palestinian refugees' differing fates in Lebanon and Jordan, and Palestinians' inability to escape death in Syria, Rosemary Sayigh (2013) posits that this is the price Palestinians pay for their stateless status. In the same vein, Abu Moghli, Bitarie, and Gabiam (2015), in an article entitled 'Palestinian Refugees From Syria: Stranded on the Margins of Law', examine the discriminatory legal framework applied to Palestinian refugees from Syria in Arab countries, arguing that such treatment is tied to the 'Israeli government's denial of the right of return of Palestinian refugees' (Moghli, Bitarie and Gabiam, 2015). Noura Erakat (2014) similarly attributes 'the inferior treatment of Palestinian refugees' to Palestinians' protracted refugee status, examining the gaps in protection Palestinian refugees suffer in their forced, ongoing displacement in neighbouring countries. In particular, she highlights the inadequacy of UNRWA and UNHCR policies for Palestinian refugees from Syria (Erakat, 2014).

At the time of writing this book, there had already been an enormous amount of academic literature produced on the Syrian refugee crisis, including feminist engagement with questions of gender issues, humanitarianism and forced migration (Freedman, 2016; Yasmine and Moughalian, 2016; DeJong *et al.*, 2017; Lokot, 2018). However, in the current 'crisis of Syrian refugees', feminist analysis of the geopolitics and power relations shaping gender and the displacement of Syrian refugees in neighbouring countries remains largely silent on gender processes in relation to Palestinian refugees' displacement from Syria, particularly within the context of Jordan. For example, in the volume *A Gendered Approach to the Syrian Refugee Crisis*, there is not even one significant reference made to Palestinian women's displacement from Syria, let alone a chapter or section dedicated to the issue (Freedman, Kivilcim, Baklacıoğlu, 2019).

Jennifer Hyndman's study (2019) is an influential analysis of feminist geopolitics; in it, she posits that the significance of feminist geopolitics is that it offers feminists an opportunity to learn from and build upon subaltern geopolitics. Hyndman argues that, in such a project, colonial and imperial histories alongside the state and society's geographical locations should be heeded (Hyndman, 2019). However, she summarizes the Palestinian case as follows: Palestinian refugees fall under a different UN agency, pushing the proportion of people living in conditions of protracted displacement to over three-quarters of the global number. The international refugee regime has not protected most refugees with these 'solutions' (Hyndman, 2019, p. 5). Furthermore, in another example, Hyndman and Giles address Palestinian displacement in *Refugees in Extended Exile* (2017) as follows:

> Palestinians residing in various countries of the Middle East remain the most protracted group of all facing displacement, having endured generations of exile. UNHCR acknowledges that while the Palestinian refugee situation is the most prolonged in the world, their plight remains outside its mandate and hence beyond its statistics. While Palestinian refugees should not be treated as a unique situation, they often tend to be considered separately because administratively they fall under the auspices of a different UN agency, the United Nations Relief and Works Agency (UNRWA) .... Many have integrated into Jordanian and Syrian society, only to be displaced again in the more recent Syrian conflict. Palestinian refugees in Lebanon are more likely to live in camp settings (Ramadan, 2013), whereas Syrians living there do not. Like most other refugees, Palestinians face an unresolved political situation where they cannot return home and often lack permanent legal status in the countries in which they reside.
>
> (Hyndman and Giles, 2017, p. 13)

In both texts, the analysis only refers to the protracted nature of Palestinian displacement, is descriptive rather than analytical, and hence highlights only the symptoms of, not the history and politics that shape, Palestinians' extended exile. In her description of UNHCR above, Hyndman does not engage with the question she herself posed in her own geopolitical study of UNHCR in the 1990s: 'At what point do charitable acts of humanitarian assistance become neo-colonial technologies of control?' (Hyndman, 2000, p. 147). Still, however, Hyndman does not address the politics through which Palestinians are excluded from international protection and also makes a further naturalizing statement: 'like most other refugees Palestinians face unresolved political situation' (2019, p. 5). Whilst Hyndman (2019) criticizes the universality of Western feminist work and advocates paying attention to the particularities of political, economic, cultural and environmental factors that differently shape people's conditions, she fails to do this herself in the case of Palestinians. While her work calls for learning from and building upon subaltern knowledge and does (at least) acknowledge the Palestinian case, it still overlooks the particularities of Palestinian displacement.

Feminist scholarship's lack of attention to or naturalization of Palestinian displacement parallels the absence of Palestinian refugee women from Syria in feminist organization and United Nations agency reports, data, and statistics on gender and gender-based violence (See UN Women GBV(gender-based violence) reports 2018, 2017, 2016; UNFPA reports; Women's Refugee Commission, 2014). A review of humanitarian responses, gender empowerment programmes and GBV reports on Syrian refugee camps and host communities in Jordan – examined in depth in Chapter 3 – reveals that no international organization or UN study has recognized the different treatment Palestinian and Syrian refugee women receive and the impact on the lives of Palestinian refugee women from Syria in Jordan. Nonetheless, the existence of such a group has been acknowledged by research 'informants', e.g. the Women's Refugee Commission Report (2014) states: 'Another vulnerable population mentioned by key informants is the Syrian Palestinian refugee population that once again find themselves as refugees, this time in Jordan' (Zaatari *et al.*, 2014, p. 13).

J. M. N. Jeffries, the *Daily Mail* correspondent in Palestine from 1917 to 1938, denoted the unnatural creation of a Zionist regime in Palestine as the cause of the entire question, which should not be complex to understand. Jeffries explained the representation of Palestinian issues as 'complex' in the following statement:

> The history of Palestine … ought not to be intricate, because it is only the so-called 'Palestine Question' which makes it intricate, and the Palestine Question ought not to be in existence. There was no Palestine Question, nor

ever would have been one, if certain statesmen had not created it. Since it was thus unnaturally created, however, it tends at times to intricacy.

(Jeffries, 2017, p. XXXIII)

A wide variety of literature continues to portray Palestinian refugees as a 'complex' case; a representation that refutes the simple fact that, like any other refugee population, Palestinians should have the right to return to the homes, villages and other places they were forced to leave. Historical studies have also largely engaged with whether refugees left of their own accord, out of fear, or by force. However, such questions only address technicalities, but they do not tackle the primary issue: if someone leaves their home, by whichever way, does that give another the right to occupy and deny their return to those homes? Representing the issue as complex, hence, is a representation of one's political understanding of the problem's origin – i.e. the 1948 dispossession of Palestinians of their lands and erasure of their history in order to establish a settler colonial project in Palestine. Thus, defining 'refugees' as the problem means the solutions sought do not necessarily address the origin of the problem, only its consequences, and lack a coherent relationship between origin and consequence. Those who have been displaced, forced to leave their homes, and dispossessed of their belongings become a 'burden'.

Action-oriented fieldwork

Between 2015 and 2019, I met with around thirty families of Palestinian refugees from Syria living in Jordan. It was not easy to find Palestinians from Syria, as they hid in the camps, afraid of arrest and deportation. In fact, some of those I spoke with had already been deported once, but managed to find their way back. The 'illegal' situation of many Palestinian refugees from Syria in the Palestinian camps made it very difficult for some to agree to be involved in the discussions and conversations. Thus, I have not included conversations with women who were unsure of whether they wanted me to share their experiences or those who insisted on identifying as Syrian not Palestinian.

I had these conversations not only with women, but also with husbands, brothers, sons, daughters and sometimes granddaughters/sons, who either took part in the conversation or sat for a while at the beginning or end. I also followed-up via Skype, Messenger and WhatsApp with some who were deported and two women who managed to resettle in Europe between 2019 and 2021. My conversations with women and their families took an unconventional form, one of open discussion rather than semi/structured around a number of questions. Six themes emerged from my first discussions: the first experience of displacement from Palestine, whether in 1948 or 1967; the displacement journey from Syria to Jordan; life in Palestinian camps and the relationship with the refugee host community; the restrictions and limitations on movement that Palestinian refugees from Syria experience in Jordan; their future aspirations of return to Syria and Palestine; and the conditions under which they live as legal or illegal refugees. As my relationship with these women grew, they also gradually expressed the issues related to their gendered experiences.

In 2017, I took the opportunity to travel to Jordan as Jordanian women's NGOs were preparing a shadow report for the 66th Session of the Convention on the Elimination of All Forms of Discrimination Against Women (CEDAW), in order to highlight and address the particularity of Palestinian refugee women from Syria. In engaging women in conversations during the writing period, many details were shared that may not have if they had not been actively engaged in the writing process. Action-orientated conversations, as a research method, not only uncover stories but also make research participants comfortable sharing their stories, especially if it takes the form of a dialogue. Our shared interest in these conversations made it possible for women to share the experiences I present in this book in greater detail. I further address the shadow reporting process in Chapter 2, particularly regarding Jordanian women's NGOs' willingness to risk their relationship with the government to address the plight of Palestinian refugee women; a position that also challenged donors and humanitarian organisations' politics and selectivity of aid.

In the gatherings and discussions that occurred during the shadow report-writing period, organized with the help of a number of small charities from various Palestinian camps in Jordan, many women were not only receptive, but engaged deeply in the process of finding more Palestinian women to share their stories, suggesting areas to address and participating in discussions with other women. As most of the women I spoke with remain in Jordan, I have changed their names, current place of residence and any other information that might reveal their identity. Still, by sharing their stories, they risked identification by the authorities, but they actively engaged because they understood the importance of taking their case to the United Nations.

During our conversations, the women were not concerned with my identity. Being a Palestinian refugee, myself, might have helped but it was not the main reason. Certainly, it was because I had been introduced by people and organizations with whom they work closely and were also participating in the writing of the shadow report. Even the police officers and guards at the Cyber City Camp (a detention centre for Palestinians refugees displaced from Syria) allowed me to enter when they understood my purpose was to find a solution, despite the prohibition on organizations and people entering the centre. Although the shadow report complicated NGO relations with the government (since the CEDAW session, the government restricted funding to organizations who participated in the report), the two concluding comments from the CEDAW committee on the particularity of Palestinian refugee women displaced from Syria and held in the Cyber City Camp resulted in the government's closure of the detention centre and moving Palestinian refugees to refugee camps with their Syrian counterparts. One woman told me that, after moving to the King Abdullah Gardens' Camp, some of their living conditions had improved – particularly, in the new camp they could live as a private family, separate from other refugees – but restrictions on mobility and movement continued to be the norm governing their daily lives.

Throughout the research period, I also conducted informal interviews with UNRWA aid workers in Syria, a number working in the Palestinian refugee camps in Jordan, and other UN agency and international organization representatives. During workshops and conferences related to refugee women in Jordan, I asked questions about Palestinian refugee women from Syria, but it was very rare for there to be any organizations – despite the fact that most of these organizations were working on refugee issues – with information about the status and conditions of Palestinian refugee women from Syria. Nonetheless, there were differences between staff working with refugees on the ground and those managing projects from headquarters and main offices in Amman. Those working closely with refugees on the ground could speak of the discriminatory practices against Palestinian refugees from Syria they had seen and experienced during project implementation, whilst those responsible for proposal writing, reporting and decision-making lacked knowledge of the particularity of Palestinian refugees from Syria. The disconnect between knowledge accumulated on the ground by frontline workers and that held by decision-makers and programme officers operating through ready-made, funded projects and models exported from other places regardless of context, extends beyond the inclusion of Palestinian refugees in the humanitarian response and context of Jordan. Research on humanitarian practice from several parts of the world showed the existence of such disconnection in various contexts (Hyndman, 2000; Malkki, 2005; Lautze and Raven Roberts, 2006; Gabiam, 2012; Mays, Racadio and Gugerty, 2012; Ticktin, 2014; Al Adem *et al.*, 2018; Besiou and Van Wassenhove, 2020; Farah, 2020; Sevastov, 2021).

Re-listening, the writing process and representation

In the late 1990s, I worked as a translator and research assistant, helping researchers who came to Jordan to study Palestinian refugees. During this time, I witnessed how researchers leave Palestinian homes with a sort of desperation, as they were mostly concerned with the living conditions and poverty in which Palestinians lived. At that time, I engaged in countless conversations with these researchers about the fact that the conditions were not only what people wanted them to take away from these interviews; rather, they were trying to impart different messages than what the researchers were gathering. Still, I found myself, in my first fieldwork experience, predominantly focused on Palestinian refugee women from Syria's hard living conditions in Jordan and, as such, developed the same sentiments I had tried to challenge all those years before. The feeling of despair as a result of their unjust and inhumane treatment made it impossible to hear clearly what the women were sharing with me. In one such conversation, a mother of four young children shared that she kept a daily journal of what each of her kids ate, explaining that this allowed her to rotate food between them. She had created a meals rota, basically, where she sometimes deprived one kid of a meal or some type of fruit or vegetable in order to feed the others. My listening stopped at that point; I could not continue to fully engage in the conversation. It was distressing to hear this story and similar accounts of the choices women were making to survive the lived reality of forced illegality and invisibility.

As previously mentioned, my fieldwork took place over five years and, during this time, I had to process women's journeys and narratives in various ways. Before starting the writing process for this book, I decided to connect with some women still living in Jordan, mostly through WhatsApp and Facebook Messenger. These short and scattered virtual conversations had a different impact on me than the first face-to-face conversations. At that stage, I had the transcripts of the first conversations, but decided to listen again to the recordings, one of which was of the mother with four young kids. Listening to her voice several times allowed me to re-hear what she was trying to tell me. 'Look how healthy they are', she said, referring to her children, 'they will grow up caring for each other … to survive and be the best they can, they need each other'. In her statements, the woman showed a sense of pride in the way she managed her kids' nutrition and prompted their feelings of responsibility for each other. Despite the difficult situation she was experiencing and the hard decisions she was making, she was not merely surviving but somehow managing and taking control over her life and children's; there was a sense of a pride I could feel in her voice.

Re-listening to women's voices, trying to carefully hear what they wanted to share and thus what I should be taking away from our conversations shifted my thinking from how I felt and what I thought was important to the women's well-thought-out imparts from their stories. Conspicuously, women do not just speak and share stories, they also measure, calculate and decide accordingly what they want to share. They have their own personal and political reasons for revealing or concealing parts of their stories. It is hence the responsibility of the researcher to hear, respect and respond to women's messages while listening and engaging in conversation with them.

In Chapter 5, I discuss masculinist manoeuvrings and the ways in which women contribute to the management of men's masculinity. Before re-listening to the recordings, I had the sense that women, particularly those with Jordanian and Syrian nationalities married to Palestinian refugee men from Syria, were trying to keep gender norms intact, but upon re-listening, it was clearer that it was the injustice against their husbands that made these women invent ways to empower them; it was a way of righting the wrongs committed against their husbands, not merely women's practices of re-enforcing masculine norms. The re-enforcing of gender norms intersected with both men's and women's legal and illegal residency as well as the politics that shaped their identity and refugee status. As a friend put it, after I shared with her stories of women trying to minimize the impact of their husbands' illegal status through masculinist manoeuvring acts and practices: 'this is an honourable position and act'. For feminists, re-enforcing gender norms cannot be seen as honourable, but considering also women's reasoning and the politics of their choices in understanding their masculinist manoeuvrings meant not only respecting women's choices but also recognizing them as active-speaking (Spivak, 2015) subjects and equal producers of knowledge, whilst at the same time acknowledging material effects of epistemic and structural violence they were exposed to.

Camps in Syria: Where have women who participated in the research been displaced from[1]

According to the UNRWA, there were 575,234 registered Palestinian refugees in Syria prior to 2011 (UNRWA, 2022b). UNRWA estimates that 438,000 have remained in Syria and over 120,000 have fled to Lebanon, Jordan and other countries. UNRWA statistics also show

> The majority of the 438,000 Palestine refugees remaining in Syria have been displaced at least once within Syria –with some having been displaced multiple times – and over 95 per cent of them remain in continuous need of humanitarian aid to meet their most basic needs. Up to 280,000 Palestine

---

[1] Check the Palestine Return Centre (PRC) website for status updates on Palestinian refugee camps in Syria (SyriaReport2019.pdf (prc.org.uk)). Al-Shabaka also publishes regular reports on Palestinian refugees from Syria that are useful in offering background information as well as analyses of the current status of Palestinian refugees from Syria, both inside and outside Syria (Refugees Archives – Page 3 of 3 – Al-Shabaka). UNRWA's database and statistics can be accessed here: Where We Work | UNRWA.

refugees from Syria (PRS) are currently displaced inside Syria, with a further 120,000 displaced to neighbouring countries, including Lebanon, Jordan, Turkey, Egypt and increasingly, to Europe.

(UNRWA, 2022b)[2]

Around 90,000 Palestinian refugees whose villages and hometowns were destroyed by the Zionist Hagans fled to Syria in 1948, mostly from the northern Palestinian districts of Safad, Haifa, Yafa, Acre, Tiberias and Nazareth. Palestinian Refugees in Syria are distributed into twelve camps, nine officially recognized and three considered unofficial. Palestinian refugee camps in Syria are located across the country, in Aleppo, Damascus, Homs, Hama, Latakia and Deraa. There are also several Palestinian residential communities that are not classified as camps, around twenty, located primarily in Damascus, Dera'a and their surrounding countryside (PRC, 2018).

Except for two women displaced from Aleppo city, all the women who participated in this research were displaced from the following camps in Syria:

Yarmouk Camp: The majority of the women who participated in this research fled Yarmouk Camp between 2011 and 2015, and two fled after the thirty-three-day military operation launched by the Syrian regime in April 2018. Yarmouk was established in 1957 and is 8 kilometres from Damascus. Although an unofficial camp, Yarmouk was the largest Palestinian refugee community in Syria prior to 2011, with approximately 160,000 UNRWA-registered refugees (UNRWA, 2022a). According to the Palestine Return Centre (PCR), only 200 families have remained in Yarmouk Camp, as the majority of its residents were either internally displaced or fled to Jordan, Lebanon or other countries (PRC, 2018).

Al-Aideen Camp: Also known as Homs Camp, it was established in 1949 to accommodate Palestinian refugees forcibly displaced by the 1948 Nakba, primarily from the villages surrounding Haifa, Tiberias and Acre. Before the conflict in Syria, the camp was home to 20,000 UNRWA-registered Palestinian refugees; now, due to the conflict, the number of refugees currently living in

---

[2] UNRWA facts and figures can be accessed here: Syria@11 | UNRWA.

the camp is around 12,000 (UNRWA, 2022a). Only one research participant, Salam, was displaced from Al-Aideen, and her entry to Jordan was made possible via a forced marriage.

Khan Eshieh Camp: It – the third largest Palestinian refugee camp recognized by the Syrian government – was founded in 1948 near the village of Khan Eshieh, some 27 kilometres from southwestern Damascus. According to UNRWA estimates, 20,000 refugees were registered in the camp prior to 2011. In 1948, Khan Eshieh Camp unofficially provided shelter for Palestinians being forcibly displaced. Then, in 1949, the camp was officially established for refugees from the northern part of Palestine. Before the conflict in Syria, the camp was home to more than 20,000 Palestine refugees. In 2012, the farms and fields surrounding the camp became active battlegrounds where heavy weapons were deployed, often indiscriminately, more than halving the population to 9,000 (PCR, 2019).

Dera'a Camp: Located in southern Syria in Dera'a City, it was established in 1950–1 for refugees from the northern and eastern parts of Palestine following the 1948 Nakba. A second wave of Palestinian refugees forced to leave the Quneitra Governorate following the 1967 War were also accommodated in Dera'a Camp (UNRWA, 2022a). In addition to the 10,500 Palestinian refugees in the camp prior to the conflict, there were also over 17,500 more refugees living in the neighbouring Syrian villages; in al-Muzeireeb town alone, there were nearly 8,500 Palestinian refugees. Both Dera'a Camp and al-Muzeireeb were largely destroyed (PRC, 2016).[3]

Organization of the book

Chapter 1 addresses the Nakba not as an event, a Palestinian experience or perspective, but as a juncture-point in history. It adopts the Syrian-Arab nationalist intellectual Constantin Zurayk's meanings of *Nakba* – the originator of the term – to address the emergence of a new moral order. The chapter outlines the theoretical framework for this book by questioning categories, experience and geography, and engaging with how and what to decolonize in

---

[3]   PRS_ClosedDoors2016EN.pdf (prc.org.uk).

a context where settler colonialism continues to shape life, but in different, not necessarily direct and connected, ways.

Chapter 2 examines the variety of ways in which settler colonial forms of epistemic violence unfold, looking in particular at the multiple categorizations of Palestinians in Jordan in order to highlight Jordan's historical interest in concealing Palestinian identity. I follow in this chapter, through Palestinian refugee women's narratives, a timeline of historical events both before and after the 1948 Nakba that shaped Jordan's politics and led to the 2013 no-entry policy. By concealing their presence, forcing their disappearance and silencing their voices, the 2013 policy further marginalized Palestinian refugees from Syria. As a consequence, this policy is not only integral to Jordan's politics of survival and search for legitimacy, but is also a continuation of politics aimed at suppressing Palestinian identity.

In this chapter's examination of the changing categorization of Palestinian refugees in Jordan, it investigates the role categorization has played – in connection to the epistemic violence that has shaped the experience of being a Palestinian refugee since the 1948 Nakba – in Jordan's politics. Here, the chapter highlights the changing politics of Palestinian categorization, from wanted to unwanted, thus showing that such has shifted based on the state's national interests and the changing relations between colonial and national projects competing in the region. Examining Jordan's 2013 no-entry policy for Palestinian refugees from Syria would not be adequate without also addressing Jordan's politics and historical involvement in the question of Palestine and its role in the settler colonial project in Palestine. To understand each category and their gendered implications on women's lives, it is important, if not vital, to understand the political moments through which the creation of each Palestinian category emerged; categories deemed necessary on grounds such as expanding Jordan's territorial borders, preserving its national identity and interests, and protecting national security.

Chapter 3 highlights and examines international organizations' humanitarian and development response in Jordan over the last eight years. In particular, it focuses on the work of UN agencies and international development organizations concerned with gender and gender-based violence, showing how the response included gender empowerment and the elimination of gender-based discrimination and violence against refugee women programmes.

However, such programmes have exclusively targeted Syrian refugee women and disregarded other refugee women's groups similarly affected by the conflict in Syria. This chapter also looks at how local actors employ strategies to confront state and organizational politics of aid, gendered empowerment and development agendas. With government and international organization exclusion of Palestinian refugees from Syria from aid and development programmes, local women's groups and frontline workers, particularly those operating in the Palestinian camps in Jordan, have tried to fill the service and programme gaps. By doing so, these groups have challenged the selectivity of aid and the politics of the gendered development approach in humanitarian settings.

Chapter 4 discusses how Palestinian refugee women from Syria, second- and third-generation Palestinian refugees, express their Palestinian identity, ideas of home, belonging to a Palestinian camp, and relationship with Palestinian communities in the camps in Syria and Jordan. Here, the aim is to examine whether the new displacement experience – shaped by Jordan's barring of Palestinian refugees from Syria, lack of humanitarian support and the abandonment of the Palestinian authority, represented by the embassy in Amman – has influenced Palestinian refugees from Syria's ideas of home and belonging to a collective group. There are two sub-groups of Palestinian refugees from Syria addressed in this chapter: those who entered Jordan legally and live in Palestinian camps and those who entered illegally and hide within one of the Palestinian communities in Jordan's camps. This chapter argues that in/visibility is determined not only by the legality of one's residency, but also by gender arrangements and norms, thus creating differing effects on women's abilities to act, have self-diligence over their activities and make new beginnings, which in turn has created a multiplicity of relationships with the camps and Palestinian community in Jordan.

Palestinian women understand their illegal status and lack of humanitarian support as an integral part of the continuity of the Nakba, a form of anti-Palestinianism. Their personal experiences are connected to what they describe as 'the Palestinian condition', which engages with the question of the human condition. In this regard, Arendt proposes the term *vita activa* (active life), which she designates to the three human activities of labour, work and action. Thus, the in/ability to act and disclosures of the self in the act create multiple relationships with the camp and Palestinian community in Jordan. In this respect, the in/ability to act and in/visibility determined the extent and degree to which the new displacement impacted 'who women are'; and, as such, its impact on their agency over their own choices differed.

Chapter 5 analyses Palestinian and Syrian refugee women married to Palestinian refugee men's narratives of entering the country, experiences at entry points, border guard practices and the lived realities of 'illegal' refugee-ness, as strictly applied to Palestinian refugee men from Syria. Such analysis aids in understanding the conditions under which gender norms can be reconstructed, displayed and differently played off during displacement, and thus how gender relations and roles challenged within families during conflict and displacement can be re-managed and manipulated through acts of masculinist manoeuvring. Masculinist manoeuvrings are defined as both the management of masculinity, in cases of men's legal vulnerability, and the ways in which men and women try to restore normative gendered traits and roles when they are challenged in practice. In this, I look at how women understand the support they provide to their husbands' reclaiming of masculinity as an integral part of reclaiming their Palestinian identity; identity not in the narrow nationalist sense, but a sense of belonging closely connected to the quest for justice.

The violation of men's rights based on nationality determines women and children's rights and access to education, health, decent work and freedom of mobility. Hence, the political is very personal for these women and necessitates a response at the private level; their support for their husbands' reclaiming of masculinity is their way to right the state's wrongdoings. Here, I discuss how Palestinian refugee women from Syria respond to attempts to subordinate Palestinian refugee men by adopting a form of masculinist manoeuvring aimed at resisting the state's prejudiced practices and policies against such men. In my interviews, this response was not articulated in relation to gender roles, as these norms are disconnected from politics, but rather by closely linking the personal and political as informed by structures of power, systems of inequalities, and questions of justice and rights. Claims for political and gender identity are entangled with the right of recognition; in Fraser's words, these are 'claims for justice'.

In Chapter 6, I further develop the idea of connecting recognition to justice by exploring another group of women amongst Palestinian refugees from Syria: Jordanian Palestinian women married to Palestinian refugee men from Syria. In order to understand the particularity of Jordanian/ Palestinian refugee women's experiences in relation to discriminatory state practices and societal GBV, an understanding of how both the misrecognition of gender and politics and the maldistribution of power at the political, legal, and socio-economic levels formed the unity of their situation. Therefore, this chapter connects analysis of GBV to questions of misrecognition and injustice, two analytical frameworks often delinked in studies of gender issues of the displacement experience. This chapter proposes that redressing gender injustice begins with an analysis of the structures and status order that organize society based on gendered and political categorization; categorization that creates subgroups within one group, ultimately leading to misrecognitions that manifest as injustices against these groups. In the case of Jordanian Palestinian refugee women and their Palestinian daughters, their experience of displacement is embroiled between settler colonialism, militarism, nationalism and gender regimes that create multiple forms of misrecognition, which in turn translates into GBV practices and discriminatory policies and laws. The only way for GBV to end is for oppressive systems to end, through destabilizing the connections tying these systems together. Freedom from GBV is not possible without justice and recognition, as the absence of latter continues to legitimize the former.

Chapter 7 is the conclusion and way forward. It returns to feminist work and agendas to suggest that, while feminist geopolitical analyses and contributions continue to engage and produce alternative modes of knowledge by accounting for human conditions, such analyses still – as it relate to the broader context of colonial and imperial histories and political and economic factors – fail to assemble a shared proposal or solidarity action that accounts for the continuity of colonialism in the case of Palestine. This is particularly true with regard to Palestinians' second displacement: the displacement from another context of displacement, such as the Syrian refugee 'crisis'.

1

Nakba: A juncture-point in history – Gender and displacement

Decolonization is 'imaginable, or achievable, for Fanon only in the process of resisting the peremptory and polarizing choices that the superpowers impose on their "client" states' (Fanon, 1961, p. xv). Bringing total disorder to the order of things is at the heart of Fanon's decolonization, causing interruption of what already exists, which could necessitate new connections and the origination of new categories. To destabilize such an order, Stuart Hall, in line with Fanon, proposes to make connections between ideology, representation and meanings in order to understand subjects' lived experience within the order of things. For Hall, ideological effect is central to the interpretation of any given experience: 'formation at any one time – which have certain effects for the maintenance of power in the social order' (Grossberg, 1986, p. 49). The significance of using ideology through the articulation of its meanings and effects is, for Hall, because such forces the continuity of thinking about the origin of a problem and 'relations of force' (Grossberg, 1986, p. 49). Articulation, hence, is the 'form of the connection that can make a unity of two different elements' (Grossberg, 1986, p. 49). It is 'both a way of understanding how ideological elements come, under certain conditions, to cohere together within a discourse, and a way of asking how they do or do not become articulated, at specific conjunctures, to certain political subjects' (Grossberg, 1986, p. 53). Countless studies, including the aforementioned, define the Palestinian Nakba only in terms of what it means for Palestinians. Although the 'two-sided-conflict' rhetoric has been challenged, the articulation of the Nakba as a perspective solely and uniquely related to Palestinian memories and descriptions of 1948 – rather than as a historical event and, as I propose, a juncture-point in world politics – continues to limit the struggle to two peoples competing over land. Articulating the Nakba as a juncture-point means looking at it not as an expression, but instead addressing its deeper, broader political implications. Juncture-point is defined by Stuart Hall as the point in history where the 'New World' is created and we continue to feel its presence in contemporary Western racism and identity politics. It is the point where people and strangers from different worlds collide; a space of continuous displacement that represents the endless ways in which people have been forced, through slavery and colonization, to 'migrate'. Hence, this juncture-point is a signifier of migration as it relates to displacement, slavery, colonization and conquest (Hall, 1990). With regard to the meaning of the Nakba (1948), Syrian-Arab nationalist intellectual Constantin Zurayk coined the term 'Nakba' in a way that corresponds to Hall's articulation of a juncture-point. For Zurayk, the Nakba signifies the emergence of a new moral order; it marks the triumph of colonial power over colonized people's right to self-determination and principles of justice; a signifier of the relations of powerful forces in contemporary world politics. Accordingly, the Nakba as a juncture-point is a defining historical moment that marked the turning of the colonizer–colonized relationship on its head, and upon which a new era of settler colonial projects is normalized, defended, and protected on one hand, and the narrative of those subjected to genocide treated as a 'perspective', a 'viewpoint of difference', 'two-competing narratives', and a 'protracted conflict' on the other.

Such representations of the normalized and systemically regulated knowledge of the Nakba is what Spivak defines as 'epistemic violence': a violence that aims to impede and actively limit the emergence of non-Western narratives by altering the historical and native social consciousness, deleting all traces of the original and overwriting with what she calls 'subjugated knowledge'. Epistemic violence offers 'an account of how an explanation and narrative of reality was established as the normative one' (Spivak, 2015, p. 67). As a method of settler colonialism, epistemic violence also aims to inflict harm on Palestinians through the discourse of anti-Palestinianism. This is evident in how Palestinians are addressed as a displaced population for whom the denial of both asylum and the right of return is naturalized.

Hence, the study of Palestinians' lived experience of displacement entails analysis of the idea of anti-Palestinianism as a form of epistemic violence, which, in line with what as Hall suggests, is a way of understanding how ideological elements, in certain political conditions, coalesce into a discourse. On the other hand, an examination of this category also helps show how the invention of certain categories can lead to their subjects' empowerment, allowing them to make some sense of the 'intelligibility of their historical situation, without reducing those forms of intangibility to their socio-economic or class location or social position' (Grossberg, 1986).

In line with Hall, categories exist to classify people and determine their entitlements, meaning that classification has material effects on those who are not entitled/excluded based on affiliation, belonging or membership to a group, be it political, ethnic or religious. If categories are identified based on difference and difference is articulated in connection with ideas (Hall, 1986), then Palestinianism as a category emerged in response to the injustice of the Nakba and the continuous suppression of the Palestinian narrative. Said offered three understandings of what Palestinianism is: a form of representation, as it works to 'replace the silence with what is now only a substitutive political voice'; a form of struggle, as Palestinianism dedicates itself to 'liberating Palestine, actually and intellectually, from the segregations and the confusions that have captured it for so long' (Labelle, 2020); and a counter ideology to colonialism, as Palestinianism is the 'witnesses to a century defined by ethnic cleansing, wars of national liberation', and migration, in restless, nomadic pursuit of freedom', 'a counterpoint ... of multiple, almost desperate dramas' (Shatz, 2021). In these definitions, Palestinianism does not merely refer to the Palestinian struggle, but it also upholds the hope of a future liberated from centuries of injustice, enslavement and colonialism. The erasure of the people living in the area called Palestine and identified as Palestinians, and the removal of Palestine itself from the world's geography, formed the core of Zionist project, creating an anti-Palestinianism based on both politics and geography, or rather race, biology or ethnicity. Palestinianism emerged in response to anti-Palestinianism, which suppresses and silences the Nakba, and stands as a representation of the continuity of colonialism and injustice through the new world order created in its aftermath. Hence, the Nakba can be seen here as a juncture-point in history, where anti-Palestinianism was borne of colonial and Zionist ideologies.

The study of how anti-Palestinianism emerged as a form of epistemic violence of settler colonialism is central to understanding the displacement experience of Palestinian refugees from Syria and first in the order of an intersectional analysis that connects the dominant episteme of settler colonialism, nationalism, militarism and global governance of refugees with social formation of gender. This helps us understand the origins of practices that classified Palestinians as a differentiated group, exceptionalized their circumstances and legitimized discrimination against them in Jordanian state and humanitarian policy on the one hand, and gender norms and structural GBV, on the other. Similar to race, class, and gender categories that determine the lived experiences of Black, poor, and women based on ideologies of racism, classism and sexism that inform systematic institutional prejudices, anti-Palestinianism is an erasure of the history and people that existed before 1948 and, hence, is the function that informs the displacement experience of Palestinian refugees. In order to understand the current displacement of Palestinian refugees from Syria, we need to connect it with oppressive systems of both the past and present that naturalized, and to a large extent normalized, the exclusion of Palestinians from humanitarian settings and interventions as othering and anti-Palestinianism processes.

Intersectional analysis of Palestinianism and gender in the displacement experience

In many of my interviews, with both women and men, gender issues and practices were not the primary concern; most of my interviewees understood and explained everything they had faced in relation to their Palestinianism. In one such discussion, Salma, a twenty-four-year-old woman, explained how things dramatically changed for her after arriving in Jordan. As her husband feared deportation, Salma had to do everything outside the house; as a woman, she was not subject to identity checks and could thus move around more freely. I asked her how this made her feel, and Salma responded: 'It's painful. It's not fair to treat us in this way. But, you know, we are Palestinian *ma benghlab* (we do not get tired of finding solutions).' 'Us' was not a reference to Salma and her husband, but rather to 'Palestinian refugees from Syria'. The feeling of being differently treated due to being Palestinian refugees from Syria was central to Salma's understanding of their displacement experience – discussed in greater detail in Chapter 3. However, in the second part of her reply, Salma referred to Palestinians in general. She expressed pain at the first instance, but then articulated the meaning of association with a collective group. Salma did not think of her situation as outside the collective conditions of Palestinians, which gave her the strength to 'guarantee or necessarily enable an enhanced sense of humanity'.

Palestinian refugees from Syria's articulation of their displacement conditions – discussed in Chapter 3 in relation to what women termed 'the Palestinian condition' – relates first to their Palestinianism and second to the result of the conflict in Syria, meaning they understand the particularity of their displacement experience and connect it to the broader question of Palestine. Hence, analysis of Palestinians' gendered experiences – discussed in depth in Chapters 2–6 – should be distinct from that of Syrians; although both are displaced from the same place, one cannot apply the same analysis for all displaced populations from Syria. Such analysis should lead to an examination of questions like: How should analysis of displacement be organized and analysed in a context where displaced populations receive different treatment based on different political grounds? How does intersectionality work in this situation? Do all categories hold the same weight or are some seen as more central than others? Here, my undertaking aims to highlight the fact that since Palestinianism is central to refugee women's own understanding of themselves and is also the basis of Jordanian government policy and the humanitarian exclusion of Palestinian refugees from Syria from receiving aid and seeking asylum, discussed in detail in Chapters 1 and 2, then any reflexive feminist research must first acknowledge and recognize the centrality of Palestinianism as a primary analytical category – a category also entangled with other modes of categorization such as gender, nationality and refugee-ness – in understanding the gendered displacement experience of Palestinian refugees from Syria in Jordan.

Anti-Palestinianism practices appear to have shaped Palestinians' sentiments, ideas and decision to leave or stay in Syria, with material, potentially life-threatening effects. Ismail, an aid worker from the Yarmouk Camp, relayed his father's sentiments: 'Do you want me to do it one more time? No. I would rather die here. No more displacement and humiliation, we Palestinians have had enough.' Not only did Ismail's father make a clear decision, he also somehow protested the protracted othering of Palestinians; what he did is representational, as a Palestinian. Over seventy years of displacement has told refugees what they represent in national, regional and global politics, thus Palestinian refugees' extremely low expectations. Mohammed (see his full story in Chapter 4) expressed a similar account:

> When I went back to the Dera'a Camp there was nothing left, the camp was totally destroyed. Some Palestinians still live in or around it, some just moved to other areas, and some were just in UNRWA schools and facilities. It was an absolutely disastrous situation. There was no hope. Some people did not want to flee again. 'Three exoduses are more than enough in one's lifetime', my uncle told me when I suggested he leave Dera'a.

From Palestinian refugees from Syria's different narratives, it seems that older Palestinian men and women – those who experienced the first and second exoduses in 1948 and 1967 – did not want to go through the experience again. Their memories of displacement have not yet faded and, perhaps more importantly, they know what it means to be displaced. They have learned from experience; an experience repeated time and again. Aminah, a Palestinian aid worker I met and spoke with several times in Jordan, said: 'I begged my mother to leave the Yarmouk Camp, and she kept saying, "a third *hijra* (exodus). A third *hijra*. No ... I am not leaving Yarmouk but for Palestine".' Despite all efforts to get her out of the camp, Aminah's mother refused to leave. 'Why bother leaving war when you know Palestinians are not going to be in a safer place?,' Aminah stated, and relayed her mother's words: 'We left our home in Yafa in 1948, our home in Jerusalem in 1967. If we leave Yarmouk, there is no guarantee we will be able to make it back.'

The statements of those who refused to leave the very catastrophic situation in Yamouk show that Palestinians' displacement experience has been shaped by what they represent as a group. This shows both the material and representational effects of anti-Palestinianism on the lives of Palestinian refugees. However, the act of not leaving, which appears suicidal, is indeed an act of defiance: a rejection of experiencing dispossession and displacement again and also a reaction to feeling unwelcome or undesirable. As Mohammed explained further:

> Many wanted to leave, but they knew they could not even try to come to Jordan or Lebanon. The road was, and still is, dangerous and the result is known: Palestinians are not welcome. We were told that clearly at the Jordanian border the first time I came to Jordan. A police officer said: 'Palestinians go back. No Palestinian will be allowed to enter'.

Said posits that any idea's effectiveness can be assessed 'when its value has been proved in reality by its widespread acceptance' (Said, 1979, p. 10). Additionally, the political actualities and impact of any idea – its force not only in theory but also in material terms – is also key to its effectiveness. Applying this to Palestinian refugees from Syria's articulation and understanding of their situation, the idea of anti-Palestinianism and its material force can be studied in two interrelated ways. First, one must look at the idea's historical basis and relation to other ideas – particularly Zionism and the settler colonial nature of the occupation in Palestine – in order to understand the lack of accountability attributed to the settler colonial state with regard to Palestinians' recent displacement from Syria and Palestinians' unity in articulating both the cause of their suffering and their sense of belonging; a result of the creation of, what Said terms, 'a practical system for accumulation (of power, land, and ideological legitimacy)' (Said, 1979, p. 11). Second, one must also look at anti-Palestinianism as an outcome of the creation of the settler colonial project and its political and material implications on Palestinian refugees, which have exposed Palestinians to further displacement, suffering and the denial of asylum and humanitarian assistance.

Geopolitics of gendered experience of displacement

> The idea that the earth is in effect one world, in which empty, uninhibited spaces virtually do not exist. Just as none of us is outside or beyond geography, none of us is completely free from the struggle over geography. That struggle is complex and interesting because it is not only about soldiers and cannons but also about ideas, about forms, about images and imaginings.
>
> (Said, 1993, p. 6)

Said's argument about the struggle over geography is in relation to the formulation of ideas about the 'Other' in terms of how 'power, knowledge and geography are drawn together in acutely physical way' (Gregory 1995, p. 448). I show throughout this book how Palestinianism emerged in women's narratives as an analytical mode. Women's experience of displacement from Syria can only be told by situating their experience within the context of the geopolitics of their displacement, their parents' first displacement and how that first experience shaped their lives. Hence, their situation can only be understood if told in relation to history and the politics of geography, not as separate, individual experiences. Joan Scott explains that understanding an experience is an 'examination of the workings of the ideological system itself, its categories of representation, its premises about what these categories mean and how they operate, and of its notions of subjects, origin, and cause' (Scott, 1991, p. 778). Experience here is not a one-time event, but instead relational to the history, politics and ideologies surrounding its existence. Speaking of experience is hence 'an examination of knowledge-making and living at the same time'. Likewise, the displacement experience, its meanings and readings cannot be understood unless studied in relation to the political arrangements made to accommodate it. In this sense, Palestinians from Syria's second displacement (for some refugees interviewed it was the third or fourth displacement) cannot be seen as a result of one event, but rather as a function of a series of fundamentally related histories – i.e. the Nakba of 1948 and the Syrian revolution of 2012 – and the incalculable historical and political moments in between that informed the current realities of their displacement experience, be it in Jordan, Lebanon, Egypt or Europe. Hence, the degree of engagement with history is determined by the depth of relationship between oppressive systems of the past and present and whether a connection – whether direct or indirect – can be made between the two as it relates to one particular experience.

In my conversations with women, they insisted on referring to themselves as 'Palestinian refugees from Syria'. For me, this self-identification has become clearer by looking at the significance of the historical trajectories of different Palestinian groups, which produced various meanings and a multiplicity of figures of the Palestinian refugee. This categorization of the self – which was not of Palestinians' own making, but rather by way of the routes they took and the journeys they went through – has become a choice; a choice to establish the group's particular relationship with two connected geographical locations, but not in the dual or fluid meaning of an 'African American' or 'Caribbean British' identity, as discussed by Gilroy (1993) and Hall. It is 'for people to categorize themselves back' (Malkki, 1995, p. 8), 'a refusal to be categorized, a refusal to be fixed within one and only one nation or categorical identity, one and only one historical trajectory' (Malkki, 1995, p. 4).

Although all Palestinians share the history of uprooting and displacement, the route each group took, the rights they enjoyed or were denied, the politics determining such rights within nation systems, and their singular, double or multiple experiences of displacement all shape and influence their perception of refugee-ness. As I will discuss in Chapter 3, even the same group of Palestinian refugee women from Syria may define their refugee status in a way distinct from the meanings Palestinian refugees gave their first displacement based on the new, lived circumstances and politics shaping the new experience. Moreover, the categorization of refugees as legal or illegal, as in the case of Palestinian refugees displaced from Syria to Jordan, can determine the connection with the collective memory and create sub-groups within the larger national group with new trajectories and imaginations of the future. This challenges the image of a universal refugee figure and suggests, in line with Malkki's argument, that the political and lived reality of the displacement experience is what defines refugee-ness, not the displacement itself. It is the politics of the displacement experience that produces different narratives of refugee-ness, belonging, home and collective identity, as I examine in-depth in the following chapters.

2

Legacy of Jordan's entanglement with the settler colonial project in Palestine

I met Aida, a sixty-eight-year-old Palestinian refugee woman, along with her twenty-eight-year-old daughter, Kefayeh and nineteen-year-old granddaughter, Tamam, in Wihdat Camp in 2017. Before the revolution, Aida had lived in Muzirib/ Dera'a in Syria with her husband, twelve daughters, five sons and three stepsons. Before I could ask any questions, Aida began talking straightaway about her two sons who were killed by the Syrian regime in 2013, and her daughter who, as Aida said, 'died from sadness after her two sons and one and only daughter were killed in 2014'. Aida also has a daughter in Switzerland, Shaimaa, who is married to a Palestinian refugee from Syria. Shaimaa had previously been detained in the Cyber City Detention Centre for five years and was then moved to the Gardens Camp until the Red Cross arranged for her resettlement in Switzerland. Two of Aida's sons managed to enter Jordan and remain in al-Zaatary Camp for six months, after which they were removed and detained in the Cyber City for about a year awaiting deportation to Syria. Another of Aida's sons took a boat from Turkey to Greece and has been a Greek camp since early 2016. Aida's fifth son is still in Syria, as he was injured and could not leave. Two of Aida's daughters were already married to Palestinian refugee men and had lived in Jordan before the war. Finally, seven of Aida's daughters have remained in Syria, as they were not able to leave Muzirib due to being married to Palestinian refugees from Syria. 'We are scattered everywhere. I live now with one daughter and one granddaughter. My husband died two years after arriving in Jordan: faqa'e min alhasrat ealaa khasarat 'abna'ih (He was heartbroken over the loss of his children).'

While recollecting her time in Syria, Aida told me, 'We had a farm in Muzirib, a big one. Whatever you desired you could find on the farm. We built our life well in Muzirib after we were forced to leave our homes in Palestine several times.' While Muzirib was not an official camp, the majority of its population was Palestinian; indeed, since UNRWA services were also available, Muzirib is considered an unofficial Palestinian camp. At the start of the revolution, as Aida recalled:

> [W]e accommodated Palestinians escaping the regime's bombardment of Dera'a camp. There were also Syrians who escaped Dera'a and lived among us. We did not think the regime would do the same to Muzirib. There were only very young boys running around chanting *hurryeh* (freedom). There were no militia groups in our neighbourhood, nothing whatsoever that could justify the ruthlessness of the regime and what it has done to us. Still, what happened in Muzirib was worse than any other place, we were basically murdered in cold blood, and for no reason.

Aida and her husband left Syria in late 2014 and managed to enter Jordan using Palestinian Jordanian travel documents (temporary passports) issued to them with the help of the Palestinian embassies in Damascus and Amman. In fact, Aida and her husband used to hold Jordanian citizenship, as her husband served in the Jordanian army. In 1972, however, after the Black September of 1970–1, he was suspended and discharged, after which he and Aida left for Syria to be close to his family: 'Three of his sons from another wife lived in Syria and he wanted to reunite the family,' Aida explained. Years passed and, in 1995, Aida's daughter got engaged to a Palestinian refugee in Jordan. In order to travel to attend the wedding celebration, Aida and her husband needed to renew their Jordanian passports; upon attempting to do so, however, they discovered – to their surprise – that they no longer held Jordanian national numbers. Their nationality had been revoked without their knowledge. Furthermore, as they had entered Syria in the 1970s using Jordanian passports, they also did not qualify for Syrian travel documents like other Palestinian refugees in Syria. Aida, her husband and children had no identity cards. As such, when the conflict intensified in Muzirib and Dera'a in 2012/2013, her husband had to approach the Palestinian embassy in Damascus to find a solution. Still, it took more than a year for Jordan to issue Palestinian Jordanian travel documents to Aida and her husband. These documents are a type of temporary Jordanian passport with no national number, but can nonetheless still be used to enter and live in Jordan. Her sons and daughters, on the other hand, were not given travel documents, so birth certificates were all the identity documents they had (and still have, for those in Syria).

Aida, her daughters and sons took different routes in their journeys. One of her daughters, who now lives with Aida, was married to a Syrian man and thus – as the wife of a Syrian man – was able to enter Jordan using just her birth certificate. When later discovered as Palestinian, however, she was removed from al-Zaatary and detained in the Cyber City. Aida's daughters married to Palestinian refugees from Syria, with Syrian travel documents, were all denied entry to Jordan. One daughter, as previously mentioned, died and lost her three children in two separate attacks, one in the bombing of the UNRWA school in Muzirib in 2014. Before her own and her sons' deaths, she had tried to enter Jordan with her family twice, but was denied entry. Only Shaimaa, Aida's youngest daughter, managed to enter Jordan with her Palestinian refugee husband, the conditions in which she was allowed to do so I explain further below. When I asked about her two daughters who are married in Jordan, Aida responded: 'their situation is not better, their husbands are from Gaza, so they too hold Palestinian travel documents'.

The stories of Aida, her daughters and sons show the complexity of Palestinian refugees from Syria's status in Jordan. In my later visits to Wihdat, the camp on the fringes of Amman where Aida now resides, I had multiple conversations with Kefayah and Tamam, Aida's daughter and granddaughter, who both currently live with her. I also had a conversation over Skype with Shaimaa, Aida's daughter in Switzerland, and spoke on the phone with Rifiqaa, one of the daughters who could not leave Syria, as she was twice denied entry to Jordan. Rifiqaa still lives in Muzirib with her husband and children. She spent around ten months in an informal camp near the Syrian-Jordanian border in a desperate attempt to be allowed entry. In this chapter, I show how Aida, each of her daughters I interviewed and other Palestinian refugee women's stories and narratives have been differently classified and the effects of this divergence on their experiences of displacement from Syria to Jordan.

This chapter examines the variety of ways in which settler colonial forms of epistemic violence unfold, looking in particular at the multiple categorizations of Palestinians in Jordan in order to highlight Jordan's historical interest in concealing Palestinian identity. In this chapter's examination of the changing categorization of Palestinian refugees in Jordan, it investigates the role categorization has played – in connection to the epistemic violence that has shaped the experience of being a Palestinian refugee since the 1948 Nakba – in Jordan's politics. Here, the chapter highlights the changing politics of Palestinian categorization, from wanted to unwanted, thus showing that such has shifted based on the state's national interests and the changing relations between colonial and national projects competing in the region. Examining Jordan's 2013 no-entry policy for Palestinian refugees from Syria would not be adequate without also addressing Jordan's politics and historical involvement with the question of Palestine and its role in the settler colonial project in Palestine. To understand each category and their gendered implications on women's lives, it is important, if not vital, to understand the political moments through which the creation of each Palestinian category emerged; categories deemed necessary on grounds such as expanding Jordan's territorial borders, preserving its national identity and interests and protecting national security.

The analysis of Jordan's multiple categorizations of Palestinians challenges the narrative that Jordan has been more receptive to Palestinian refugees than other Arab countries, as Palestinian refugees in Jordan have been naturalized and carry Jordanian passports. Through women's narratives, this chapter argues that Jordan's categorization of Palestinians cannot be studied outside its colonial legacy or disconnected from the settler colonial project in Palestine. Thus, understanding the differing treatment Palestinian refugees from Syria receive, as 'unwelcome' and 'undesired refugees', implies an analysis of Jordan's multi-categorization within the context of the epistemic violence of settler colonialism that created the conditions and atmosphere of anti-Palestinianism, as discussed in the introduction.

Although this chapter explores the political factors that contributed to this multiple categorization of Palestinian refugees, it is beyond its scope to detail the myriad of historical factors or analyse those addressed in greater depth. Rather, this chapter creates a timeline of historical events that link Jordan's politics and policies to both its colonial legacy and the settler colonial project in Palestine. Any special attention paid to certain political moments is solely based on the narratives of Palestinian refugee women's displacement, movement from one place to another, and relocation in camps in Palestine, Jordan and Syria. Therefore, the chapter follows their displacement routes, each of which is tied to the 1948 Nakba. The Nakba theorized as a 'juncture-point' (see introduction) where Jordan nationalism, settler colonialism, colonial power interests, and Arab nationalism meet, compete and also potentially re-enforce one another.

UN documents, Jordanian statistics and the archives of the setter colonial state of Israel all differently estimate the number of Palestinians forced to leave their homes in 1948–9. The larger the number, the more it challenges colonial propaganda – e.g. 'A land without a people for a people without a land' – used to legitimize the establishment of a home for Jews in Palestine; the smaller the number, the more it serves settler colonial propaganda. Thus, the settler colonial state estimates around 500,000 to 600,000 Palestinians were forced out in 1948, numbers considerably lower than Palestinian estimates. As for the UN and Jordanian estimations, it is not the number itself that is most noteworthy, but the definition of a Palestinian refugee (versus the Jordanian, for example) that can shed light on the origin of classification and, hence, the epistemic violence that set the stage for anti-Palestinian sentiments and policies.

Under the UNRWA's operational definition, Palestine refugees are 'persons whose normal place of residence was Palestine between June 1946 and May 1948, who lost both their homes and means of livelihood as a result of the 1948 Arab-Israeli conflict' (United Nations, 1950). Based on this definition, UNRWA estimates the number of Palestinian refugees from 1948 at 957,000. Whilst this number is higher than the 726,000 often cited in various literature (Barakat, 1973), it still does not recognize movements of Palestinians to neighbouring countries or elsewhere prior to 1946; it does not recognize that pre-1946 events – such as the Great Palestinian Revolt (1936–9) and the confiscation of lands by the British imperialist authorities and Jewish Agencies, as Palestine had come under the British colonial rule in 1921 – also led to the displacement of Palestinians (Sakran, 1948). Furthermore, the UN figure negates the fact that not all displaced Palestinians immediately registered with UNRWA or were accommodated in refugee camps (Hollis, 2000). Due to existing kinship connections between the populations of the

Levant, many Palestinians were hosted by relatives in other parts of Palestine, as well as in Jordan, Lebanon, Syria, Egypt and other Arab countries. The UN estimate also does not acknowledge the thousands of individuals who were either working or studying outside Palestine at the time and could not return home. This issue is particularly important to the case of Jordan and was pointed to repeatedly in my interviews; for instance, the case of Aida's husband and the decedents of those recruited to the Jordanian-British army prior to 1948.

In one of my interviews, Rania – a thirty-four-year-old Palestinian refugee woman displaced from Khan Eshieh Camp in Syria, who was detained in the Cyber City and then moved to the Gardens Camp until her family finally managed to get her released – told me that neither she nor her husband has ever had an identity card, be it Palestinian, Syrian or Jordanian. The only document they had was a *quid nofus* (birth registration) from the Palestine Liberation Organization (PLO) branch office in Syria, as neither Rania's father nor her father-in-law had any official documentation of their refugee status to pass on to their children. From the early 1940s, both Rania's father and father-in-law, who were close friends, had served in the Jordanian army. In the early 1970s, however, both were detained and discharged on the grounds of disloyalty to Jordan. Then, in the later 1970s, they joined the revolution in Lebanon, moving to Syria after the settler colonial state of Israel's 1982 invasion of Lebanon. As a result of their political affiliation with Fateh, both had their Jordanian nationality revoked; but, because they were residents of Jordan prior to 1946, the UN considered them Jordanian, not Palestinian refugees. This meant that neither man qualified to register with UNRWA. In the proceeding sections and chapters, I discuss the implications of this on Rania's life, and that of her family. For now, both her and Aida's story show how their lives were impacted by both events that led to the 1948 Nakba and the politics that shaped Jordan's formation, such as the Jordanian-British army's recruitment of Palestinians and its impact on their refugee status, their Jordanian citizenship rights and their current displacement from Syria.

From the establishment of Transjordan, both the British authorities and Amir Abdullah I sought to recruit Palestinians into the country's army and newly established civil service. While Jordan became an independent kingdom in 1946, two years before the Palestinian Nakba, Britain continued to rule in matters related to foreign, domestic and military affairs through a network of advisers and military commanders until 1956 (Tal, 1995). Britain's direct influence over Jordan was the reason Jordan's application to join UN was rejected, especially by the Soviet Union and the United States, but for different reasons. Indeed, Jordan did not become a UN member state until 1955, when King Hussein expelled British army officer Major John Glubb. Thus, it follows on that all of Jordan's pre-1955 policies were largely shaped by British foreign policy; a foreign policy that only began to weaken in the early 1950s as a result of American ascendancy and the rapid spread of Soviet influence in the area. Hence, the role of Jordan, specifically the Hashemite family, should not be seen outside the British colonial legacy and gradual, increasing US foreign policy influence, particularly in managing the relationship between the two newly established states, the Jewish one in Palestine and the Arab in Transjordan.

Amir Abdullah I's life-long ambition of uniting Greater Syria, which he foresaw as his empire, is another important factor that shaped Jordan's policies towards Palestinians both prior to and after 1948 (Achilli, 2014, p. 237). The Amir's role 'was to mediate the interests of the British and the Arabs of Transjordan in such a way to keep the local social structure intact along with his position at its pinnacle' (Wilson, 1987, p. 37). However, the Amir was not content with the role the British had assigned him. In his eyes, he was the amir of an area of no particular significance to either the West or the Arabs, and thus his goal was to expand his realm; a goal that shaped his policies towards Palestinians both prior to and after 1948 (Brown, 1970; Kazziha, 1979; Wilson, 1987; Tal, 1995; Massad, 2001; Soh, You and Yu, 2016).

The throne Abdullah envisioned primarily included Syria and Iraq; Palestine did not enter the equation until 1937, 'when Britain suggested that Palestine might be partitioned between Arabs and Jews and that Abdullah might rule the Arab part' (Wilson, 1987, p. 38). In the minds of the British, the formation of the Emirate of Transjordan in 1921 served two ends: to lessen the Arab resistance to the Palestine Mandate and to compensate the Hashemites, whose promised rule over Greater Syria was first delayed and then betrayed by giving Syria to France (Jeffries, 2017). Britain's role in determining Jordan's borders and policies relevant to the establishment of the settler colonial project was to maintain the myth of Transjordan's independence while, simultaneously, keeping Abdullah under control (Jeffries, 2017). As Kazziha argues, 'by appointing a ruler on whom he could bring pressure to bear, to check anti-Zionism. The ideal would be a person who was not too powerful, and who was not an inhabitant of Transjordan, but who relied upon His Majesty's Government for the retention of his office' (1979, p. 244). The newly established Emirate of Transjordan, and the Hashemite throne, was completely dependent on the British government for protection; a reality that characterized Jordan's relationship with both Palestinians and the Zionist movement at the time (Wilson, 1987; Massad, 2001; Soh, You and Yu, 2016), as well as continues to shape its politics and foreign policy to the present day. In Abdullah's 'early dealings with the Jewish Agency ... The source of his attitude towards partition was not an uncanny foreknowledge of Palestine's future. Rather, it was his own understanding of the inherent weakness in the structure of his and Transjordan's dependence on Britain' (Wilson, 1987, p. 44).

The colonial pattern and legacy of Jordan's relationship and entanglement with the settler colonial project in Palestine was reflected in the British Parliament's debate of Jordan's annexation of what later became known as the 'West Bank', the remaining Palestinian-held parts of historic Palestine after the 1948 Nakba. On 27 April 1950, a parliamentary debate was initiated by a private notice asking the secretary of state for foreign affairs whether King Abdullah of Jordan had consulted Britain before annexing the Arab-held parts of Palestine and if he would be making a statement. Mr. Younger, the minister of state, answered:

His Majesty's Government in the United Kingdom have been officially informed by the Government of the Hashemite Kingdom of Jordan of the union of the Kingdom of Jordan and of that part of Palestine under Jordan occupation and control .... This action is subject to explanation on two points. The first of these points relates to the frontier between this territory and Israel. This frontier has not yet been finally determined. The existing boundary is the line laid down in the Armistice Agreement signed between Israel and Jordan on 3 April 1949, and is subject to any modification which may be agreed upon by the two States under the terms of that Agreement, or of any final settlement which may replace it. Until, therefore, the frontier between Israel and Jordan is determined by a final settlement between them. His Majesty's Government regard the territory to which the Anglo-Jordan Treaty is applicable as being bounded by the Armistice Line, or any modification of it which may be agreed upon by the two parties.

(HANSARD 1803–2005, 1950)

The British position on King Abdullah's annexation of the parts of Palestine not under settler colonial occupation was based on the 1949 Armistice Agreement between the Zionists and the Hashemite Kingdom of Jordan, which led to the Zionists gaining Palestinian lands previously held by Iraqi forces, from which around 20,000 refugees were forced to leave (Hollis, 2000). Hence, Britain's support for Transjordan's 1950 annexation of the West Bank was entirely based on the assumption that the two created states would serve British interests. The annexation plan, according to Ilan Pappe (1994, p. 115), was first floated by the British in 1936, during the Great Palestinian Revolt, when the Amir and Zionist movement agreed to solve 'the question of Palestine by annexing densely Arab populated areas to Trans-Jordan'.

In 1954, a few years after annexation and two years after King Hussein II took the throne, Jordan amended the Transjordan Nationality Law of 1928 to grant citizenship rights to Palestinian refugees in Jordan and Palestinians born in the West Bank: 'All those who are habitual residents, at the time of the application of this law, of Transjordan or the Western Territory administered by the Hashemite Kingdom of Jordan, and who hold Palestinian nationality, are considered as having already acquired Jordanian nationality and to enjoy all the rights and obligations that Jordanians have' (Massad, 2001, p. 39). Through this, Palestinians in Jordan and Palestine were unified as part of the Jordanian population, not Palestinian. On the one hand, this marked the beginning of Jordan's policy of Jordanization, a process facilitating homogenization, while on the other, it entailed the absence of Palestinian identity and nationalism and led to the emergence of two categories: the Jordanian of Palestinian origin and the 'Palestinian refugee-Citizen' (Soh, You and Yu, 2016).

Jordanization versus Palestinianism

Pre- and post-1948 recruitment of Palestinians – into both the Jordanian army and state institutions – was integral to Amir Abdullah's ambitions for Palestine and also 'meant to strengthen the Palestinian-Transjordanian relations' (Kádár, 2019, p. 94). In the 1950s, however, during King Hussein II's reign, Jordanization took on a different trajectory: strengthening Eastern Jordanian nationalism as the conduit through which the true Jordanian identity could be created. This shift was not purely directed against Palestinians, as growing nationalist sentiments in Syria and Egypt and the unity of these countries were also targets; the regime in Jordan perceived such as fundamental threats to its existence, a matter also connected to Cold War regional divisions (Brown, 1970; Kazziha, 1979; Massad, 2001; Soh, You and Yu, 2016; Kádár, 2019). As it pertains to Palestinians in Jordan, King Hussein II pursued policies that increased Eastern Jordanians' presence in the army and official posts and the narrative of 'Palestinians as threat to Jordanian national identify' began to emerge (Kurd, 2014). After defeat in the 1967 Six-Day War, Jordan did not change its policies for refugees from the West Bank, as this area remained under Jordanian administration (Soh, You and Yu, 2016). However, Jordan did not extend nationality and citizenship rights to Palestinian refugees from Gaza who, until being displaced by the war, had been under Egyptian administration (Masalha, 2003). Since then, Palestinian refugees from Gaza have remained in a special refugee category, known as 'Gazans' (Pérez, 2011). Gazans were given only temporary two-year passports and excluded from citizenship rights such as education, health and employment, as they were restricted from certain jobs. As such, refugees from the Gaza Strip – even those not originally from Gaza, but displaced there from nearby villages destroyed in 1948 – live in very precarious conditions in Jordan. Of the 140,000 refugees from Gaza, based on the government's estimates, the majority were displaced to Gaza in 1948 (Sabaghi, 2015).

The Jordanian government argued, as its reasoning for withholding citizenship rights from refugees from Gaza, that refugees from areas occupied in 1967 in the annexed West Bank were already Jordanian, but Gazan refugees had been living in areas governed by Egypt until 1967 and thus were not

Jordanian. This was perhaps the start of Jordan's multi-classification of Palestinian refugees, clearly distinguishing between different categories. Jordan asserted (and continues to assert) that it should not be solely responsible for dealing with the refugee 'problem': these refugees should be returned to either Gaza or Egypt. The categorization of 'Gazan' refugees has not only had an impact on those who live in Jordan, but also – as several research participants explained – on refugees from Gaza who moved to live in Syria, as they were not equally treated to other Palestinian refugees in Syria.

Amal, for example, explained that her father and grandparents were forced from their village in 1948 and displaced to camps in Gaza. In 1967, again, they were forced to flee the camp to the West Bank and then Jordan. As they were considered refugees from Gaza, they were given the two-year Jordanian passport. The family lived in hardship in Jarash Camp, the camp for Gazans, until 1969, when they decided to move to Syria and reunite with relatives displaced there since 1948. In Syria, they could not own property, their house was registered under Amal's uncle's name, as Palestinian refugees from Gaza were excluded from rights granted to other Palestinian refugees in Syria. Amal could not get any form of identity document and, despite having a degree in nursing, could not work in any public hospital. When Yarmouk Camp came under the regime's heavy bombardment, her father and mother managed to flee and enter Jordan with their expired temporary passports. In Jordan, Amal's father renewed his passport and tried to apply for temporary passports for his seven children, but the passport was only granted to Amal's sister, who was under eighteen at the time. Amal and her other five siblings were left to find another solution:

> Before my father left Syria, he prepared a pack of documents for each one of us. The pack included copies of our land registers in Palestine; each one's birth certificate; a copy of a statement signed by my uncle, under whose name our house in Yarmouk is registered, declaring that my father owns the house in Yarmouk, not him; and a copy of his UNRWA card and Jordanian temporary passport. These were all the documents we have had, and my father wanted to make sure that if something happened to him or any one of us, the others could keep these documents safe. If my father had not done this, I would never have had the opportunity to leave anywhere. My husband

is a Palestinian refugee from Syria, he could go to Lebanon, but I had nothing. We tried the Jordanian borders several times together, but it did not work, we were told to go back. My husband then suggested that I and my nine-months-old baby try without him. I spoke to border officers, showed them the copy of my father's passport, claimed I lost mine. The officers were very sympathetic, one of them told me to wait, and I waited for maybe 10 hours or so. Then, an officer came to me and told me to go with him. I was asked to stay in a room and waited again for a couple hours, until an officer came and asked me questions about my husband. I said I did not know where he was. After an hour of interrogation, I was taken by bus to el-Bashabsheh Camp in Ramtha, then to Cyber City', where she stayed for a few months until her father managed to get her out by arranging *kafalah* (sponsorship) by a Jordanian.

Aida also pointed to this issue in our conversations, when she spoke of her two daughters married to Palestinians from Gaza: 'I sometimes send them some of the donation I get. My poor girls and their children, they are suffering a lot.' It was distressing to hear Aida, who had very little herself, say that she shared the infrequent donations she received with her daughters who hold temporary Jordanian passports, alongside her need for concern not only about her children displaced in multiple places and those still under bombardment in Syria, but also for her daughters who hold temporary Jordanian passports. Gazan refugees' legal status and precarious living conditions cannot be isolated from Jordan's post-1967 political decisions. Jordan, which welcomed refugees in 1948–1950s, when its objective was to expand its borders, increase its population and unify its kingdom, did not do the same when the West Bank was occupied and it lost its power over the territories it annexed in 1950 (Soh, You and Yu, 2016). In Jordan's political decisions, 'the beginnings of a definite pattern in the relationship between Jordan and Israel may be discerned. This pattern emerged in Abdullah's time and is still with us today despite the 1967 war. It is set by the common interest of both countries in containing Palestinian nationalism' (Wilson, 1987, p. 41).

Nonetheless, the territorial loss was not the only reason Jordan chose to exclude refugees from Gaza, there are a myriad of geopolitical political factors and aspects of the Palestinian-Jordanian relationship that are important to understanding the multiple displacements, relocations and revocations of citizenship in the narratives of Palestinian refugee women from Syria who held either temporary Jordanian passports or Jordanian citizenship that was revoked between the 1970s and late 1980s. The first such factor was Egyptian-Syrian unity, led by Egypt's Nasser, and his support for the developing Palestinian national movement (Brand, 1988). This facet is also linked to the second point, the rise in Arab and international support for the PLO, established in 1964. The growing tension between Nasser and Jordan's king in the 1950s and 1960s also reflected Jordan's relationship with imperialist powers and its siding with the United States during the Cold War. 'Jordan's role at this historical period was to form a counterbalance to Nasser and to preserve the common interests it has with the Settler Colonial project in Palestine in the need to contain Syrian and Egyptian armies and nationalism' (Bunch, 2008, p. 57). However, prior to 1967, there had also been a growing tension with the settler colonial state in Palestinian due to frequent attacks on Jordan's borders – justified as retaliation for armed Palestinian guerrilla operations – which King Hussein believed undermined Jordan's power in the West Bank. With little US support for Jordan's position, the king began doubting his main ally's intentions. Tensions, Jordan's change of sides in 1967 (Brown, 1970; Bunch, 2008; Achilli, 2014; Kurd, 2014), and a difficult economic situation – with an increase in unemployment and the loss of half of Jordan's agricultural and fertile lands after 1967 – made it necessary for the king to play 'the refugees' card. The refugee card has become one of Jordan's most systematic and deliberate strategies in responding to both internal and external tensions; hence, 1967 refugees from Gaza were not given citizenship rights and those from the West Bank were distinguished from those from 1948 as *Naziheen*, 'displaced people'. After the disengagement of the East and West Banks in 1988, this classification, as I discuss shortly, would determine citizenship revocation criteria.

Besides the loss of life and lands and the displacement of people, the separation of families in the East and West Banks and the inability of thousands of Palestinians working abroad, especially in Gulf countries, to return to Palestine were other direct impacts of the 1967 war on Palestinians. The case of Palestinians working in the Gulf emerges later as another classified group, particularly 'Palestinians from Kuwait', who were expelled from Kuwait after Saddam's invasion in 1990. In my discussion with Rania, she explained that, due to his work in the Jordanian military, her father remained in Jordan while her mother, who lived in Palestine prior to 1967, stayed in Palestine. The family spent a few years apart until her mother managed to cross the bridge between Jordan and Palestine in 1970. However, only a few months after arriving in Jordan, Rania's mother found herself in the middle of another war. Tension between Jordan and the PLO over the representation of Palestinians reached its peak in September 1970, in what was later to become known as 'Black September'. King Hussein felt threatened by PLO and Palestinian factions' control over the camps, which he saw as undermining his power and an attempt to renew Palestinian identity, weakening his efforts to Jordanize Palestinians (Massad, 2001). Thus, in September 1970, Jordan initiated a military campaign against Palestinian guerrillas in the camps; a campaign in which thousands of Palestinians lost their lives.

Although Rania did not live the events, as she was not yet born, she did recall some of her mother's memories of Black September: 'My mother told me that Jordanian tanks were in the middle of the camp, shooting indiscriminately. Our house was raided in search of guns, there were dead bodies in the streets. It was hell-like, as she described it.' An agreement was later reached in which the PLO moved it headquarters to Lebanon and the Palestinian factions withdrew their armed resistance from the camps. Following Black September, the king discharged many Palestinians from the army as both a step of precaution and still part of the earlier policy of replacing Palestinians either in favour of loyal Jordanians or due to their direct affiliation with Palestinian factions. Whilst Rania's father was affiliated with the revolution, and his discharge – along with the discharge of her father-in-law – was on this basis, Aida's husband was discharged without having had any affiliation with Palestinian factions. Rania's father followed the revolution to Lebanon, but her mother stayed behind in Jordan. In 1985, Rania's father moved from Lebanon to Syria, and her mother followed in 1988. On the Jordanian-Syrian border, intelligence security officers interrogated Rania's mother about her husband's affiliation with the armed resistance. She was held at the border for hours and then her passport was stamped with 'leave without return'. It was also during this time that Aida and her husband's citizenship was revoked.

The revocation of both Aida and Rania's mothers' citizenship was founded solely on Jordan's masculinist national identity, the impacts of which I discuss in Chapter 5. In Jordan's nationality law, Jordanian women were left out, only considered followers of their husbands; only the wives of Jordanians were seen as Jordanians (Jabiri, 2016). Replicating the British Nationality Law, the 1928 Jordanian Nationality Law stated: 'The wife of a foreigner is a foreigner' (Massad, 2001, p. 46). Despite amendments made to the law in 1961 and 1963, it was only in 1987 that women married to foreigners were allowed to retain their Jordanian nationality (Massad, 2001; Jabiri, 2016). Consequently, the revocation of their citizenship was founded on gender as well as Palestinianism. Aida does not know the exact date her citizenship was revoked, but she estimates sometime between 1988 and 1995, as she neither visited Jordan nor used her Jordanian passport during this period. Rania's mother's citizenship was revoked the day she left Jordan in 1988. Both estimated dates were after amendments made to the Nationality Law in 1987. While the amendment meant that Jordanian women married to non-Jordanians could retain their Jordanian nationality, Aida and Rania's mothers were treated according to old norms and laws due to the revocation of their husbands' citizenship being founded on political grounds, especially after the disengagement decision of the East and West Banks.

Disengagement policy: The Jordanization and denationalization of Jordanians of Palestinian origin

On 31 July 1988, thirty-eight years after his grandfather's annexation of the West Bank, King Hussein II delivered the Disengagement from the West Bank Statement to the nation, announcing his dismantling of administrative and legal ties between the West and East Banks of the United Kingdom of Jordan. In his opening remarks, the king first sought to define the Jordanian nation and then appealed to hearts and minds: 'I am pleased to address you in your cities and villages, in your camps and dwellings, in your institutions of learning and in your places of work. I would like to address your hearts and minds, in all parts of our beloved Jordanian land.' In this address, the king clearly defined the Palestinian camps in Jordan as Jordanian; a deft distinction between Palestinians living in Jordan, even if in camps, and those in the West Bank (King Hussein Disengagement Statement, 1988). He, furthermore, affirmed that this disengagement decision was in line with God's Will – a matter important to the legitimacy of Hashemite rule in Jordan, as grandsons of the Prophet Mohammed – and one made after a thorough study for the benefit of Palestinians: 'after seeking God's assistance, and considering a thorough and extensive study, a series of measures with the aim of enhancing the Palestinian National Organisation and highlighting the Palestinian identity. Our objective is the benefit of the Palestinian cause and the Arab Palestinian People' (King Hussein Disengagement Statement, 1988, p. 2). The king reminded the nation of Jordan's role in protecting the Palestinian cause, outlining the timeline of events that led to the decision, including the establishment of the PLO and Arab recognition of it as the sole legitimate representative of the Palestinian people, leading Jordan to sever ties with Palestinians in the West Bank. The king also affirmed that this disengagement was merely triggered by the Arabs and Palestinian leaders desire to establish independent Palestinian state on Palestinian soil, and that the unity of any two nations should, first and foremost, be equally sought by the two nations. Thus, disengagement was not a reversal of Jordan's position, but a response to the PLO's wishes. Through this, the king sought to justify Jordan's measures by blaming the PLO and Arabs who supported the plight of Palestinian self-determination, and reaffirm Jordan as an independent state with sovereign power over its lands and people.

The defining of Jordanian citizens and the status of Palestinians in Jordan was one of the definitive messages of King Hussein's address:

[I]t has to be understood in all clarity, and without any ambiguity or equivocation, that our measures regarding the West Bank, concerns only the occupied Palestinian lands and its people. They naturally do not relate in any way to the Jordanian citizens of Palestinian origin in the Hashemite Kingdom of Jordan. They all have the full rights of citizenship, and all its obligations, the same as any other citizen irrespective of his origin. They are all an integral part of the Jordanian state. They belong to it, they live on its land, and they participate in its life and all its activities. Jordan is not Palestine; the Palestinian independent state will be established on the occupied Palestinian lands after its liberation, God willing. There the Palestinian identity will be embodied and there the Palestinian struggle shall come to fruition as confirmed by the glorious uprising of the Palestinian uprising under occupation.

(King Hussein Disengagement Statement, 1988, pp. 9–10)

This statement affirms that Palestinians with Jordanian citizenship are Jordanian, belong only to Jordan, and all forms of Palestinian identity should remain in Palestinian lands, thereby making a clear and unequivocal distinction between both Palestinian and Jordanian identities and Palestinians in Jordan and those in Palestine. In other words, the statement powerfully declared that there is no place for competing identities or the Palestinian struggle on Jordanian soil; any signs of the Palestinian struggle for liberation in Jordan go against Jordanian nationalism. This pronouncement clearly meant that the Palestinian identity and resistance threaten Jordan's unity and security, which the king vowed to protect as a 'sacred duty that will not be compromised' (King Hussein Disengagement Statement, 1988, p. 10).

The king's address also affirmed that Jordan's unity, as a national state like any other, is based on shared identity, but even more significant is the importance of this unity to Jordan's security, economic development and prosperity: 'national unity is precious for any country; but in Jordan it is more than that it is the basis of our stability, and the springboard of our development and prosperity. It is the foundation of our security' (King Hussein Disengagement Statement, 1988, p. 11). The king's carefully crafted and calculated messages continued using a 'carrot and stick' approach, promising prosperity if people abided by national unity and harmony, laying the groundwork for punishing those who do not. While the king's address sounded like a statement of independence from Palestinians, it also simultaneously affirmed Jordan's good will in trying to find a just solution for Palestinians. However, as the Nationality Law has never been amended to reflect the Disengagement Statement's new policies, the definition of a Jordanian National in the constitution remains ambiguous (Frost, 2022). In 1988, general regulations were issued reflecting the core issues of the king's statement; while these were not translated into law, they were nonetheless issued to facilitate the revocation of Jordanian nationality from citizens of Palestinian descent (Frost, 2022).

The decision to reduce links between Jordan and the West Bank led to hundreds of thousands of Palestinians losing their citizenship – not only those who were in the West Bank before 31 July, but also some displaced in 1967 who still had family in Palestine had to 'correct' their position and show proof of residency in Jordan. Thus, there were changes to their passports, as they were now regarded as Palestinian, and their five-year passports were replaced with two-year temporary passports. After the disengagement decision, Jordan introduced the dual yellow and green card system to differentiate Palestinians living in Jordan from those living in Palestine. While the system was originally introduced for the purposes of crossing the border between Jordan and the West Bank, it has now become an identifier of Palestinian origin. The yellow card is given to Palestinians who left the West Bank before 1 June 1983, and allows its holder to visit Palestine due to family ties, but not to live there; a yellow card holder is still entitled to citizenship, a national number and five-year passport. Green cards, on the other hand, are given to Palestinians who were living in Palestine prior to 1988, and entitles its holder to either the two- or five-year passport, but without a national number, and the right to visit Jordan and stay for a maximum of two months.

At the time, this differentiation based on place of residency put many Palestinian families scattered across the West and East Banks in a difficult position. However, the impact of this policy on the lives of Palestinians has not been addressed; indeed, there are only a few studies looking at King Hussein's motives, the effects of the disengagement decision and the policies that followed on the Palestinian leadership and revolution, and Palestinians' response to the policy (Robins, 1989). Although this decision put the PLO leadership in a difficult position, nationalist Palestinians applauded it, as they opposed Jordan's annexation of the West Bank and advocated for an independent state. Yazid Sayigh summarized this position as follows:

> Jordan's new policy enunciated at the end of July 1988, concerning the severance of legal and administrative ties with the West Bank, and the justification given, to the effect that this action would make the PLO and the Palestinians in general more credible in struggling for the independence of the Occupied Territories, is the only explicit and coherent statement of policy regarding such independence. But even in this case, the cynics have not failed to express the concern that the policy may in the end prove to involve political double entente. Indeed, it is fair to say that the only shift in the BPR [balance of power] that has occurred within the Arab countries as a

result of the Intifada has precisely been the new Jordanian policy. Whatever the motivation behind it, it certainly has energized the search by the PLO (and the leadership network in the OT) for a political formula to assert the eligibility of the OT for independence, and of the Palestinian people as a whole for a state of their own, on Palestinian soil.

(Sayigh, 1988)

The announcement of cutting ties with the West Bank, made after one year of Palestinian Intifada (uprising), generated fears in Jordan of another mass expulsion of Palestinians from the West to East Bank. The 1967 war had resulted in a mass expulsion and displacement of Palestinians in Jordan, but those displaced were not perceived as refugees, as they had moved from the West to East Bank; hence, the population of the East Bank increased sharply, with Palestinians comprising over 65 per cent. Furthermore, the king's fear was also triggered by his loss of more territories to the settler colonial state in Palestine and having to deal with the consequences of expulsions without sufficient help from the United States, especially given there was a 'growing proportion of Israelis coming to believe that the "transfer" of the Arab population from the West Bank to the East Bank was the best possible solution. The maintenance of an organic link between the two banks had fuelled this view' (Robins, 1989). In this sense, the king's decision was intended as a message to the PLO leadership, the settler colonial state and the United States when he declared: 'Jordan is not Palestine' (King Hussein Disengagement Statement, 1988; Robins, 1989). Once again, Palestinian lives were caught between multiple and competing nationalist and colonialist projects (Sayigh, 1989).

Aida and her family held no cards, and Aida believed that the revocation of her and her husband's passports was due to the fact that her husband's second wife was still in Palestine with her children. Aida's husband was married to three women before 1967; as result of war and expulsion, the first went to Syria in 1967 and the second remained in Palestine. Aida, the third wife, joined her husband in Jordan. As they moved to Syria in the 1970s, Aida and her husband did not realize the need to 'correct' their legal status in Jordan. Thus, their citizenship was revoked in abstentia, which was also true for many Palestinians not present in Jordan or Palestine at the time of the announcement of the disengagement plan and introduction of the dual yellow-green card system.

A few years later, this issue arose again when Kuwait expelled thousands of Palestinians after Saddam Hussein invaded. Unlike other nationals working in the Gulf before the war, Palestinians could not be repatriated to their homes in Palestine, and thus around 300,000 Palestinians arrived in Jordan in a matter of months (van Hear, 1995; Le Troquer and al-Oudat, 1999). This was considered 'the third major forced population influx that Jordan has experienced in little more than four decades' (van Hear, 1995, p. 352).

Jordan's treatment of Palestinians from Kuwait, and other Gulf countries, largely depended on the classification systems developed from 1948 to 1988: those with five-year passports with national numbers were considered Jordanians returning home; those who resided in the West Bank before 1 June 1988 were considered Palestinians and had to undergo status corrections; the majority were given two-year passports with no national numbers; and Gazans with Egyptian travel documents were dealt with on a case-by-case basis, and predominantly denied entry. What was striking about the case of Palestinians from Kuwait was the strong presence of messages from the king's disengagement speech in governmental, media and nationalist narratives: the 'Jordan is not Palestine' and 'Jordan first' narratives. The economic aspect of the mass influx took most attention, as Palestinians from Kuwait were blamed for the increase in unemployment and worsening economic conditions; conditions Jordan was experiencing prior to the Gulf War due to International Monetary Fund and World Bank restrictions and conditionalities on its economy (Le Troquer and al-Oudat, 1999). Palestinians from Kuwait were, nonetheless, blamed, despite the fact that they – and Palestinians from other parts of the Gulf – contributed to the economy in significant ways. Indeed, as 'returnees repatriated their capital from Kuwait, capital transfers rose sharply in 1991–92', and

> In 1991, the construction, commerce, and service sectors registered growth rates of 10.5 percent, 29.3 percent, and 15.8 percent, respectively. But that same year, growth in GDP was only 1.8 percent at factor cost. In 1992, all sectors of activity showed growth, especially agriculture; manufacturing and utilities (electricity and water) grew by at least 9 percent. Growth in real GDP rose to 11.3 percent, before slowing down to 6 percent the following year.
>
> (Le Troquer and al-Oudat, 1999, p. 43)

The distorted image of the negative impacts Palestinians from Kuwait were having on Jordanian society coupled with an environment already hostile to Palestinian refugees since the disengagement decision, Jordan's experiences in the 1967 war, and Kuwait and other Arab states' refusal to repatriate Palestinians at the end of the 1991 Gulf war, led to the marginalization of Palestinian refugees from Iraq affected by the US invasion of that country in 2003. Palestinian refugees from Iraq were trapped for years between the borders of Jordan and Iraq, in 'no man's land', with neither Jordan nor Iraq accepting any responsibility for their displacement or hardships living in the desert. Some Palestinian refugees from Iraq's stories, only queried in a handful of studies, resembled those of Aida and Rania in terms of having their citizenship revoked after moving to Iraq from Jordan (Enders, 2008). Palestinian refugees from Iraq fled the war between 2003 and 2006, like hundreds of thousands of Iraqis, to Jordan, but the Palestinians were denied entry (Wengert and Alfaro, 2006). Indeed, a Human Rights Watch statement on the status of Palestinian refugees from Iraq on the borders of Jordan was quite indistinguishable from one issued in 2014 about Palestinian refugees from Syria: 'Jordan is slamming the door in the face of a small but desperate group of people, who have seen their relatives murdered in Baghdad. Jordan should not treat Iraqi Palestinians fleeing persecution more harshly than other Iraqis fleeing violence, who have generally been allowed to enter Jordan' (cited in Wengert and Alfaro, 2006, p. 20).

The case of Palestinian Iraqi refugees presented a legal challenge for UNRWA: it has no mandate in Iraq, as the country refused UNRWA assistance in its dealings with Palestinian refugees and pledged to treat them equal to Iraqis, except for nationality. Furthermore, as Palestinians in Iraq were not under any UN agency mandate, they did fall under the protection of the UNHCR. Thus, Palestinian refugees in Iraq, estimated at around 34,000 by the UNHCR, had no option but to remain in Iraq, as all UNHCR efforts to exercise options available to other refugees failed. The first option was voluntary repatriation to country of origin. The UNHCR approached Israel about allowing those displaced from Gaza and the West Bank in 1967 and with ties in these territories to return, but all such requests were denied, despite these areas being under the administration of the Palestinian Authority. Assimilation in neighbouring countries was also not an option, as Jordan and Syria closed their borders to Palestinians. They were also excluded from resettlement in other countries. Around 24,000 Palestinian refugees were internally displaced in Iraq and in camps along the borders, and 5,000 remained in 'no man land' between Jordan and Iraq for over five years (Human Rights Watch, 2006). In 2003, a royal decree granted 386 Palestinian refugees entry to al-Ruwayshed Camp in Jordan, but only those married to Jordanians were granted this temporary asylum with their families. However, their freedom, right to work and ability to leave the camp were restricted, forcing many to return to Iraq (Human Rights Watch, 2006).

The UNHCR statement below about the small number admitted to al-Ruwayshed Camp shows the gravity of the situation and the unwillingness of most states, save a few, to include Palestinian refugees from Iraq in resettlements plans for Iraqi refugees:

> UNHCR is grateful for a generous offer by the Government of Brazil to resettle an estimated 100 Palestinian refugees who formerly lived in Iraq. Most of the Palestinians have been living in Ruwayshed inside Jordan – 60 km from the Iraq border – for the past four years. There, they have faced extremely harsh conditions in a dusty and scorpion-infested desert camp with nowhere to go. In recent years UNHCR has repeatedly appealed for a humane solution for this group. Until this latest response from Brazil, only Canada and New Zealand – which took 54 and 22 Palestinians respectively in recent years – had come forward to help this desperate group.
>
> (UNHCR, 2007)

While the Brazilian resettlement plan included 100 Palestinian refugees from Iraq, most Palestinians preferred to stay in al-Ruwayshed than move to Brazil, a country with which they had no connection (Schiocchet, 2019). Schiocchet's article on the difficulties this group of Palestinians had integrating into Brazilian society confirms the fears of those who chose not to go (Schiocchet, 2019).

The case of Palestinian refugees from Iraq confirms that it is not only the international legal protection gap that leads to Palestinian exclusion from the UNHCR mandate and options available to other refugees (voluntary repatriation, assimilation and resettlement). Indeed, as this case shows, even when they qualify for international protection and fall under the UNHCR mandate, Palestinian refugees are still excluded and treated differently. In explaining Jordan's reasoning for Palestinian refugees from Syria receiving different treatment and the 2013 no-entry policy, officials used justifications similar to those used against Palestinian refugees from Iraq. For example, former Jordanian prime minister Abdullah Ensour, in an interview with *Al-Hayat* on 11 January 2013, described Jordan's ban on Palestinian refugees entering the country as follows:

> There are those who want to exempt Israel from the repercussions of displacing the Palestinians from their homes. Jordan is not a place to solve Israel's problems. Jordan has made a clear and explicit sovereign decision to not allow the crossing to Jordan by our Palestinian brothers who hold Syrian documents. Receiving those brothers is a red line because that would be a prelude to another wave of displacement, which is what the Israeli government wants. Our Palestinian brothers in Syria have the right to go back to their country of origin. They should stay in Syria until the end of the crisis.
>
> (JPC News, 2013)

Shaimaa, Aida's daughter who currently lives in Switzerland, explained the severe effects of this reasoning on Palestinians' lives. Shaimaa arrived to Jordan in winter of 2012 and, along with her husband and children, was detained in the Cyber City for five years. In 2017, she and her family were moved to the Gardens Camp for a few months before finally being granted asylum in Switzerland. She described her journey and experience on the Jordanian border as follows:

> We left Dera'a earlier than my family. We lived in an area called Dera'a Almatar, near Dera'a airport. My husband was involved in the revolution with his two brothers. After one of them was caught and the bombing of our area had become continuous, we decided to leave. We took a taxi to the point nearest the Jordanian border, then continued on foot. It was very cold and muddy, and we arrived at the border hungry, thirsty, and exhausted; we perhaps walked for 10 hours or more. My daughter was one month old, and I had not yet recovered from labour. I was 17 when I gave birth, so my body was not strong enough. There were many people, mostly Syrians but also some Palestinians. My husband and I were asked to go back to Syria. We were told Palestinians were not allowed to enter Jordan. We refused and stood at the entrance of the Jordanian border-crossing. After two hours, a

Jordanian army officer approached us and whispered to my husband, 'your wife is bleeding, her dress is covered with blood' and left. My husband looked at me and could not say a word, it was very embarrassing. I tried to hide the blood by throwing my jacket around my waist. Shortly after, the officer approached us again and said, 'Now, some officers will come and ask you to leave. Do not leave. Stay close and I will see what I can do.' We did what he said and refused to move. Some officers were very sympathetic with us, they did not push or try to force us to leave. After another two hours of waiting, the officer came back and took us to an office. There, we were offered water and another officer interrogated us for three hours. They asked about my father's release from the army and so many questions related to his move to Syria, which I did not have any information about. After that, we were taken to the Bashabsheh Camp near Ramtha.

Until 2012, as mentioned previously, Palestinians from Syria were dealt with on a case-by-case basis. As such, there were conditions – such as those of Shaimaa and her family – under which border officers would manoeuvre and try to help. However, since the 2013 no-entry policy was adopted, it has become even more difficult for Palestinians from Syria to enter Jordan. Those who crossed before 2013 without residency rights in Jordan, like Shaimaa, they were detained in the Cyber City for years, I discuss the Cyber City in further detail in the next chapter.

In our conversation, Shaimaa recalled when, during her stay in the Cyber City, one of the humanitarian organizations told her and her husband that their only option was to be resettled in Brazil. 'Some people accepted, but no one was moved to Brazil while I was there,' Shaimaa told me. Shaimaa was 'lucky', and her resettlement in Switzerland was set in motion by exceptional circumstances. As she explained, her family's resettlement was arranged after a group of European organizations, along with someone from the Swiss embassy, visited the Cyber City. The case of Shaimaa's family, two parents and three little kids living in one room with another family, separated only by a curtain, with no access to health or educational facilities, must have elicited the visitors' sympathies. Shaimaa's eldest daughter was one month old when she and her husband fled Syria, and her two sons were born in the Cyber City. As their resettlement was based on humanitarian grounds, due to being 'stateless', Shaimaa recalled the moment she saw the three Xs next to her nationality on the resettlement papers: it was 'devastating. The moment of joy, to finally have the hope to leave the drastic situation we had lived for five years, was ruined. My Palestinian pride was prompted, and I angrily told the case worker: "My home is not xxx. I am Palestinian". I discuss this issue in humanitarian response and practice at length in Chapter 3.

Rima, a Palestinian married to a Syrian man and former aid worker in Syria, further explained the strict nature of the no-entry policy, as she only managed to enter Jordan via smuggling:

> We stayed in Syria until mid-2014. We had no plans to leave but my husband's business was nearly ruined. That's when we decided to leave and come to Jordan. We arranged for everything: we got a car, paid a group of people to facilitate our trip, and my husband transferred his money to Jordan. The journey from Damascus to the Jordanian border, despite all the arrangements we made, was still not easy. We had to bribe the regime's soldiers and the militia groups several times so they would let us pass, but we were finally there. At the border, they asked for our passports and my husband presented his and my kids' Syrian passports and my Palestinian Syrian travel document. The officer asked me, 'Is this the only travel document you have?' When I answered 'yes', he looked at my husband and said: 'You and the kids can pass, but she has to return to Syria.' We tried to convince him, but it did not work. We decided that my husband would take the children and go to Amman and then we would figure out how I could join them, but my children grabbed my dress and started shouting. I could not leave them there, so the kids and I went back to Syria and my husband carried on to Amman. We had to pay a lot of money for me to enter the country and be with my husband again.

The border officer's position here was completely different from those in Shaimaa's narrative; here, the officer ordered a woman to experience a very dangerous situation on her own. She was treated as equal to a Palestinian man, her legal position as 'dependent' on her husband – under his guardianship – was not reason enough to grant her entry. Her Palestinian travel document was more important than both her life and the gender roles 'normally' advocated by the Jordanian state as part of its authentic Islamic culture, an issue I engage with in greater detail in the following chapters. The government's justification – represented in the former prime minister's statement and various other official statements – for its discriminatory practices against Palestinian refugee women clearly indicates the continuity of Jordan's politics from the 1970s and 1980s, which aimed to distinguish Jordan as an independent state, with one national identity, apart from that of Palestine. In Jordan's response and official statements, the invocation of concepts such as 'national interests', 'demographic threat', 'security threat' and Jordan's sovereign power also meant to locate Jordan's policies within a modern state narrative of nationalism. Such issues were directed at both allies and non-allies, who commonly make use of the same narrative; in this regard, Jordan appears not to be an exception, but rather following the international norms of national state power, sovereignty and security.

The other reason Jordan's officials cite as justification for its policies, i.e. the threat of contributing to another Palestinian displacement if Palestinians from Syria are allowed to enter, is nonsensical. These people are already displaced from Palestine; allowing them in Jordan would not alter their legal status as refugees. Furthermore, Ensour, in another interview, spoke more specifically about Jordan's treatment of Palestinians, emphasizing that the burden of hosting Palestinian refugees should be shared between Jordan, Lebanon and Syria (JPC News, 2013). For him, if Palestinians from Syria were to become permanently displaced in Jordan, then Jordan would be dealing with the question of Palestinian refugees almost entirely alone, unaided by neighbouring countries. Not only would this weaken Jordan's position in negotiating a solution for Palestinian refugees, but it also poses a threat to Jordan's demography and national identity. Nonetheless, in Jordan's negotiation of the 1994 Wadi-Arabeh peace agreement with Israel, there was no mention of refugees in Jordan, the justification being that the refugee question was too big to be dealt with solely by Jordan. This statement reflected both the tension between Jordan and its neighbours and, particularly, its discontent with the PLO's lack of coordination and consultation both before and after the 1993 Oslo Accords, which Jordan saw as further marginalization of its position and the regional and international leadership role it had historically played in the question of Palestine. The 1993 Oslo Accords also relegated the issue of refugees to a sub-clause (Hollis, 2000), left unresolved and marginalized by Israeli-PLO bilateral negotiations. The refugees, the discussion of whom was a PLO and Jordanian precondition to opening negotiations, were left out of the two bilateral negotiations. Moreover, the issues mentioned in the prime minister's statements do not apply to all Palestinian refugees in Jordan equally, as it solely addressed those from Syria and those holding Jordanian Palestinian travel documents, like Gaza refugees. Indeed, the number of those addressed by the prime minister's statement is insignificant when compared to the number of Palestinians naturalized as Jordanian in 1949–1950s and their decedents, who continue to carry Jordanian passports. Hence, some questions addressed in the literature, such as what has changed in Jordan's policy, can be misleading.

Conclusion – Continuation of politics suppressing Palestinian identity

This chapter was not concerned with what happened to Palestinians in 1948, but instead how do we make sense of the political relevance of 1948 in Jordan's treatment of Palestinian refugees from Syria. Thus, this chapter sought to answer the question: how does the epistemic violence of settler colonialism appear in the action patterns and policies closely associated with Jordan's colonial legacy and how do these patterns continue to reproduce the dynamics of epistemic violence through Jordan's multiple-categorization of Palestinians? In trying to understand the politics behind Jordan's 2013 no-entry policy, I followed – through Palestinian refugee women's narratives – a timeline of historical events from before and after the 1948 Nakba that shaped Jordan's politics and led to this policy. By concealing their presence, forcing their disappearance, and silencing their voices, the 2013 policy further marginalized Palestinian refugees from Syria. As a consequence, this policy is not only integral to Jordan's politics of survival and search for legitimacy, but is also a continuation of politics aiming at suppressing Palestinian identity.

For the last seventy-four years, such politics have created sub-groups among Palestinian refugees in Jordan: Jordanians of Palestinian origin, citizen-refugees originally displaced to Jordan in 1948; West Bank temporary citizens of 1967; temporary refugees from Gaza with temporary passports; and illegal, invisible Palestinian refugees displaced from Syria. In Chapter 3, I show how Palestinians attempted to supersede such categorization and forced disappearance through choosing to hide in Palestinian camps, using kinship and marriage relationships to remain connected to a collective group, and how this in turn has created more sub-categories. In the coming chapters, I also discuss the gendered implications of both old and new categories of Palestinians in Jordan. However, in this chapter, while the gendered effects of multiple-categorization are clearly present in Jordan's nationality law and border-crossing practices, I simply highlighted – through women's stories – its long-lasting politics of multiple-categorization as both gendered and Othering processes. This analysis paved the path for an exploration of how Jordan's policies and politics not only denied Palestinian refugees entry and the right to escape death, but also, as is shown in Chapter 2, how that – along with the politics of aid and refugee/asylum governance – informed humanitarian aid and practice.

The brief history of the connection between the establishment of the settler colonial project in Palestine and the Jordanian state discussed here was not an in-depth engagement with the history, as it was used more to show their relation and mutual interest in concealing Palestinian identity; an interest that largely springs from a deep, cumulative and continued thirst for legitimacy that both entities demand from Palestinians. In different historical moments, the longing to validate both projects as legitimate states with sovereign powers at the expense of Palestinians took different forms, as the chapter demonstrated. However, throughout the history of both projects, the Nakba has been a juncture-point that connects them, as both regimes remained concerned about the development of Palestinian identity in that such bears witness to the colonial legacy of their historical creation. However, as I show in Chapter 3, the suppression of Palestinian identity by forcing the disappearance of Palestinian refugees does nothing but recharge the Palestinian sense of belonging – 'knowing thyself as a product of the historical process' (Gramsci, 1971) – connected to their first displacement, even if they might not have experienced that displacement first-hand. Subsequently, the epistemic violence of the settler colonial presence apparent in Jordan's multiple-categorization and discriminatory practices is far from reaching its end pertaining to Palestinian sense of belonging.

3

Governance of refugees: Life-long precarity and anti-Palestinian policies

UNRWA estimates that of the 20,000 Palestinian refugees from Syria in Jordan, 10 per cent are residing illegally (UNRWA, 2022a). To register with UNRWA, Palestinian refugees from Syria must show documentation proving their eligibility for UNRWA services. However, some Palestinians I met said they had to get rid of their UNRWA card and anything else showing they were Palestinian in order to enter Jordan using fake Syrian identities. Such are not registered or included in UNRWA data. As Jawad, a director of an UNRWA emergency centre, told me: 'due to entering illegally, there are many not registered with UNRWA. There are undocumented marriages; kids born under these conditions have no birth certificate. This is a huge challenge for us as UNRWA workers'. Jawad also shared a case he was dealing with at the time of our interview in 2019. He narrated the story as follows:

> A man and his family were smuggled into Jordan at the end of 2012. They lived illegally for three years before the man was caught by the police and deported back to Syria (*Qadhef* [hurl] is the word refugees and the director used for deportation to Syria). His wife and four children remained in Jordan illegally. Later on, the man managed to reach Europe through the deadly boats. After he was deported, it took two years for him to apply for family reunion. To do this, we had to first document the marriage and then get the children's birth certificates. This took a long time and can only be done informally, via personal efforts and connections, not UNRWA services. When all of this was done, he applied for family reunion. But, we just discovered yesterday, there is a 25,000 JOD fine for his wife and kids' illegal residence that has to be paid before they can travel. UNRWA cannot pay this, nor can it intervene in these cases; this is not part of its mandate.

In these cases, we try to find informal ways and independent legal firms
or organizations that provide legal aid, but it is still not easy, as legal aid
for refugees is mostly governed by UNHCR rules. The legal protection of
Palestinian refugees or facilitation of resettlement arrangements – in the
rare case it happens – is not part of the UNRWA mandate, or any other
agency for that matter. For us, the main problem is how to support those
not registered with UNRWA and not eligible for UNHCR – or any other
organization – protection; they live in limbo.

Jawad further explained the UNRWA services and emergency plans available,
which included emergency food and cash assistance, protection and
psychosocial support to vulnerable refugees. He also confirmed that women
in Jordan illegally, even if registered with UNRWA, cannot seek help from
organizations providing protection for women exposed to GBV. In such cases,
UNRWA officers listen and try to give women social and psychological advice.

In the previous chapter, I examined the changing politics of the categorization
of Palestinians in Jordan. Through analysing the multiple-categorization of
Palestinians and the political moments through which the creation of each
category emerged, this analysis aimed to explain Jordan's 2013 no-entry
policy for Palestinian refugees from Syria. The significance of identification
categories in humanitarian practice is the focus of this chapter, as it examines
how humanitarianism that seeks to provide assistance to those in need and
alleviate suffering not only does the opposite, but has also – by aligning itself
with both state nationalism and settler colonialism – helped to create the
conditions under which settler colonial epistemic violence is prolonged and
linked to practices of structural and gender-based violence.

Here, I use Gayatri Spivak's 'epistemic violence' to assess the humanitarian
response to Palestinian refugees, as compared to refugees from Syria in
Jordan, and examine how power politics work in dismissing Palestinians'
'provincial knowledge' as a silenced and marginalized group. This silencing
and marginalization of Palestinian knowledge led to the emergence of
anti-Palestinianism, which is conceptualized in this book as the denial of
the Nakba as a juncture-point in history, where a new moral order denying
Palestinians the right to self-determination signifies a new colonizer–
colonized relationship. Here, the continuity of the order created in 1948 is
examined in relation to humanitarian practice in the response to refugees

from Syria in Jordan to show how the politics of the 1948-juncture underlines humanitarianism's current acts of exclusion. The chapter looks at both elements of epistemic violence: silencing and inflicting harm. Palestinian refugee women from Syria's voices are silenced through the creation of the 'UNRWA refugee' category and the use of 'displaced population' language in reporting mechanisms. The harm inflicted on Palestinian refugee women is discussed in terms of actual, material and epistemological harm. The exclusion of Palestinian women from services available to Syrian and Jordanian women have exposed them to various forms of structural and GBV, both linked to the denial of Palestinians' existence in the response to refugees from Syria. This chapter links gender and UN and international agencies' humanitarian approaches that – by adopting a feminist universality-based analysis of GBV within the Syrian refugee crisis – define gender and GBV in terms of cultural and social norms. As such, these approaches actively aid in perpetuating structural violence against women and the settler colonial epistemic violence of anti-Palestinianism.

Nonetheless, while this chapter acknowledges the significance of issues raised in the literature, it is beyond its scope to engage with the broader humanitarian response to Syrian refugees in Jordan, and thus largely focuses on the case of Palestinian refugees within that response. In the first section of this chapter, I examine the response of humanitarian organizations and the representation of Palestinian refugees within this response in relation to the question of Palestine in general terms and the creation of the 'UNRWA refugee' category specifically. The section provides the foundation for the analytical analysis of the succeeding sections. In the second section, I focus on the actions of humanitarian organizations; actions such as excluding Palestinian refugees from assistance, silencing women's voices in reports and normalizing Palestinian refugees as a 'displaced population'. Such are seen here as acts of settler colonial epistemic violence. This analysis helps to demonstrate how settler colonialism works through the actions, regulations and strategies of international aid organizations, particularly UNHCR regulations, which have become the 'example' informing humanitarian practices around Palestinian refugees. Further, the analysis here also points to how the settler colonial epistemic violence of organizations effectively contributes to the precarity of Palestinian refugee women from Syria's lives, arguing that the epistemic violence of settler colonialism as a framework of analysis underscores Palestinians' protracted, extended and multiple displacements and exclusions. This understanding should be coupled with any analysis of GBV and gender issues in the case of Palestinian refugee women; an analysis specifically absent when referencing Palestinians' multiple displacements. Throughout this chapter, I shed light on the attempts and challenges of local women's groups and frontline workers when trying to fill services gaps created by the exclusion of Palestinian refugee women from the response.

Through interviews with Palestinian refugee women from Syria residing in Palestinian camps in Jordan, women activists in these camps, UN representatives, aid and international development organizations and informal conversations with representatives of women's organizations, this chapter offers an analysis of how humanitarian subjects are prioritized through categorization and formal and informal conditions placed by international donors on local women's organizations to implement a selective approach in assisting and empowering refugee women in Jordan. The chapter also shows how everyday activities of humanitarian, aid and gender empowerment programmes make it necessary, if not imperative, to analyse humanitarian practice within the framework of settler colonial epistemic violence.

As mentioned above, this chapter does not provide an in-depth profile or analysis of the critique of the humanitarian response to the crisis in Syria and its failure to protect Syrian refugees. This issue is examined both in general terms and in Jordan in various literature (Cohen, 2013; Achilli, 2015; Alhayek, 2016; Culbertson *et al.*, 2016; Ferris and Kirisci, 2016; Tobin, 2016; Kattaa and Byrne, 2018; Martin *et al.*, 2019; Tsourapas, 2019; Shanneik, 2021). This chapter also does not conduct a specific analysis of the situation of the Palestinian refugees in relation to international resolutions, conventions and mandates, whether related to Palestinian refugees or refugees in general; such is addressed by the various literature I reference throughout the chapter. Instead, this chapter simply seeks to provide a baseline of analysis for assessing the significance of the 1948 Nakba as a juncture-point in the history-making of global refugee governance and its epistemic, material and actual impacts on the case of Palestinian refugee women from Syria in Jordan.

Palestinian refugees as a differentiated category in humanitarian practice

'As a Palestine refugee, you are already born with a tag that says "displaced",' said UNRWA Commissioner-General Philippe Lazzarini. 'If you are a Palestine refugee in Syria, then you are at least doubly displaced and most likely living in extreme hardship' (UNRWA, 2021). Statements like the above are familiar in their description of Palestinian refugees as a 'displaced population', without reference to the context, politics, or forces that continue to deny Palestinian refugees the right of return or the protection of the international community. When mentioned by UNRWA representatives, or other agencies on rare occasions, no reference is made to the forces responsible for Palestinians' forced displacement. This is unlike the case for Syrian refugees, as the Syrian regime – whether rightly or not – is commonly held responsible for the crisis.

This selective approach to neutrality, apoliticism and impartiality in some cases but not others has been addressed by a wide range of literature, albeit derivatively, in relation to humanitarian practice (Loescher, 2001; Barnett, 2005, 2009; Beardsley and Schmidt, 2012; Sliwinski, 2020). Further, the shift in humanitarian practice has also been criticized for its incorporation of politics in adapting to the environment in which it operates (Loescher, 2001; Ayoob, 2004; Mills, 2005; Barnett, 2009; Ticktin, 2014; Hanafi, 2020), despite the fact that 'humanitarian actors have held that humanitarianism and politics are separate endeavors, have asserted that their ability to relieve suffering is dependent on being viewed as outside of politics, and have labored to keep humanitarianism and politics apart' (Barnett, 2009, p. 623). In this vein, a wide range of literature from various contexts demonstrates that humanitarian action has increasingly become a manifestation of the international order and politics of time (Ayoob, 2004; Mills, 2005; Barnett, 2009; Ticktin, 2014). In the context of this research, I argue that the exclusion of Palestinian refugees from Syria from the actions of humanitarian organizations and the Jordanian state have corresponded with one another. Rather than humanitarian practice adapting itself to the context in which it works, it has instead, since inception, maintained and perpetuated the world order established at the 1948

Nakba juncture-point. This is not a coincidence, as such coincided with the emergence of humanitarianism in the post-Second World War era, but also the humanitarian response built its policies around Palestine based on the pre-Nakba, British colonial history.

In July 1922, the League of Nations approved the Balfour Promise in the British Mandate of Palestine (Adelman, 2001; JAD, 2007; Miller, 2010), which stipulated the 'establishment in Palestine of a National Home for the Jewish people' (cited from Adelman, 2001, p. 10). The League of Nations' approval of the Promise, as Qustantain Zurayk noted in *The Meaning of Nakba* (1948), was the international community's first betrayal of its own principles, as the League's mandate pertained to people's right to self-determination. The United Nations' 1947 Partition Plan of Palestine was, for Zurayk, the second important indicator of the birth of the new international moral order. The Plan not only endorsed the Balfour Promise but also gave the indigenous people – the majority at the time – less than half the land they already owned. This meant not only the acceptance of Palestinian displacement from the land 'gifted' to European Jewish immigrants, but also the UN's active role in legitimizing Palestinians' forced displacement.

Various mechanisms, notably the 1950 Statute of the United Nations High Commission for Refugees and the 1951 Refugee Convention, aided in the development of an institutional humanitarian response and international regime of refugee protection. During the drafting of both the UNHCR Statute and 1951 Convention, the situation in Palestinian was discussed extensively (Akram, 2002, p. 40). Indeed, Palestinians were the only refugee population to be mentioned/singled out in both documents (Akram, 2002, p. 40). From the onset, the UNHCR's primary duty has always been to provide legal protection for refugees in compensation for their loss of national legal rights (Jacques-da-Silva, 1966). However, such was not applied equally to all refugees, as Palestinians were explicitly excluded based on their status as a category differentiated from those 'of concern' to UNHCR.

In Arendt's chapter on refugees, she theorizes refugees as people who experience three types of loss – of home, of government, and of human rights – and looks at how this trifecta of loss places refugees as exceptions to the norm, even though mainly recognized as displaced populations:

The term stateless at least acknowledged the fact that these persons had lost the protection of their government and required international agreement to safeguard their legal rights. The postwar term 'displaced persons' was invented during the war for the express purpose of liquidating statelessness once and for all by ignoring its existence. Nonrecognition of statelessness always means repatriation, i.e., deportation to country of origin.

(Arendt, 1951, p. 365)

Exceptionalizing Palestinians from the norm as a 'displaced population' and the politics of Palestine's pre-Nakba colonial history can clearly be seen in the UNHCR's yearly Global Trends Reports. In these reports, Palestinians are not noted as a population with one of the greatest numbers of refugees globally. Instead, the reports present Palestinian refugees in a category apart from other refugees, under the term 'UNRWA refugees', and estimate their number at 5.7 million (Trends, 2020). As discussed in Chapter 1, however, this number still does not reflect the correct figure, as the data has been affected by the classification of Palestinians under various categories and dependence on UNRWA's definition of a Palestinian refugee. The reports also highlight Jordan as third in the world in its refugee–citizen ratio. But, aside from these two pieces of information, the reports mention nothing else about Palestinian refugees in general or Palestinian refugees in Jordan. Further, while the country from which both Syrian and Palestinian refugees have been displaced is the same, the annual reports – which, since 2013, have counted Syria as an origin country from which one of the highest number of refugees (4.9 million) have fled – fail to present data on Palestinian refugees' displacement from Syria.

The significance of the UNHCR's annual reporting is its centrality in disseminating information about developments pertaining to displacement and, hence, its influence on decision-making processes around aid assistance, durable solutions, shelter and accommodation distributions (Krause, 2022). However, such processes are largely conducted via selective and vague approaches related to numbers and figures; an issue critically addressed in various regions (Marlowe and Elliott, 2014; Tappis *et al.*, 2021; Krause, 2022; Palattiyil *et al.*, 2022). Krause explores the quantification of refugee accommodation in eighteen Global Trends Reports, arguing that 'the way in which quantifications subsume the dynamic social surroundings of so many people worldwide in some numbers, disregarding their experiences, histories, practices, mobilities, and wishes, and leading the reader to believe that authorities are omniscient and in control' (2022, p. 149). For Krause, the vital question is how do 'quantifications produce (non)knowledge and link with the humanitarian landscape?' (2022, p. 141). She argues that vague language, undefined accommodation and unclear calculations led to gaps in reports. Despite the fact that reports display knowledge about refugees locations and whereabouts, this is really, as she conceives, a form of non-knowledge production (Krause, 2022). Freier (2022) addresses the second issue in the Global Trends Reports, the 'power of categorization', arguing that the creation of 'Venezuelans displaced abroad' as a special category led to treating Venezuelans as migrants rather than refugees, with real repercussions on policymaking, state recognition of their refuge-ness and their inability to self-identify as refugees.

Both the quantification of refugees and power of categorization issues apply to the situation of Palestinian refugees in these annual reports, in addition to the inclusion of Palestinian refugee numbers without any analysis or attention, thereby normalizing Palestinian displacement. Palestinians are given an epistemological representation that both acknowledges and denies their existence at the same time. Indeed, despite acknowledging 5.7 million Palestinian refugees, the presentation of this number as a category differentiated from other groups implies no action needs to be taken, as it is enough to categorize Palestinians as 'UNRWA refugees'. This is also despite the fact that UNRWA has no protection or legal mandate, an issue I will come to shortly, but the one-line statement about Palestinians being under UNRWA's mandate fails to say this and even makes it sound as if UNRWA offers the same protection and solutions as the UNHCR, which is both misleading and naturalizing of Palestinian displacement.

In the same vein, On 17 December 2018, the United Nations General Assembly adopted the Global Compact on Refugees (GCRs): a 'framework for more predictable and equitable responsibility-sharing, recognizing that a sustainable solution to refugee situations cannot be achieved without international cooperation'. The framework affirms its most important guiding principle is that it 'is entirely non-political in nature, including in its implementation, and is in line with the purposes and principles of the Charter of the United Nations'. Nonetheless, in the 2021 GCRs report, the one-line statement of 5.7 million Palestinian refugees under the UNRWA mandate is mentioned only once (UNHCR, 2021). In discussing the protracted refugee situation, the report affirms: 'Based on UNHCR's definition of a protracted refugee situation, where 25,000 or more refugees from the same nationality have been in exile for at least five consecutive years in a given host country, it is estimated that some 15.7 million refugees (76%) were in a protracted situation at the end of 2020' (UNHCR, 2021, p. 21). In a footnote, it states 'excluding Palestinian refugees', although the report gives no reason for this exclusion. Indeed, it is the GCRs' grounding 'in the international refugee protection regime, centred on the cardinal principle of non-refoulement, and at the core of which is the 1951 Convention and its 1967 Protocol' that is the reason the longest protracted refugee situation is excluded (UNHCR, 2021). The 1951 Convention has long been understood to apply neither to refugees who benefit from the protection or assistance of a UN agency other than UNHCR – such as refugees from Palestine, who 'fall under the auspices of the United Nations Relief and Works Agency for Palestine Refugees in the Near East (UNRWA)' – nor to refugees who have a status equivalent to nationals in their country of asylum. As previously mentioned, UNRWA has no legal or protection mandate, and its relief mandate is woefully disassociated from the idea of repatriation or legal protection. Hence, by continuing to place Palestinians under a different category, despite the fact that UNRWA cannot fill the protection gap, humanitarian organizations see relief and humanitarian assistance as the only rights Palestinian refugees have access to at the international level. Thus, since there is no international agency dedicated to finding a sustainable solution for them, Palestinians are left in a particular legal predicament and protection gap (Akram, 2002; El-Abed, 2009; Tareh, 2020).

On the other hand, Palestinians' right of return – thoroughly examined in works such as Mallison and Mallison (1980), Khalidi (1992), Akram (2002), Al-Hardan (2012), Shalhoub-Kevorkian and Ihmoud (2014), and Siklawi (2019) – is perceived as a political right, which must be dealt with through political negotiations and the so-called peace process, and hence fall outside humanitarian response. Nonetheless, the right of return is only stipulated in non-binding resolutions. Despite the UNHCR's affirmation that it is bound by both binding and non-binding UN resolutions, on Palestinians' right of return the UNHCR is exempt from these commitments. In addition, the right of return is also drafted in vague language and a manner intended to skew the origin of the question of Palestinian refugees. For example, United Nations General Assembly Resolution 194 (Dec. 1948), paragraph 11, stipulates: 'refugees wishing to return to their homes and live at peace with their neighbours should be permitted to do so' (United Nations, 1948). There are no other UN documents that place conditions on the right of refugees to return to their homes. This statement, and the entire resolution in fact, never overtly points to 'Israel's' responsibility for Palestinian displacement and obligation to allow the return of refugees, instead emphasizing living 'at peace with their neighbours' as a condition for refugee return. The burden of return is placed on Palestinians, conditioned on their willingness to live in peace with their neighbours. Such language constructs a new history, where the 1948 Palestinian Nakba is denied and replaced with the language of a conflict between two peoples, two neighbours. This stipulation, which still holds weight in the UN narrative of two peoples competing over land, is politically determined because, as Said posits, Zionism was able to accomplish this aim and gain international support through the natives' 'excluding presence' in its narrative. Hence, this exclusion and language is crucial to the epistemic violence of settler colonialism.

Moreover, there are different conceptualizations and understandings of the right of return for Palestinians displaced in 1948 and those displaced in 1967, after the occupation of the remaining parts of Palestine. For example, United Nations General Assembly Resolution 3089 C affords different statuses to 1967 refugees, those expelled from the Gaza Strip, and those who experienced double displacement in both 1948 and 1967. This resolution recognizes and affirms the right of return for those first displaced in 1967, but not for those first displaced in 1948. For the double displaced, the resolution calls only for their return to refugee camps, not their homeland: 'the right of the displaced inhabitants, including those displaced as a result of recent hostilities, to return to their homes and camps' (Mallison and Mallison, 1980, p. 130). Unlike Resolution 194, which does not indicate Zionist Haganah's (the Zionist Military Organization) role in the displacement of Palestinians, Resolution 3089 C demands 'the Government of Israel to take effective and immediate steps for the return without delay of those inhabitants who had been displaced since the outbreak of hostilities in June 1967'. The main distinction between these two resolutions is that Israel is considered an occupation authority with regard to 1967 refugees, but not 1948 refugees, hence its responsibility for both the displacement and return of 1948 refugees is ambiguously stated.

Without any enforceable UN resolutions or protection mechanisms, the 'displaced population' language in UN reports naturalizes the perception that there is no solution for Palestinians, as repatriation or voluntary return to their country of origin is not possible, or too 'complex', resonating with the core narrative of the settler colonial project in Palestine. In addition, limiting UNRWA's assistance to only meeting their basic needs – 'food, clothing, and shelter – but none of the protections for a wide range of human rights and fundamental freedoms that were to be guaranteed by the 1951 Refugee Convention and UNHCR' (Akram, 2002), leads to Palestinians, as non-nationals, being denied both asylum – the internationally recognized right of any refugee – and the legal protection that comes with it. This has crucial implications for the idea of return as, if the right to asylum is granted based on Palestinianism, this would entail repatriation, integration or resettlement and such is in opposition to the interests of the state established on Palestinian lands, the state that denies their existence.

The logic of categories in responding and reporting GBV

In an interview with a representative of an international organization that provides aid and assistance to Syrian refugee women survivors of GBV in Jordan, I shared Shaimaa and other women's stories and asked whether their organization's programmes assist Palestinian refugee women displaced from Syria. 'There are not many of them in Jordan,' she replied, 'how many are you talking about? There are maybe a few families, perhaps a hundred or so?' Her response revealed her complete lack of awareness of the issue, so I followed up: 'Based on UNRWA's statistics, there are around 17,000 Palestinians who fled from Syria to Jordan.' She responded:

> Well, I am certainly not aware that there are thousands, but if they are residing legally in Jordan, then they will be treated equally to Syrian refugees.

You know, we are bound by the government's policies and cannot offer assistance to those who are undocumented or enter the country illegally. My understanding that those in the Cyber City Camp illegally entered Jordan.

Akin to other contexts (e.g. Lautze and Raven-Roberts, 2006), this conversation confirmed aid and development organizations' obsession with numbers and figures; the quantification of human suffering, which is only prioritized when it occurs on large scale and denotes a crisis (Malkki, 2005). Additionally, the statement makes clear that the response of such organizations is heavily reliant on state politics that define who deserves help and who is an undesirable refugee. Operating in line with state politics is a complicit and deliberate choice to tolerate its politics of exclusion. Aid organizations' acceptance of such state policies not only impacts the assistance undocumented groups receive but also contributes to further hiding their predicament and impinging their right to narrate their own stories.

Jordan's humanitarian response is coordinated by the UNHCR and applied through what is called 'the Inter Sector Working Group (ISWG)', which is chaired by the UNHCR. There are eight sub-sectors of the response divided into working and sub-working groups, which are chaired and co-chaired by the UNHCR and other partners providing information, advice and advocacy to high-level decision-making bodies in Jordan. The UNHCR's work in Jordan is managed through the 1998 Memorandum of Understanding (MoU) signed between the UNHCR and Jordanian government. The MoU underscores Jordan and UNHCR collaboration around refugee policy for non-Palestinian refugees (Cohen, 2013; Baylouny, 2020). Palestinians' exclusion from the MoU is based on the deliberate misinterpretation of articles in the UNHCR Statute and 1951 Convention, previously mentioned, that exclude refugees covered by other UN agencies and specifically single-out Palestinians. Although the 1951 Convention and UNHCR mandate were updated in the 1960s and 1970s to fill gaps around the definition of refugee, gender issues and other areas (Dumper, 2009), the gap in Palestinian refugee protection has never been revisited. The displacement of Palestinian refugees from Syria should be addressed on different grounds, particularly as UNRWA does not have the mandate to deal with the protection issues resulting from either the first or second displacement. While UN agencies and INGOs apply a universal approach to the 'Syrian refugee crisis', they have excluded Palestinian from this approach. Hence, current UNHCR policies continue to reflect the logic and politics created by the 1948 Nakba juncture-point. In Jordan, as a leader of the response, UNHCR policies govern and are also applied to other UN agencies and international organizations' work and policies. As I show in this section, not only are policies related to durable solutions (repatriation, integration and resettlement) applied, but also the UNHCR mandate that excludes Palestinians is applied to programmes related to women's empowerment, cash and medical assistance and GBV protection.

One of the eight sectors of the response is the Gender-Based Violence Sub-Sector, co-chaired by the UNHCR and the United Nations Fund for Population Agency (UNFPA), with the International Organization for Migration (IOM), other INGOS and Jordanian governmental, royal and non-governmental organizations taking part in the sub-working group. The response includes programmes around gender empowerment and the elimination of gender-based discrimination and violence against refugee women, along with cash assistance to GBV survivors and medical and mental health support. Whilst representatives of UN and donor organizations insisted they do not distinguish between women based on nationality or refugee status in cases of GBV, Samira, a Palestinian woman working in a small women's organization, shared her frustration at how local aid workers are meant to distinguish between refugees and distribute aid based on nationality.

> We are supposed to include Jordanians and Syrians in our programmes. Of course, all Jordanians in the area we serve are Palestinians, but the idea here is that we should make sure those who benefit from our programmes are either Jordanian citizens or Syrian refugees .... I know many Syrian refugees in the area are not Syrians; they are Palestinians from Syria, but they claim to be Syrian to receive aid and access services. Whenever we can, we simply do not ask the nationality or refugee status question.

However, there are cases when Samira's organization cannot but ask about a person's nationality or refugee status, mostly in UNHCR-funded projects or when funds are specified only for Syrian refugees. As Samira said, 'We have to ask for either a nationality number or refugee document if the programme targets both Jordanians and Syrians. We are obliged to send a list of programme and aid beneficiaries with a copy of an official document that shows their eligibility to receive aid.'

At one of women's community centres, via the case of Abeer, I had first-hand experience of what Samira described. Abeer is a thirty-eight-year-old Palestinian refugee woman from Syria who carries a two-year Jordanian temporary passport for Gazan refugees. She is married to a Palestinian refugee from Syria and had lived in Syria for ten years before the revolution. She met her husband through family friends when he was visiting Jordan, and moved with him to Syria after marriage. Abeer and her husband left Syria in late 2011. When I met her, Abeer was visiting the centre to ask after her application to a medical assistance fund the centre was implementing on behalf of the IOM. In that visit, Abeer received the news that she was not eligible for medical assistance. She had made the application to help with her thirteen-year-old daughter's medical expenses, who suffered from chronic anaemia. Abeer also has three other children, two with physical disabilities, and her husband suffers from a range of medical issues and cannot work. With four children, one with a chronic disease and two with disabilities, Abeer's ability to work is minimal, but she does some cleaning from time to time. As she explained: 'With my husband and children's conditions, we thought moving to Jordan would make it easier to access health services, as things were hardening on us in Syria.'

But Abeer did not hold a Jordanian passport with a national number, and her daughter was a Palestinian refugee from Syria not a Syrian refugee, this is why her application was rejected. The programme to which she applied aimed to equally support Jordanian and Syrian refugee women, but Abeer did not belong to either of these categories. Still, however, some of the centre's workers accepted to send her application to the IOM, as they were fully aware of the direness of her situation. The IOM's final decision read: 'We need either a refugee status or a national identity number to approve any application.' When discussing Abeer's rejection, staff at the centre realized that a case like Abeer's should never have been submitted for assessment in the first place; the project's eligibility criteria were clear, so this refusal was the centre's responsibility. The project officer, Arwa, the staff member who had sent Abeer's application, felt guilty to have given Abeer false hope. 'I thought since you were displaced from Syria, you would still be eligible,' she told Abeer, while apologising for putting her in this position. Arwa, a young woman in her early twenties, took responsibility for what happened, coupled with a sense of guilt.

I spoke with Abeer for an hour. She shared her story and how the difficult economic conditions placed her in a vulnerable situation. She was particularly frustrated by her family, neighbours and charity representatives treating her as an inferior because of her financial situation: 'Everyone claims control over my decisions, family member or not. When people provide you with financial support, they think you need support in everything else, basically they treat me as a minor or somebody who lacks rationale.' Abeer was discontented with everything and everyone around her, including her parents, siblings and husband: 'Everyone demands something from you. I spend my days knocking on doors to either find assistance or a decent, flexible job. Yet, I am always made to feel guilty. People, including members of my family, always say: "there must be something you can do". But when I ask, "what would you suggest?", nobody answers.' Still, Abeer was very appreciative of the support she received from the women's centre in the camp and the role it played in her life, which I explain in the next section.

As she explained, Abeer's lack of basic support exposed her to various forms of abuse and exploitation. In Chapter 4, I share Abeer's story in further detail, but here, her story shows how UN-agency practices contradict core principles of gender equality and the human rights-based framework. The IOM, for example, stipulates in its Institutional Framework for Addressing GBV in Crisis that its '30 missions are developing a contextualized mission-wide action plan to address gender-based violence' (IOM, 2018). It is unclear what contextualized mission means or whether it includes an analysis of politics, economics and other issues that intersect with gender. From the framework's definition of GBV, however, it is evident that context-specific considerations are limited to cultural practices, where the understanding of GBV is 'an effort to acknowledge that such violence is primarily rooted in gender inequality, and perpetuated by patriarchal law institutions, heteronormative cultures and harmful social norms'. The framework emphasizes that GBV should not be considered as an ad hoc or isolated act, but rather a continuum of violence, and its understanding of a GBV continuum is in reference to 'the effects of discriminatory, gendered stereotypes, expectations and behaviours grounded in gender inequality primarily affecting women and girls. However, they can also result in violence being perpetrated against other categories of individuals, due to their sexual orientation, gender identity, gender expression or sex characteristics.' Addressing GBV as a continuum, discussed in greater detail in Chapter 5, should not be limited to gender issues as inseparable from power and politics. Cockburn (2004) offered an understanding of the GBV continuum in war and conflict by linking household and battlefield violence to gender power 'seen to shape the dynamics of every site of human interaction, from the household to the international arena'. The emphasis put on gender identities, expectations and culture in the framework means that structural issues related to and directly intersecting with gender – such as class, nationality, refugee status and in the case of this research, Palestinianism – have not been acknowledged in defining root-causes of GBV, even though addressing these root-causes is one of the framework's main objectives.

Although the framework defines GBV interventions as 'activities that can remedy, mitigate, or avert direct loss of life, physical or psychological harm and threats to a person's dignity and well-being', it does not acknowledge threats and harm inflicted on those excluded from its programmes and assistance. The framework's key objective 'is to ensure that the safety, dignity and well-being of all crisis-affected persons, especially women and girls, and their equitable access to services are prioritized, integrated and coordinated across all IOM crisis operations'. It is not clear what the framework means by 'equitable access', who should be equal and to whom? Still, if practices such as those experienced by Abeer exist, equality in access here only means in relation to the criteria set for assistance eligibility; criteria that are first and foremost defined by the politics and new (im)moral order created in the aftermath of the 1948 Nakba juncture-point.

In terms of the denial of services based on nationality and refugee status, Abeer's case was not exceptional; in Chapters 4 and 5, I discuss other cases related to GBV, medical assistance, and food and other aid distribution. Some such distributions were associated with awareness-raising campaigns related to GBV and women's empowerment. In Chapter 4, I discuss the case of Samar, a Syrian refugee woman married to a Palestinian refugee man. Samar shared an experience of attending a lecture on GBV by an organization funded by an INGO contracted by the UNHCR to distribute food packages to Syrian refugee women and their families. In Samar's case, she was only eligible for a single package, not a family package, as her Palestinian husband and children were ineligible. Commenting on this practice, Samar asked: 'What do they think? Would I consume food on my own and leave my children and husband starving? Nonsense.' Indeed, this practice makes even less sense if one considers UN-agency critiques of gender inequality in Jordan, which often relate to inequality in the country's constitution and legal framework. Yet, this practice shows that UN aid and food distribution stems from the same rationale: that men are head of the family and, thus, Syrian women married to Palestinians have no responsibility for their families.

Other agency practices of silencing Palestinian refugee women's voices in general, and Palestinians from Syria specifically, can be found in UNFPA reporting on GBV trends and activities related to the humanitarian response to Syrian refugees (UNFPA, 2019). The UNFPA chairs the national reproductive health sub-working group, and co-chairs the national GBV sub-working group. In the UNFPA's GBV response, the agency states clearly that its programmes assist 'GBV survivors and women at risk of GBV – including Jordanians, Syrian refugees and refugees of other nationalities – within the framework of GBV case management' (UNFPA, 2021a). While no exclusions are mentioned in relation to nationality, a recognized refugee status is determined by the UNHCR's definition and categorization of refugees mentioned in the Guidelines for Case Management. In various UNFPA reporting on its GBV-related programming, the agency only acknowledges the existence of Syrian refugees in Jordan and, although it underscores that Jordan is a country that hosts one of the greatest number of refugees, it – like GCR and UNHCR annual trends reports – does not clarify this figure:

> As of 2020, Jordan is host to more than 1.35 million Syrian refugees (most of whom reside outside of camps) in addition to other vulnerable populations that are dependent upon humanitarian assistance to meet basic daily needs. Jordan has the second highest share of refugees per capita in the world with 10% of its population being refugees.

In providing further information on refugee populations in Jordan, the UNFPA's 2021 GBV Trends Report states:

> In Jordan, close to 80.5% of registered refugees live outside the camps, primarily concentrated in urban and rural areas in the northern governorates

of Jordan, with lesser population in the southern governorates. The remaining Syrian refugees live in camps, mainly in Zaatari Camp (± 80,708), Azraq Camp (± 43,936) and the Emirati Jordanian Camp (±6,667). Jordan also hosts refugee populations from other countries. The total number of Yemenis registered with UNHCR is 12,777. They are to be added to the multiple other refugee populations that Jordan hosts, including 66,362 Iraqis, and more than 7,972 from Sudan, Somalia, and other countries.

The statement 'Jordan also hosts refugee populations from other countries' does not implicitly mean Palestinians, as it further elaborates the number of refugees from Yemen, Sudan, Iraq and Somalia. However, the number of refugees from other countries shows how the labelling of the humanitarian response in Jordan as the 'Syrian refugee response' neglects other refugee populations, and, as Tobin rightly put it, shows how 'neoliberal governance of the Syrian refugees has resulted in both the privatization of the refugee experience and attempts at cultivating new moral subjects and, indeed, the "ideal refugee"' (2016, p. 5). The failure to mention Palestinians in Jordan is an attempt to conceal their case. Thus, universalizing an ideal refugee image and account is connected to ideologies and relations of force, it is not an abstract act.

The UNFPA's 2021 GBV report specifies the nationalities of survivors who sought help in the year, of which 66 per cent were Syrian, 27.4 per cent Jordanian, and 6.5 per cent were survivors of other nationalities, mainly Iraqis, Yemenis and Sudanese. The report outlined that the data was gathered from the UNFPA's partner organizations: the Jordanian Women's Union (JWU), the Noor Al-Hussain Foundation (NHF), the Jordan River Foundation (JRF), International Rescue Committee (IRC), Arab Women's Organization (AWO), and the UNHCR.

However, JWU reports from 2015 to 2021 – which I closely studied and analysed during my work helping JWU develop its GBV data – count Palestinian refugee women as having the third highest number of GBV survivors. In my interview with two frontline workers from the Noor Al-Hussein Foundation, both confirmed that they receive Palestinian GBV cases and, as the only organization working in the Cyber City Camp until it closed at the end of 2017, had gathered information and data on GBV-related issues in the camp. Both Noor Al-Hussein Foundation representatives were unsure if the Cyber City data had been shared with the foundation's partners, even though the JWU's reports had been shared with the UNFPA on a quarterly basis. Hence, the choice not to include data about Palestinian refugee women in the reports is a deliberate act of silencing.

The UNFPA's GBV Information Management System (2021b) categorizes GBV into six broad categories: rape; sexual assault; physical assault; forced marriage; denial of resources/opportunities/services; and psychological/emotional abuse. In line with previous years, the main types of GBV reported were psychological abuse (53.9 per cent), physical assault (24.4 per cent), and denial of resources, opportunities or services (9.4 per cent), mainly in the context of domestic violence/intimate partner violence (UNFPA, 2021b, p. 7). If denial of services is considered a form of GBV according to UNFPA classification, then the denial of aid and assistance must also be, if GBV at the structural and epistemic level is acknowledged. But, similar to the IOM definition, the UNFPA defines GBV in six categories that mainly reflect certain acts of violence perpetuated by gender norms ad hoc and inseparable from the context.

The report also uses national data from the 2018 Demographic and Health Survey (DHS) to put additional emphasis on culture and social norms: 'social norms in Jordan are still permissive of GBV, with 69 % of men and 42% of women believing it is justified for a man to beat his wife in some circumstance's' (UNFPA, 2021b, p. 4). The DHS is an international tool, designed in a universalist method, which uses standard data definitions that do not account for context-specific issues. For example, in the survey, men and women 'Respondents are asked if they agree that a husband is justified in hitting or beating his wife under each of the following seven circumstances: she burns the food, she argues with him, she goes out without telling him, she neglects the children, she insults him, she disobeys him, and she has relations with another man' (Department of Statistics, 2019, p. 283). The last justification, 'she has relations with another man', scored the second highest percentage of agreement by both women and men, with 45 per cent of women and 65 per cent of men agreeing that a husband is justified in hitting or beating his wife if she has a relationship with another man (Department of Statistics, 2019, p. 283). However, by not having a 'none of these reasons' option, the survey does not include data on how many women disagreed with wife beating in general terms, highlighting the fact that the survey was designed on the assumption that men and women agree on at least one justification for wife beating. The highest percentage justification is 'Any of these reasons', which also includes 'relations with another man'. In a society where, outside marriage, relationships between men and women are prohibited and considered adultery – and punishable by law – the figure that truly is notable is the 54 per cent of women (more than half those surveyed) who did not believe that relations with another man, despite being punishable by law and considered a shameful act according to societal norms, justified violence, specifically in a context where they are answering questions for an official national survey.

Nonetheless, relying on data that uses universal standards to understand women's perceptions takes these perceptions out of context and neglects certain aspects of the data, thereby attributing GBV to cultural practices and social norms rather than highlighting structural violence. The cultural explanation limits analysis to issues related to domestic violence without linking that violence to power and the politics of gender that – particularly when studied in relation to refugee populations – must address and interlink political processes and relations between forces that contribute to perpetuating GBV violence.

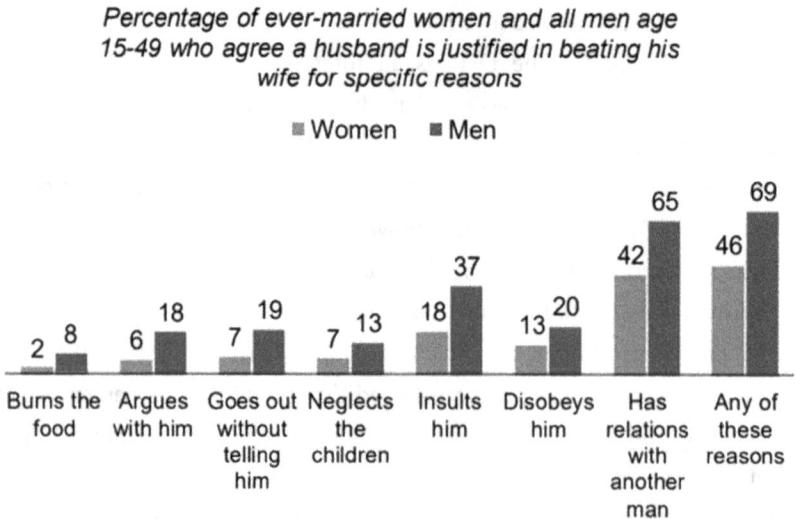

Percentage of ever-married women and all men age 15-49 who agree a husband is justified in beating his wife for specific reasons

■ Women   ■ Men

	Burns the food	Argues with him	Goes out without telling him	Neglects the children	Insults him	Disobeys him	Has relations with another man	Any of these reasons
Women	2	6	7	7	18	13	42	46
Men	8	18	19	13	37	20	65	69

Figure 1 Department of Statistics (2019) 'Jordan Population and Family Health Survey 2017–18'. Department of Statistics, p. 238.

Reporting that disregards structural violence and root-causes embedded in social, political and economic forces is, in and of itself, a form of epistemic violence when linked to the Palestinian case. As the history and experiences of Palestinian refugee women have been completely disregarded and rendered invisible, their case cannot be analysed without linking it to the epistemic violence of both the settler colonial project in Palestine and Jordanian state nationalism, both of whose roles were discussed in the previous chapter in creating anti-Palestinianism.

The epistemological nature of this violence appears clearly in feminist literature aimed at addressing connections and complicities in humanitarian practice, but still nonetheless re-enforcing its discourse and narrative. For example, in their book on gender issue in the Syrian refugee crisis, Freedman, Kivilcim and Baklacioglu state: 'refugees who are not registered with UNHCR, or who have lost their registration status and have thus become irregular residents in neighbouring countries are particularly marginalised and vulnerable. Women with irregular status are increasingly vulnerable to sexual and gender-based violence as they cannot rely on the local authorities for protection' (2019, p. 2). By referring to all undocumented refugees under the category of irregular residents, not addressing why and in which cases this type of vulnerability occurs, and highlighting what has been excluded from the humanitarian aid assistance discourse, such literature contributes to the naturalization and normalization of certain refugee populations as irregular, undocumented, and hence falls into the trap and logic of categorization. In other words, feminist theory and the practice of aid speak to one another in a way that their actions of concealing the particularity of Palestinians amount to 'frames of settler colonialism'.

Local workers spoke to me of non-UNHCR-funded programmes that require organizations to provide a list of Syrian refugee women 'beneficiaries' for not only aid, medical and cash assistance, but also women's empowerment and the elimination of GBV programmes. The stories and experiences shared from local NGO perspectives reveal the hierarchy and order within the global refugee governance response in Jordan. As the main UN agency concerned with the protection of refugees, those 'of concern' to the UNHCR become the only refugees worthy of international protection (Dumper, 2009). The UNHCR's rules, policies and practices have become the norm dictating other organizations' practices in relation to funding, establishing criteria for eligibility, defining women accessing services as 'beneficiaries', and policing NGOs' implementation of funded programmes. Through this, the UNHCR 'sets the benchmarks by which refugee programmes are judged' (Dumper, 2009, p. 568).

When I spoke to UN and international organization representatives about the eligibility criteria and exclusion of certain groups of refugees, most responded that they had to prioritize. This prioritization was explained mainly in terms of numbers and scale of the problem, but also the funds available to certain groups of refugees. Nonetheless, the discriminatory development and humanitarian agenda revealed in their response to the Syrian refugee crisis generally, and in Jordan specifically, explains how also other refugees – such as Yeminis, Iraqis or Somalis – have been made invisible in the response to Syrian refugees. One response to the criticism of humanitarian organizations' obfuscation of other refugees is that such organizations were working in line with Jordan's state policy, which aimed 'to render Syrian refugees as visible as possible to the international community, while also aiming to inflate their numbers' (Tsourapas, 2019, p. 469). However, if these other refugees were 'of concern' to the UNHCR, they have not been excluded from the response altogether. Recognized refugee women can still access services established under 'the Syrian refugee response' and funded by the UNHCR, but if funds for organizations are specifically tied to Syrian refugee women and do not come from the UNHCR, then even recognized refugee women can be excluded. In the case of Palestinian refugee women, they can be excluded from both UNHCR – and non-UNHCR-funded projects. Palestinian refugee women from Syria noted a number of organizations that had denied them access to services; one such case is mentioned in Chapter 4.

Local NGOs have responded to the hierarchy of the refugee humanitarian response in Jordan differently, mainly according to the type of contractual relationship between the UNHCR and INGOs on the one hand, and local NGOs on the other. Indeed, NGOs with pre-existing gender equality and GBV programmes can negotiate their terms of reference with funders, reject conditions based on eligibility criteria, or trick international funding systems. Smaller NGOs, or those that established their GBV and empowerment programmes through temporarily funded UNHCR projects, have less capacity to challenge or negotiate eligibility criteria. Primarily, such NGOs implement projects on behalf of UNHCR implementing partners, including: other UN agencies, such as UNFPA and UN Women; INGOs, such as Care International and Save the Children; royal NGOs; and a very small number of national NGOs, such as the Jordanian Women's Union, Arab Women's Organization and Sisterhood Is Global-Jordan. Fundamentally, smaller NGOs or those operating in rural or deprived communities rely heavily on the funds of such implementing partners, and are thus indirectly contracted by the UNHCR. In such cases, both the UNHCR and implementing partner's funding regulations apply to the projects. This indirect relationship stems from the notion that such NGOs do not have the capacity to manage funds and hence a middle, mediating partner is needed to manage reporting process.

Despite operating in areas where intervention is needed to reach refugee women, small local organizations are not trusted to manage funds themselves. In an area near one of the Palestinian camps, where the majority of people living are Palestinian, organizations were only funded to serve Syrian refugees relocated there, thus transforming the work of organizations receiving this type of funding. 'Before Syrian refugees arrived, we used to serve everyone in the area who needed our services. Now, we must prioritise Syrian refugees,' Amal, the manager of a small organization, said. Before, her organization's focus was charitable, distributing food and aid assistance linked to gender empowerment. It conducted awareness-raising campaigns and lectures on issues related to gender equality and GBV and gave food packages to women who accessed these programmes as an incentive. However, for programmes aimed at Syrian refugees' integration into Jordanian society, a complete attendance list is required and should clearly show each woman's eligibility, a UNHCR-recognized status, or Jordanian citizenship. This list is then shared with donors and the UNHCR as evidence of compliance with funding criteria, as well as to ensure there is no duplicity in aid distribution.

The manager explained that, at the beginning of the project, it was a challenge to serve only Syrian refugees, but when integration with Jordanians became possible, that eased their mission: 'It was hard to work in a very deprived community and distinguish between people based on their nationality. The community also started to be hostile towards Syrian refugees, accusing them of taking all the funds in the country.' Basically, policies aimed at empowering refugee women came at the expense of a deprived community, contributing to the creation of tensions between refugees and host communities in Jordan. When I asked the manager about Palestinian refugees from Syria, she replied: 'those with Jordanian citizenship, the majority of who we serve, are considered Jordanian. And if the funds are available to Syrians and Jordanians, then they are by default included. We only have problems with those with no refugee status residing illegally, or Gazan refugees. We mostly refer them to the UNRWA centre nearby.' I asked her if referring them to UNRWA meant they were refused access to her organization's programmes and she replied: 'Sadly, yes. But we cannot violate donor regulations.'

In my interview with the director of one of the biggest NGOs in Jordan, Nadia Shamroukh, she stressed the importance of the organization's ability to make independent choices. The JWU is one of the oldest and biggest women's NGOs in Jordan, with a long history of opposition to government policies. The JWU established its various GBV programmes in 1996, which include a hotline, legal aid, and psychological and social support for women exposed to GBV. It has branches in ten locations across Jordan and centres in six Palestinian camps, all of which include services and programmes for women. Since the start of the response to Syrian refugees, the JWU has taken a major role in GBV and refugee women's empowerment programmes. The JWU has two types of project funding: through an implementing partner and contract based. Thus, the JWU is not merely reliant on UN agencies for funding, it also has established partnerships with other INGOs and donors. The combination of various funds helps the organization manage its work with refugees in an independent way. As Nadia Shamroukh confirmed:

> The availability of funds from multiple donors allow us not to differentiate between women. In contract-based projects, where we only provide donors with access to those who are in need, like our partnership with IOM in medical cash assistance for Syrian refugee women, we mainly have an intermediary role between women and the IOM. However, even in the case of a woman who applies for medical cash assistance but she is considered not eligible by the IOM, we find other ways to assist her.

She then gave examples of projects funded by other UN and INGOs, stating: 'These projects fund our programmes, and we determine eligibility criteria not the donors. When we apply for funds, we make sure the fund is tailored to achieve our vision and aims, not a temporary project that ends at the end of a funding cycle.' However, even a well-established organization like the JWU is challenged by the rigidity of the criteria when dealing with UNHCR projects.

When I spoke to Nadia, she was in the middle of negotiation process with the UNHCR, as the UNHCR had conditioned funds for a GBV programme in one of JWU's branches only for Syrian refugee women. Nadia was adamant: 'Our programmes are open to every woman in the country. We cannot in this branch make it exclusive to Syrian refugees and contradict our own ethics and principles. This is not acceptable. If the UNHCR continues to insist on only serving Syrian refugee women, we will simply reject the funds.' I am aware – from my own experience working for JWU between 1996 and 2001, as a member of the organization for the last three decades, and in my now more occasional involvement in different capacities since joining academia – of numerous instances of the JWU rejecting funds that do not meet its vision or would cause it to compromise its principles, even if such decisions put the organization in a difficult financial position. Although I do not know whether the UNHCR project was implemented or not, knowing the organization and its feminist practice, I am sure that Nadia's insistence on rejecting the funds if the UNHCR would not change the eligibility conditions as a possible outcome of the negotiation. Whether the JWU rejected the funds or implemented the project on their own terms, their practice is quite exceptional. The organization's broad outreach and work grounded in a feminist vision, alongside its close contact with women on the ground, make it possible for the JWU to negotiate and set their own agenda in this way. But this is not the case for most organizations, especially small local ones and charities working in deprived communities, rural or urban.

However, whilst the JWU can (relatively) set the agenda for work on the ground, its work at the policy and knowledge-production levels is still compromised. In JWU reports and GBV data, Palestinian refugee women are present, but these figures are still not reflected in the UNHCR and UNFPA data. Hence, although the JWU can set its own agenda and serve Palestinian refugee women despite the funding challenge, by combining data received from all implementing partners – the majority based on UNHCR funding eligibility criteria – only cases of GBV against Syrian refugee women end up being reported. This shows that humanitarian agencies hold an epistemic power crucial to the perpetuity of an uneven knowledge-production hierarchy, resonating with what Escobar termed 'global coloniality': 'the heightened marginalization and suppression of the knowledge and culture of subaltern groups' (2005, p. 207). By continuing to enforce resolutions and conventions that exclude Palestinian refugees from international protection, naturalizing and normalizing accounts of their displacements, humanitarian organizations take an active role in institutionalizing and perpetuating the epistemic violence of settler colonialism against Palestinians.

Categories and life-long precarity in and beyond the Cyber City 'Camp' in Jordan

After Jordan implemented its strict no-entry policy in 2013, any Palestinian refugees who did manage to enter Jordan were detained at the Cyber City Camp, in the north of Jordan, if caught. The case of Palestinian refugees from Syria detained at the Cyber City Camp shows how the limiting of UNRWA's mandate to relief and aid and exclusion of Palestinians from the legal protections of the UNHCR place Palestinians in a precarious situation. Indeed, atrocities and discrimination against Palestinian refugees at the Cyber City Camp have been documented by both Amnesty International (2013) and Human Rights Watch (2014).

The Cyber City Detention Centre was a six-floor building with ten rooms on each floor. Until its closure in 2017, the Cyber City Detention Centre restricted Palestinians' freedoms, denied them access to services and only allowed visitors with official permits. The facility was initially built to house the Cyber City's Bengali workforce, but the workers protested the inadequate conditions and were moved to better accommodation. As I was told by UNRWA representatives, the agency can only work with refugees in the Palestinian camps and, hence, those in the Cyber City fell outside its mandate. Furthermore, the UNHCR's deliberate misinterpretation of both its mandate and the 1951 Convention – deeming both inapplicable to Palestinians – meant that Palestinian refugees in the Cyber City also fell outside of its mandate. Indeed, only the royal and semi-governmental Noor Al-Hussein Foundation worked with refugees in the Cyber City, but the reason why it was the only organization that could gain access, albeit sporadically and on an ad hoc basis, is unclear. Interestingly, its status as a semi-governmental organization may have been a compromise to facilitate funding for programmes for those who fall outside all available UN mechanisms and international protections.

In order to get to the Cyber City building, I had to go through two police checkpoints. During one visit in December 2015, I asked a guard: 'When was the last time any organisation had access to people inside the centre?' He replied: 'The last time we allowed assistance in was during Ramadan in July.' According to Jamal, a Palestinian activist in Hussun Camp, people were denied basic rights in the Cyber City: 'Even when we manage to get food packages and aid, the authorities won't allow us to distribute in the centre.' Jamal and other activists from a nearby Palestinian camp shared stories of trying to smuggle in food, books and toys for children – in collaboration with the Bengali workers, who lived close by – after the police refused to allow in such assistance. At the time of my visit, the centre was accommodating around 600 Palestinian refugee families and a few Syrian refugees. Palestinian refugees told me that the government accommodated a small number of Syrian refugees in the centre, estimated at less than 100, so the camp would not be known as another Palestinian refugee camp.

Although I was not allowed to enter the building itself, the policemen guarding the place allowed me to look inside the main door and meet with a group of Palestinian refugees, men and women, outside the building. The guards clearly sympathized with the refugees and were kind enough to allow these conversations to take place even though I had been unable (despite much effort) to secure government permission. From these conversations, I learnt that people could only leave if they had official permission – through what is called the 'bail-out system' – for health checks or family visits, and only for a short time. One woman said: 'the luckiest of us are those who frequently get sick. It is the only way to get out of the centre and smell fresh air'. Not everyone I met was able to leave, even when their families outside had applied for family visits. Three women I met had multiple pregnancies while in the centre; they had no access to health centres during their pregnancies and only one-day's permission to leave for the labour. In fact, a man even told me that he had deliberately injured his son so that he could go to the hospital and say goodbye to his dead brother. 'I only did this after I begged and begged but no one listened to me. I had to do this. I love my son, but the burial of my brother without saying goodbye was unbearable.' In explaining daily life in the centre, Abu Kamal, in his late sixties and the centre's unofficial spokesperson, said: 'If you see the kind of fights that take place on a daily basis among the centre's residents over basic things, you will not believe it. The other day, a huge fight erupted as the police were brought in for a silly reason. Men, children, and women were injured because whenever the police interfere, things normally get worse.'

Conversations during visits to the Cyber City were quite general but, after the centre's closure in 2017, I managed to have in-depth conversations about life there with a number of Palestinian refugee women who had either moved to the King Abdullah Gardens Camp, been allowed to live with a family member (especially in cases of daughters of Jordanian mothers), been deported back to Syria, or been resettled in a third country. When I asked them about violence, most responded along the lines: 'of course, every day and night, there was nothing but violence in the centre'. When I asked about sexual violence, they often answered '*ma taedish*' (innumerable).

'Gossip was the most common reason for a woman to be exposed to violence. Men had nothing but to talk about women,' Shaimaa – who was resettled with her family in Switzerland after living in the Cyber City from 2013 to 2017 – told me, and then described one of the times her husband beat her badly. Three days prior to the incident, Shaimaa had been in the hospital for an appendectomy. Upon her return to the Cyber City, a man whispered ' I am sure you had a good time wherever you were,' insinuating she may have been somewhere else, doing something illicit, not in the hospital. She told him, 'that's your dirty mind speaking' and, although not close enough to hear what the man originally said, her husband did hear the man respond to Shaimaa: 'you are a bitch'. A verbal fight between the two occurred but other men in the camp managed to calm things down. After, Shaimaa's husband took her inside their room and beat her severely, hitting her on the surgery site purposefully as she screamed loudly. The police were called. However, when her husband told them Shaimaa had been speaking to a man in a disrespectable manner, the policeman responded: 'you have the right to hit her. And you, looking at me, should not put yourself in such a shameful position nor should you scream like a disrespected woman if your husband hits you.'

In the previous chapter, I discussed Shaimaa's story in detail, showing how exceptional circumstances – i.e. she, her husband, and their three young children's sharing of a room with another family eliciting the sympathies of a group of European visitors – led to her resettlement in Switzerland. Shaimaa's eldest daughter was one-month old when she and her husband fled Syria, and her two sons were born in the Cyber City. While her family was one of the very few successful Palestinian resettlement cases, their story also shows how falling outside international protection mechanisms results in humanitarian organizations' categorization of Palestinian identity as 'xxx' or 'undefined country of origin' even in the rare instances when they are granted resettlement. As discussed in the previous chapter, the undefined country of origin or three-Xs status continues to complicate Shaimaa's Life in Switzerland her life there: 'Wherever you go or when you apply for anything, if you are not Swiss you need to fill in your original country. There is no country on my identification card, and applying neither through digitalised systems nor in person will solve the problem, because honestly it makes no sense.' For Shaimaa and others in a similar position, the precarity of life for the differentiated refugee extends beyond the detention centre; it is life-long.

And indeed, this life-long precarity is also gendered. When I asked Shaimaa about her husband's violence and whether it continued after they resettled in Switzerland, she said:

> I wish I could tell you things are better now, but they are not. I think of leaving him every day, but then I look at the type of person he is transformed into after the experience we had in Jordan and can do nothing but to endure and try to reduce his violence. He has not left home for months, smokes non-stop like a chimney. What keeps me from leaving him is only the short but good life we had together in Syria.

I try to conceptualize statements such as the above – discussed in greater detail in Chapter 4 in relation to masculinist manoeuvrings and how such practices connect GBV to structural violence against Palestinian refugees – but, I must say, I struggled to understand. Such statements are, on the one hand, not reflecting a passive choice and, on the other, contributing to re-enforcing gender norms. Bringing this example here is simply to show that the perpetuity of GBV is connected to the life-long precarity created by the categorization of Palestinians as a differentiated category within the humanitarian response to Syrian refugees in Jordan.

The overall categorization of Palestinians as 'UNRWA refugees' leaves them without any mechanisms of protection; even in the exceptional cases, when they are provided resettlement, their identity and national existence is categorized as 'nothing' or 'xxx'. This shows humanitarian organizations' complicit consent to the narrative of the settler colonial project in Palestine and, hence, are one of its frames perpetuating epistemic violence against Palestinians in a way similar to Butler's discussion of media coverage as frames of war. Her use of the term connects ideology, relations of power and materiality: 'the ways of selectivity carving up experience as essential to the conduct of war' (2016, p. 26). For Butler, frames are necessary for the continually manufactured disposition of material reality.

> [O]ur visual apprehension of war is an occasion in which we implicitly consent or dissent to war, or where our ambivalent relations is formulated, where we also are able to pose questions about what and how war is presented, and what absence structures and limns this visual field. If the visual field ratifies the target as a way to conceptualise precarious populations, can we read the frame as participating in the production of precarity, inducing precarity?
>
> (2016, p. xvii)

Precariousness is not an 'existential condition of individuals', it is an effect in which political demands and principles transpire out of a social condition (2016, p. xxv).

The precariousness resulting from Palestinian refugees' classification as a differentiated category and displaced population also resonates Feldman's work on Palestinian refugees in the context of Gaza, in which she argues that 'definition creates a discursive and material framework for action and opportunity, and is also a source of constraint' (2012, p. 388). Further, she also considers 'definition not just as a starting point for the delivery of aid (though it certainly is that), but as an aid practice in its own right', as it generates decisions with wide-ranging effects on refugees' daily lives: 'These decisions also shape people's experiences of displacement. People live their lives in part through the categories into which they fall and as those categories shift, so too do the possibilities of those lives' (Feldman, 2012, p. 392).

As shown in preceding chapters, acts of exclusion in either reporting or service-delivery inflict direct harm on Palestinian refugee women by denying them the chance to narrate their own stories, access services, escape violence and excluding their voices from decision-making processes in humanitarian response. In this case, in Edward Said's words, 'Palestinians [have been] denied their primordial rights ... they were also denied those rights in history, in rhetoric, in information, and in institutions. So, we have the case today, unique in history' (1981, p. 32). This is done in such a way that makes UN agencies, in particular, escape scrutiny and accountability, as nowhere in the above-mentioned reports is there reference to the exclusion of Palestinian refugees; their presence is either denied or merely noted as a differentiated category, 'UNRWA refugees'.

Through programmes imbued with universal concepts – such as gender equality, empowerment and the integration of Syrian refugee women – and aimed at bringing together Jordanian and Syrian refugee women, international aid organizations have not only stabilized the refugee-citizen binary, but also concealed and covered up the denial of services to other refugee populations in the country; refugees not recognized by the UNHCR or those living 'illegally' in the country. Such an act is defined as a form of GBV when perpetrated on women by their family members, but not when done on a larger scale, at the structure level.

4

The Palestinian condition: Gendering multiplicities of dispossession

As the opening of this book indicates, researching Palestinian refugee women from Syria was not planned or envisioned as a research project in the beginning. It started with conversations among Palestinians with different identifications alongside their Palestinian one: Palestinians from Syria, Palestinians from Jordan/Palestinian Jordanians, and Palestinians from Lebanon. All, including myself, were refugees, were raised and worked in Palestinian camps in Syria, Lebanon and Jordan, and been involved in humanitarian work with UNRWA. These shared experiences made our conversations very personal, to the extent that listening somehow was not distinguishable from the act of speaking. At times, I felt as if I were listening to myself when others spoke, but at others, tensions arose from differentiating one's own experience as distinct, more challenging or harsher than others. Palestinians with a Jordanian passport, even if born in refugee camps, are seen as more privileged by those with no passport, such as Palestinians from Lebanon, Syria or Gazan refugees, who only have travel documents. The relative freedom of mobility related to holding a Jordanian passport and citizenship, when compared to the limitations placed on other Palestinians, placed me and other Jordanian Palestinian refugees in an oppositional position to those who held no passport. The binary of holders/ non-holders of passports led me to think of categories and the ways in which the categorization of Palestinians in Jordan, their different legal and illegal statuses, works as a process of differentiation. However, the question of categorization became even more important in my conversations with Palestinian refugee women from Syria. Their narratives as discussed in Chapter 2 revealed that many Palestinians who chose to move to Jordan had, either themselves or their parents, previously lived in Jordan, were former Jordanian passport holders or, indeed, still held temporary Jordanian passports. In the second chapter, I followed a timeline of historical events based on women's narratives and experiences of these events, tracing the political origin of differentiation between Palestinians through the creation of various categories. I also looked at whether this process is somehow linked to what Palestinian refugees from Syria are experiencing in Jordan today and, more broadly, anti-Palestinianism as a form of epistemic violence.

During these conversation, this sense of privilege yielded an awkwardness for Palestinians refugees with Jordanian citizenship, and shows how an oppressive system can privilege and other one simultaneously (Lugones, 2016). This also triggered my thinking about Jordan's national system and the effects of its differentiation between citizen/non-citizen, authentic/non-authentic Jordanian on Palestinians. At the start of conversations with my family and friends about this research, many of whom are Palestinian refugees, I was initially struck by some of their indifference to Palestinian refugees from Syria's right to seek refuge in Jordan, the blame they placed on Syrian refugees for the economic crisis or, indeed, any bad thing happening in Jordan at the time, and the lack of meaningful political solidarity with both Palestinian and Syrian refugees. While many appreciated the fact that they were citizens and thus would not be subject to the same treatment as Palestinians in Syria, due to their only holding a Palestinian travel document, many also shared, as conversations developed, that simply holding a Jordanian passport did not grant them full citizenship. They pointed to examples of discrimination in education, employment, health care and others; it was quite striking, their insecurity around their status as Jordanian citizens. Indeed, one important aspect of this insecurity was directly connected to the atmosphere since Jordan's 1988 decision for disengagement, ending the unity between the west and east parts of the Jordan River (discussed in Chapter 2) and subsequently revoking citizenship for various reasons since then. This decision has had severe impacts for Palestinians in the West Bank, Gazan refugees, those displaced by the Gulf War (whether in Iraq or other Gulf states), and the current status of Palestinian refugees from Syria. The awareness of what happens to Palestinians without Jordanian citizenship, national numbers and cards created a sense of insecurity, alongside the feeling that citizenship is a privilege that can be lost. This is perhaps why some Palestinians in Jordan, while they have accommodated and helped shelter Palestinians from Syria, align themselves with the narrative of the state and have not shown overt political solidarity with Palestinians from Syria.

'Jordan has enough refugees,' an activist said in a discussion around the absence of political solidarity with Palestinian refugees from Syria. 'But aren't you a refugee?,' I asked her. 'Yes, but I am Jordanian as well,' she replied. This was not the only reason, however, this particular activist took this stance on refugees, whether Syrian or Palestinian; there was another political aspect. Indeed, she believes there is a global war on Syria due to the regime's position on normalization with the settler colonial project in Palestine, and hence views refugees escaping war in Syria as 'traitors to their country'. While the majority of Palestinian refugees I met and spoke with sympathized with the Syrian people, recognized their right to demand freedom and, as I show throughout this book, offered refuge in Palestinian camps to both Palestinian and Syrian refugees, Palestinian activists in Jordan – both in and outside camps – were sharply divided over how to describe what is happening in Syria: a revolution, a conflict, war in Syria, war on Syria? Support for the Syrian regime mostly hailed from political elites who might find a new cause in the crisis in Syria that could renew or empower their political positions, while nationalist Palestinian elites mostly aligned themselves with the Jordanian regime's narrative of 'Palestinian refugees as a threat to Jordan's demography' through their refusal of *twatin* (resettlement), and hence argue that 'Palestinian refugees from Syria should not have left their camps', as that only 'serves the Zionist project', as one activist put it. Be it due to alignment with the Jordanian and/or Syrian regimes or the insecurity triggered by their fragile status in Jordan, Palestinians in Jordan dropped Palestinian refugees from Syria from their political agenda, leaving the latter with no political representation to ensure their voices are heard.

In previous chapters, I discussed how the settler colonial technique of anti-Palestinianism is displayed in both the Jordanian State's no-entry and detention policies and international humanitarian organizations' denial of asylum and humanitarian assistance to Palestinian refugees from Syria. This demonstrated that the settler colonial project of Palestine extends beyond both the territorial boundaries of Palestine and the practices of the settler colonial state of Israel. The intersection of the oppressive systems of settler colonialism, militarism, nationalism, and global asylum and refugee governance highlights the ways in which relations between these systems continue to create new categories and processes of othering. Jordan's 2013 no-entry policy, which prevented Palestinian refugee from Syria from entering Jordan, is part and parcel of its long-time categorization of Palestinians as a threat to Jordan's national harmony and identity. This policy, first, has served the interests of the settler colonial state through further marginalizing Palestinians by erasing their presence, forcing their disappearance and silencing their voices. Secondly, this policy has created sub-groups among Palestinian refugees in Jordan: the legal, established refugees originally displaced to Jordan in 1948 and 1967; temporary refugees from Gaza with temporary passports; and the illegal, invisible Palestinian refugees displaced from Syria. Whilst this policy has severely impacted Palestinians' well-being, access to services, mobility and freedom, I demonstrate in this chapter that policies of subjugation and marginalization, whether by the state of Jordan or international humanitarian organizations, have failed to detach Palestinian refugees from Syria from their collective sense of belonging to Palestine.

Palestinian refugees from Syria's insistence on identifying as: 'Palestinian refugees from Syria', shows their conception of multiple pasts and homes, rather than the past being only the first experience of displacement and home being only Palestine. This multiplicity of belonging is characterized by two timeframes of displacement, where the second is connected to the first and neither displacement is privileged over the other. This means that Palestinian refugees from Syria understand their present displacement experience within the framework of a sequence of events, as a trajectory rather than an isolated event. This idea is confirmed in scholarship such as Gabiam and Fiddian-Qasmiyeh (2016), which concludes: 'forms of attachment and belongings to places other than Palestine do not necessarily come at the expense of refugees' sense of connection with the Palestinian homeland or their political activism in relation to the homeland' (Gabiam and Fiddian-Qasmiyeh, 2016, p. 19). On the other hand, the new displacement experience has created a sense of distinctiveness based on the multiplicities of dispossession(s), the trajectory of displacement and the accumulation of loss, and hence reproduces new narratives of Palestinian refugeeness and its relation with the camp community in Jordan. This challenges the notion of a universal refugee figure and suggests, in line with Malkki (1996), that it is the political and true lived reality of the displacement experience – rather than the displacement itself – that reproduces different narratives of refugeeness, in terms of the subjective meaning of belonging, home, and the relational or distinctive sense of national identity as products of war.

In this chapter, I discuss how Palestinian refugee women from Syria, second- and third-generation Palestinian refugees, expressed their Palestinian identity, in relation to the interconnectedness of the meaning of home, belonging to a Palestinian camp, and intra-relationships with Palestinian communities in the camps in Syria and Jordan. Here, the aim is to examine whether the new displacement experiences – shaped by Jordan's barring of Palestinian refugees from Syria, lack of humanitarian support and the abandonment of the Palestinian Authority, represented by the embassy in Amman – has influenced Palestinian refugees from Syria's ideas of home and belonging to a collective group. There are two sub-groups of Palestinian refugees from Syria addressed in this chapter: those who entered Jordan legally and live in Palestinian camps and those who entered illegally and hide within one of the Palestinian communities in Jordan's camps. The chapter argues that in/visibility is determined not only by the legality of one's residency, but also by gender arrangements and norms, thus creating differing effects on women's abilities to act, have self-diligence over their activities and make new beginnings, which in turn has created a multiplicity of relationships with the camps and Palestinian community in Jordan. In this respect, the in/ability to act and in/visibility determined the extent and degree to which the structural frameworks of displacement impacts 'who women are' as agents. The ability to act, engage in activities inside the camp, define their roles in the struggle, and have self-diligence over their actions influenced the relationship between Palestinians from Syria and Palestinians in Jordan, generating divergent ways of belonging to the camp as a Palestinian space.

I argue in this chapter that, while all Palestinian refugees share a history of forced uprooting, the subjective experience of belonging to a collective memory, the meaning of refugeeness and camp belonging might differ from one Palestinian refugee group to another due to their historical trajectory of displacement, the rights enjoyed or denied, the politics determining the denial or confirmation of rights within nation systems, and the singular, double or multiple experiences of displacement. In what follows, I engage with how, in the camps in Jordan, the possibility for personal diligence and the ability to act, as a Palestinian, has generated a stronger sense of belonging to the collective group, and how the intersection of gender and Palestinianism in experiences of displacement has shaped ideas of belonging, home and their relationship with camp residents. Here, the definition of refugee–refugee relationship is not fully relational (e.g. Agier, 2002; Fiddian-Qasmiyeh, 2016b; Bjørkhaug, 2020; Farah, 2020), but both relational and specific, in terms of attachment to the collective group and with respect to their own experiences, history, trajectory, and the changing social status, gender norms and roles that shaped not only their experience but also informed their ability to be present in the space through action, respectively.

The Palestinian condition, collective belonging and plurality of action

Palestinians understand their status of illegality and lack of humanitarian support as an integral part of the continuity of the Nakba, a form of anti-Palestinianism. Their personal experiences are connected to what they described as 'the Palestinian condition'; in Malkki's words, a 'historicizing condition that helped to produce a particular political subjectivity' (1996, p. 378). In my discussions with women, expressions of home, camp identity, and belonging to camps in Syria and Jordan were strongly present and thus cannot be avoided. Nonetheless, I questioned how I should represent the multiple accounts of home, identity, and the relationship between this group of Palestinians and established Palestinian refugees in Jordan.

During discussions with women, they generally began narrating their stories as they related to the Palestinian Nakba. They all expressed strong views against the camps in Jordan as well as a strong sense of belonging to a Palestinian community and were doubtful about a return to Palestine. They also spoke of a future entangled with the idea of return; and held a very strong sense of home as a multidimensional place, the one in Palestine, the camp in Syria and Syria itself, but also home expressed in a sense of a continuum of losses. As all the women with whom I engaged are third- or second-generation Palestinian refugees, they expressed their loss in terms of both their parents/grandparents' loss of the homeland and their own loss of home in Syria, illustrating an accumulation of loss. They referenced their loss of home in Syria in terms of a multiplicity of dispossessions, reflecting more complexity than their parents, as they did not have the ability to envision what would happen next. This was clearly voiced through statements such as: 'I know one day we will return to Palestine, maybe I won't but my kids will. I do not know if this is true for my home in Syria.' The loss of home in Syria is different than the loss of the homeland in Palestine, as expressed through the possibility that the Syrian home might be nonreturnable. Many also wondered, return to what, as some camps – like Yarmouk and Dera'a – were destroyed and are now unliveable. For example, the number of refugees living in Yarmouk, the largest Palestinian camp, decreased from 400,000 to 3000 people (UNRWA, 2021). Furthermore, as the Syrian regime's plan remains unclear, with reports emerging that plans for the camp's reconstruction are still vague (Rollins, 2020). Palestinian refugees are also feeling that their ownership of their homes in the camps in Syria may now be in question.

There was also variation in expressions related to the legality of their stay in Jordan and its impact on their relationship with the new spaces they occupy in Palestinian camps. Those with legal residency, who are very few, could envision a new life in Jordan, but even they have yet to come to terms with the new space as a Palestinian one to which they relate. Women, particularly those who moved to camps through marriage and kinship connections, mainly expressed discontent with their lives through continually describing it as 'different from in Syria'. In articulating the difference between camp life in Syria and Jordan, gender norms were present, defining the relationship with the camp and belonging to a Palestinian community. Those with illegal status, who hide themselves in the camps and rely solely on the support of neighbours and the camp community, spoke of the camp and Palestinian refugees in Jordan with more gratitude, voicing a closer relationship with the camp as a space to which they belonged and without which life in Jordan would be intolerable. Here, the ability to be invisible as part of a collective group provided a sense of being seen. For women in this group, the ability to be active and take charge of their own and their families' lives meant the camp has provided the cover they need to conceal themselves from the authorities and, at the same time, a space where their identity is evident and cannot be hidden. Between the two groups, accounts of the camp as a space of either the appearance or disappearance of the self, as an acting being, generated differing meanings of home, camp identity and belonging to a collective group.

'Sometimes my neighbours in the camp recommend me for teaching private Arabic lessons to their friends' kids outside the camp, but people outside the camp never know who I am', Thuryyah – a former Arabic teacher with twenty years' experience in UNRWA schools in Syria – stated (See Chapter 4 for Thuryyah's full story). Unclear on what she meant, I followed up, 'do the people whose kids you teach know you are Palestinian?' 'Yes', she replied, 'they know I live in Irbid camp, so it is understood that I am Palestinian. But they do not know that I am a Palestinian refugee from Syria. Unless I am among *nasnaa* and *ahlna* (our people) in the camp, I do not reveal my story.' Although Thuryyah used *nasna* and *ahlna* to describe her relationship with people in the camp, as a group related by their association to Palestine, this is not all that she represents; this type of identification does not tell her story and, hence, it is not who she is. At the same time, all the women I spoke with shared the same explanation for the exceptional treatment of Palestinian refugees: what many of them coined as *alzarf alfilastini* 'the Palestinian condition' (sometimes also referred to as *al-hlaat al-falistiniah* or *alwade'a alfalasitni*). The Palestinian condition determined how they narrated their stories in connection to what has happened in Palestine, their choice to move to a Palestinian camp in Jordan, and their plans to either return to their homes in Syria, stay in Jordan, or try to seek refuge elsewhere. When asked directly what they meant by the Palestinian condition, the answers were varied, but the most common response referred to the reasons for their forced disappearance from among Syrian refugees. For most, the no-entry policy, lack of humanitarian assistance and denial of the right to apply for asylum are all intended to suppress the Palestinian issue, reflecting the continuity of injustice against Palestinians.

The Palestinian condition was also explained in terms of the women's own relationship with the Palestinian struggle. 'To exist as a Palestinian is, in and of itself, enough for our case to continue to live, but we aim to do more than that. We work hard to preserve our case and sow seeds for our kids' future', Um Walid, whose story is presented below, stated. Um Walid defined what it means to exist as a Palestinian in general terms, i.e. to exist as a Palestinian is a way of being that involves carrying on the legacy of her grandparents while continuing to exist and work for a better future for the next generation. Life – as it is linked to past, present and future – is a form of remembrance; the continuity of Palestinian existence against the forces that sustain the Palestinian condition are present in their acts and hopes for the future. For a Palestinian, life means to exist. It is a form of self-appreciation for one's past and the collective group to which they belong; a valuation of the self that appears important to their endurance for their difficult, mundane lives. This outlook is not nationalistic, as it was not developed in contrast to other groups' identities. As Hannah Arendt posits, 'human distinctiveness is not the same as otherness' (2019, p. 176). Thus, in the case of Palestinians, it is their endeavour to show their unique case and maintain power against the systems working to make them disappear; it is an act of resistance and, what Palestinians refer to as, *sumood* (steadfastness).

Hanna Arendt posits that humans 'are always conditioned beings', in other words situated in relation to forces, relationships of power, hierarchy, and order (2019, p. 9). In the *Human Condition*, she explains: 'whatever centres the human world of its own accord or is drawn into it by human efforts becomes part of the human condition. The impact of the world's reality upon human existence is felt and received as a conditioning force' (2019, p. 10). To engage with the question of the human condition, Arendt proposes the term *vita activa* (active life), which she designates to the three human activities of labour, work and action, each of which has its own characters (Buckler, 2011). The human condition of labour, likened in her analysis to the biological process of the human body, feeds and produces all vital necessities for life. Hence labour is life itself, while work is the opposite of nature; it is but the wordily human activity that produces the 'artificial' world of things. Arendt criticizes the interchangeable idea and use of labour and work, where no distinction is made between the two: 'the work of our hands ... distinguished from the labor of our bodies' (2019, p. 136). Labour, for Arendt, defines all human activity and serves as the maintenance of life, responding to the requirements of biological necessity (Buckler, 2011); work, on the other hand, is only the product of human activity, 'man-made of things'.

Although work is more distant from nature than labour, both are requirements for biological life. Further, as both are characteristics shared by all human species, they are not how a human being's active life should be measured. Through this, Arendt distinguishes between human species and human beings. In terms of an active life, for Arendt, 'What is certain is that the measure can be neither the diving necessity of biological life and labour nor the utilitarian instrumentalism of fabrication and usage' (2019, p. 174). Indeed, it is the third category, action, that measures and distinguishes a human being's active life. Action defines the human condition of plurality (2019, p. 7), which is the condition of all political life. It is not the work of human hands (work) or the body (labour), but human action that makes the uniqueness of one's own self and identity. Unlike labour and work, action means the human capacity to begin something new through the ability to uniquely act.

What made me look to Arendt's *Human Condition* was the need to understand how Palestinian refugees from Syria have managed to articulate a sense of shared belonging and identity with Palestinians more broadly alongside a feeling of their distinctiveness as refugees from Syria through the idea that action is a realm of plurality, where humans interact and engage with each other through their unique sense as individuals. As Arendt argues, 'plurality is the condition of human action because we are all the same, that is human, in such a way that nobody is ever the same as anyone else who ever lived, lives or will live' (2019, p. 8). Arendt presents a sophisticated and philosophical analysis of the three characteristics of the human condition – labour, work and action – from ancient Greece to the Modern Age. My intention is not to engage with these as philosophical questions, but instead to apply her description of these conditions, particularly action and the realm of public appearance, to accounts of Palestinian refugees from Syria in order to explain this group's self-identification as distinctive among Palestinian refugees and the conditions under such individuals have identified their relationships with the collective group in the Palestinian camps.

Labour and work in Arendt's analysis resemble Palestinian refugees' general association with Palestinian identity and collective memory. Born in a Palestinian camp, in a Palestinian community or somewhere else in exile, essentially means inheriting the Palestinian condition and characters. For Palestinians, it is something like labour, a necessity of life. Preserving the collective memory is the production of the Palestinian narrative, and is shared by all Palestinians by virtue of being Palestinian. The way in which Palestinians identify themselves, as Palestinians, and retain their connection with Palestine through carrying the legacy and narrating their stories is like work and labour, both defining the question 'what are they?' These are qualities shared by all Palestinians; they are the perquisites for life itself. To exist for Palestinians is to define and situate themselves within the historical and political conditions that uprooted them and are the reason for the displacement tag they carry wherever they go.

This, however, is a form of a passive existence, as it does not reflect the words and deeds of the individual, only the inherited characters. Active existence, as clearly expressed by Um Walid is what individual Palestinians do in the present, creating their own presence without disproving the past. As Arendt posits, both words and deeds point to who somebody is: 'no other human performance requires speech to the same extent as action … in acting and speaking, men show who they are, reveal actively their unique personal identities and thus make their appearance in the human world, while their physical identities appear without any activity of their own' (2019, p. 179). As Thuryyah stated, it is clear that she is Palestinian because she is living in a camp, but that is not enough for her to feel visible; she still cannot reveal her full story, the story that she herself lived. In this sense, it is not the identity itself, but the revelation of the actor in the act. If the agent in the act does not disclose, Arendt posits, 'the action loses its specific character'. Therefore, we cannot know who somebody is only through knowing the story of which 'he is himself is the hero-his biography, in other words; everything else we know of him, including the work he may have produced and left behind, tells us only what he is or was' (2019, p. 186). Arendt's analysis of action and differentiation between 'what' and 'who' – as the first represent the qualities shared by everyone and the latter is the actions that allow the appearance of the agent in the act – corresponds with Palestinian women's self-identification as simultaneously both Palestinian and Palestinian refugees from Syria, who have a shared but distinctive history and narrative.

The public realm is the space of appearance and ability to be visible that humans need in order to appear, where there is a disclosure of deeds and words that cannot be done anonymously or covertly. As Arendt states, 'without a space of appearance and without trusting in action and speech as a mode of being together, neither the reality of one's self, of one's own identity, nor the reality of the surrounding world can be established beyond doubt' (2019, p. 208). Palestinian refugees from Syria's choice to live in refugee camps in Jordan is an action, a form of resistance against their forced disappearance as a group of Palestinian refugees distinct from both Syrian refugees and Palestinian refugees in Jordan. The camp in Jordan is a space of appearance, where Palestinian refugees from Syria can perform their Palestinian identity within the collective group but can also easily hide from the authorities. Through the collective appearance, they can resist their invisibility without repressing their own distinct identity as Palestinian refugees from Syria. It is also a place that allows them to regain power over their own selves; living together with other Palestinian refugees, as Arendt suggests, 'makes the potentialities of action present and for power to remain within them and hence it is the most significant material necessity for power' (2019, p. 201). A human being's existence in the public realm is relayed through the power of acting and speaking. In this respect, power is different from force and strength because it is independent of material forces but relies heavily on the existence of other people. The refusal to be made invisible by joining the larger group is an act of preserving what they are against the forces working to supress their existence, as Palestinians. However, the act of distinguishing themselves from other Palestinians in Jordan is a form of protest against the potential loss of their homes in Syria and to maintain the unity of their displacement situations, connecting past and present experiences, as well as preserving their refugee status in Syria.

In her article 'The Palestinian Identity among Camp Residents' (1977), Sayigh projected that it was unlikely that Palestinian refugees in camps in Lebanon would lose the Palestinian colour of their identity 'Even if they take another Arab citizenship, or emigrate' (Sayigh, 1977, p. 4). This vision, proved correct by various research (e.g. Peteet, 1992, 1998; Abdo, 2005; Sayigh, 2007; Achilli, 2014; Shalhoub-Kevorkian and Ihmoud, 2014; Fiddian-Qasmiyeh, 2016a; Holt, 2016; Loddo, 2017; Lindholm, 2020), addressed Palestinians' sense of self and identification and was made based on extensive research in one of the camps near Beirut. Sayigh's findings revealed that there are several foundational bases for the development of Palestinian identity: a history that largely differs from that of other Arab peoples; a situation of displacement; ambiguity of and discrepancy in Arab support; the development of other Arab identities; resistance movements; and indigenous factors, such as solidarity amongst kin and neighbour networks, and their historical experience of self-reliance and survival (Sayigh, 1977, p. 21). All these are shared bases and were also clearly expressed in my discussion with Palestinian refugee women from Syria. However, the new displacement experience shaped by geopolitical developments, Jordan's differing treatment of Palestinian refugees from Syria from other refugees (whether Palestinian or Syrian), and the enforced status of illegality and invisibility (discussed in Chapter 2) have generated new bases for self-identification not shared with other Palestinian refugees. This has, thus, created a sense of distinctiveness from Palestinians in the camps, Jordanian citizens and Syrian refugees.

The research of Lindholm (2020) on Palestinian refugees in Sweden also demonstrates that refugees create a shared understanding of identity as Palestinians as well as internal gaps, splits and contradictions shaped by the different processes of displacement that led to their residence in Sweden, their former places of residence, and increasing racism in Sweden. The act and expression of distinguishing themselves as a unique group of Palestinians is not an act of division; rather, it corresponds with their desire to maintain a sense of authority over both what and who they are, which strengthens their connection with Palestine, without losing sight of their own specific case and story. As Arendt posits, human power corresponds with the conditions of plurality, as 'power can be divided without decreasing it, and the interplay of powers with their checks and balances is even liable to generate more power, so long, at least as the interplay is alive and has not resulted in a stalemate' (2019, p. 201). This general analysis of the choice of Palestinian refugees from Syria, as a distinct group of Palestinians, to live in Palestinian camps in Jordan partly explains individual cases of refugees' self-identification and relationship with established refugees in the camps, even if it does not take into account how these experiences – aside from the Palestinianism that shapes their illegal status in Jordan – are also informed by other positions, such as: gender, economic status, solidarity and kinship relationships.

The camp as a Palestinian base and connecting space

One of the most common responses to my questioning why Palestinian refugees from Syria would choose to live in a Palestinian camp was: 'When you are in a Palestinian camp, you do not feel *enak taftaqir 'iilaa asas*, you lack a base.' Whilst some have relatives and connections in the camps they chose to live or hide in, many had no previous relationship with people in the camps in Jordan. Most women I interviewed explained that they knew where they wanted to live when arriving in Jordan, as they had already identified a camp prior to leaving Syria. However, it was only when they had kinship and friendship connections to a camp that they were able to go there directly; most women and their families had to move several times before settling in one of the Palestinian camps. The majority settled in camps near the borders, e.g. the Irbid, Jarash and Huson camps in northern Jordan, waiting to return to their camps in Syria. Some have also moved to camps in Amman – such as the Wihdat and Hussein camps – and Al-Zarqa city, such as Al-Zarqa and Shinilar camps.

In trying to express their familiarity with the Palestinian camps in Jordan, some spoke of a strong connection between the camps in Syria and Jordan: 'You know, sometimes I feel as if I was in the Dera'a camp. Things are quite similar here.' The choice to live in a camp was deliberate, as they wanted to rebase themselves within a Palestinian community. In my discussions with Palestinian refugee women from Syria, the simple answer of having a base was rather complicated, however. Despite the connection to and familiarity of Palestinian camps, it was clear the women wanted to convey both that they are 'refugees from Syria' and the 'camps in Jordan are different than in Syria'. For these women, there is an order of belonging that starts with Palestine, the camps in Syria, and then Syria; in their narratives, the camps in Syria are represented as both a connecting space to Palestine and the context of their own stories. The camps in Jordan, on the other hand, for those living illegally, are but temporary places that allow them to melt in a Palestinian community with which they share a collective sense of belonging to Palestine. The idea of melting did not mean assimilation, but rather the ability be invisible and continue living, which means, simultaneously, to exist as a Palestinian.

In women's narratives, the camp, as a base, allowed their existence by providing a space of disappearance that facilitated their access to necessities such as work or health services. Indeed, access to health services was a primary example the women gave to explain how living in a Palestinian camp has helped them overcome the lack of support Palestinian refugees from Syria receive from the Jordanian state and humanitarian organizations:

> I was pregnant with my second child. I had some medical issues but I could not go to hospital. I needed either a Jordanian national number or a refugee certificate to access medical services from organisations that help refugees. I tried a medical clinic for one of relief and humanitarian organisations near Irbid Camp, but that did not work either. My neighbour, who was also pregnant, offered me her medical card and this was the only way I could access medical assistance.

There is also the example of Ro'a, discussed in Chapter 5, who spoke of using her neighbour's medical card in order to get her child hospital treatment.

Fiddian-Qasmiyeh's work (2015, 2016b, 2020) addresses what she terms 'refugees relationality', and demonstrates how Palestinian refugees in camps in Lebanon actively provide support to other refugees (2020). Fiddian-Qasmiyeh, furthermore, shows that Palestinian refugee camps in Lebanon have become safe spaces for other refugees; spaces where they form a 'broader refugee nation' and practice acts of solidarity and togetherness (2016c, p. 27). In this sense, newcomer refugees choose to live in camps in order to avoid being treated as outsiders in Lebanese cities. Indeed, my research participants all acknowledged and shared the acts of solidarity, support and local aid provided to them by Palestinian refugees in Jordan. Some said that their neighbours fully furnished their houses or provided them with food on a daily basis, while others shared that their neighbours had helped them find jobs or offered an orientation to the services in the camps and surrounding areas. Thus, the sense of solidarity in the camps in Jordan is similar to that discussed by Fiddian-Qasmiyeh (2020, 2015, 2016a) with regard to Lebanon's Palestinian refugee camps.

Although Fiddian-Qasmiyeh acknowledges the complex hierarchy within refugee camps, her conclusion about newcomers' sense of insider-ness was expressed differently by my research group. These women have chosen to live in Palestinian camps, on the one hand, because of their desire to remain within a Palestinian community, but, on the other, intentionally and persistently identify themselves as 'Palestinian refugees from Syria'. This distinguishing of themselves from established Palestinian refugees in Jordan was very significant to them. While there was a sense of familiarity, a need for a base and a desire to belong to a collective group, their choice to live in the camp was also about concealing their identity from the authorities and retaining their sense of distinctiveness. Through this, they are neither insiders nor outsiders, but instead both simultaneously. Living in a Palestinian camp is not enough to define who they are. For example, as Um Walid shared:

> Here we are renting a house; in the Yarmouk camp, we have our own. It is almost destroyed, what remains is only the skeleton, but this house encompasses our life and our memories. People in the camp have been good to us. Really, there is too much sympathy with us, but, you know, it's different when you are in the place you have history with and with the people you have built your life with.

Um Walid's words reveal her feelings of *gurba'* (exile) in the Palestinian camp in Jordan. Sympathy is clearly appreciated, but relationships based solely on sympathy or solidarity, without equal conditions and rights between two groups, create a hierarchal structure and a greater sense of inequality that affects the equality of relationships between the two. In 2018, Um Walid took a dangerous trip back to Syria to check on her house and belongings, describing her return journey as follows:

> After five years in Jordan, I decided to go back to Syria. I made all the arrangements and was prepared for anything. When I approached Yarmouk, I shockingly started running towards the ruins of the camp. I lost my way and managed to avoid the first two military checkpoints. When I arrived to the third, a solider approached me asking: 'what are you doing here and how have you managed to arrive to this point?' I replied, 'I have no clue, it seems I lost my way. Do you know where the centre of the camp is? I need to check on my house.' The soldier asked me to leave but I insisted on seeing my house. He pointed in the direction of the camp's centre, and, for some reason, let me continue on my way. I finally arrived somewhere I recognised and then was able to reach our building. I entered my house, nothing was left but the skeleton of the building. All our belongings had disappeared, even

the pictures we hung on the walls had been taken; our closets were empty and the kitchen was destroyed. My 30 years of living in Yarmouk had been completely erased. It felt as if we had never existed in that place. I am not sure they will allow us to rebuild our houses in Yarmouk. Nothing is certain now, but I hope we will be allowed to return to Yarmouk sometime soon.

The rebuilding of Um Walid's house, among others, would be a restoration of her past existence as a refugee in Syria. Her insistence on going back to Syria to check on her house, despite risking not being able to return to her children in Jordan, shows her strong connection with her home in Syria and the Yarmouk camp. When describing her arrival to Syria, her eyes were full of tears and joy. Without her past in Syria, her life would be disconnected, fragmented, and insufficient for creating social and political ties with nationhood and belonging to a collective identity on equal footing with Palestinian refugees in Jordan. The return to Palestine, for Um Walid and other Palestinian refugees from Syria, can only be via Yarmouk, as this route is also related to refugees' resilience and resistance in the face of attempts to erase the history of their original displacement from Palestine.

Palestinian refugees from Syria's decision to simultaneously connect with and distance themselves from established refugees in Palestinian camps in Jordan is an act that seemingly reinstates them into Palestinian nationhood as equal to, but also distinctive from, other Palestinian refugees, rather than painting them merely as victims of yet another tragedy. This distinction to achieve 'equality of condition' appears to be 'the working principle' of Palestinian refugees from Syria, which, in Arendt and Baehr's words, is 'a basic requirement for justice' (2000, p. 75). To have equality of conditions with other Palestinian refugees means to also protect their legal status as Palestinian refugees from Syria.

The empowering power of acts in a space of dis-appearance

I met Um Walid in al-Hussein Camp in Jordan. She left Yarmouk in late 2013, entering Jordan legally, but has been unable to apply for residency since the introduction of the no-entry policy; hence, she has been living without legal status. Um Walid has four sons and one daughter. One of her sons does daily-wage work in the camp, 'sometimes he works in shops, other times in construction, whatever available for him he does'. Two of her other sons and her daughter attend the camp's UNRWA school. As she arrived prior to the ban on entry, she was allowed to register with UNRWA and thus access the camp's services for Palestinian refugees. Um Walid is connected to charities in the camp, and she and her daughter try to help out. Her fourth son, the eldest, was caught and deported back to Syria. Walid refused to smuggle him back to Jordan, he decided to go to Lebanon and from there travelled to Europe. At the time of our interview, Um Walid did not know where her son was. She thought he might be in a camp in Greece, but was not sure. 'Walid was caught outside the camp. I warned him not to take work outside the camp, but he did not listen,' she explained.

Throughout our discussion, Um Walid tried to articulate the significance of living in a Palestinian camp: 'I want my kids to continue to be connected to Palestine. It's easier to do this when you live in a camp'. The Palestinian camp in Jordan is where she can maintain and strengthen her kids' relationship with Palestine. Um Walid felt a sense of self-appreciation and achievement in her ability to successfully reach the camp, live in it for over five years, and manage her three sons' and daughter's work and education despite their forced disappearance. She defies the forced disappearance imposed by Jordan's no-entry policy through her choice to live in a Palestinian camp in Jordan and her ability to actively engage in the camp's activism. Through this, she confronted the authority and turned her disappearance into presence, where she can act and appear in her act, be active and have interactions with the community. For Um Walid, the camp's centrality as a Palestinian base and, at the same time, a space of dis/appearance that allows for her existence was very important. She is clear that she does not only want to live, to be alive, to be seen – she also wants to perform the life of a Palestinian.

In the course of our interview, Um Walid explained that she was not a stranger to al-Hussein Camp, where now she lives, and that is why she chose it. Her grandparents were first displaced from Isdud/Gaza to Egypt and then to Jordan. In the 1970s, her father left for Lebanon when the PLO moved its base from Jordan to Lebanon after what is known as 'Black September' (Black September, which began in September 1970 and lasted until July of 1971, was a fight between the PLO and Jordanian Armed Forces). Thousands lost their lives, mostly Palestinians, and it ended with the PLO's departure from Jordan and relocation to Lebanon [for more details, see Singh, 2015]). Um Walid's grandparents, aunts and uncles followed her father to Lebanon, as they feared reprisal from the Jordanian Armed Forces due to his high status in the PLO. Although only a child at the time, she could still relate to the place through the memories of her mother and grandparents. In 1982, her father moved to Syria with one of the Palestinian factions. Um Walid joined the same faction at the age of eighteen and was an active member in Yarmouk Camp, where she also met her husband: 'We were comrades first then we got engaged.' Her husband died from cancer a few years before the revolution in Syria. Um Walid continued to be active in the camp, but she disagreed with her faction's sympathies for the Syrian regime: 'We, the Palestinians, should not accept the regime's injustice against the Syrians.' This position ended her relationship with the Palestinian faction, and she then chose to distance herself from their politics.

In Um Walid's narrative, there were multiple locations, political events, and positions that summarized the unity and connection of her story with the history of Palestinian displacement and resistance. She strongly insisted on positioning herself as a Palestinian refugee from Syria, an affiliation that will allow her to return to Syria. Her illegal status in Jordan makes it difficult to envision any future there. Still, for Um Walid, living in a Palestinian camp and the ability to be active, although on a smaller scale, fulfils her existence as a Palestinian and human being. As she explained, 'if not for the charity work I do, life would have been unbearable. I am used to doing something. I believe I should never stop or sit at home with my hands on my cheeks, that would be the end of me.'

Although Um Walid has memories of Lebanon, she does not affiliate herself with the country; the place where she was active. She had a role in the camp and her involvement in resistance to the colonial settlers repressive laws, meant more to her. Um Walid's self-perception, relates to multiple homes and pasts, and the importance of one's particular experience shows the significance of analyses as discussed by Peggy Levitt and Nina Glick Schiller (2004). In their work they take the simultaneity of the migration experience into consideration in their challenge of the automatic equation of society with the boundaries of a single nation state or identity. Palestinian refugees from Syria's strategy of using the camp in Jordan as a temporary base that permits both their disappearance and existence at the same time, making clear linkages with Palestinian refugees in Jordan, as Palestinians, and simultaneously remaining distinct, as refugees from Syria as well, reveals the complex interconnectedness of their particular contemporary reality, past experience, historical trajectory of displacement, and state politics and power structures. In this sense, it is important to understand different 'combined actions of ways of being and ways of belonging in different contexts', alongside the interplay between ways of being and belonging in certain contexts and how such contexts interconnect with historical and political trajectories of displacement (2004, p. 103).

Another form of being, for Um Walid, is implicit in her ability to act, appear and to be heard. For her, Life without activism and doing things would not be a life, hence her involvement in charity work and having an active presence in the camp can overcome some of the consequences of her illegal status. She confronts the attempt to force her disappearance, the erasure of her presence, as a Palestinian refugee from Syria, through her active-presence within the refugee community in which she lives. Her sense of belonging to this community, despite distinguishing herself from it, is stronger than those who cannot find a position in the camp that allows for them to manage their own lives through their own self-diligence and action, as discussed in the following section.

The inability to act and articulation of a space of appearance

I cannot adapt to life in Jordan. Life in the camp here is quite different from what I had in the al-Aideen (returnees) camp near Homs City in Syria. We are more open and flexible. I do not know if it is my family-in-law's customs or everyone else's here. They are ultraconservative and sometimes I feel as if they are counting my breaths. We are different. We had a beautiful life in Syria. I could stay out with friends until 2am with no fear of anything. (Salam, a 25-year-old Palestinian refugee woman married to a Palestinian refugee in Jordan)

Salam lives legally in a Palestinian camp in Jordan, arriving there in 2015 by marrying the son of her mother's friend. Before getting married, Salam had never met her husband, but her mother knew his family very well. The arranged marriage was part of Salam's family's escape plan from Syria. A year before the marriage, Salam's sister had an arranged marriage with a cousin in Denmark. Her two brothers were sent to Lebanon, travelled from there to Turkey and then took the boat to Greece. They are also now settled in Denmark. Such arrangements were necessary due to Salam's uncle's involvement in the revolution. 'We tried to be neutral,' Salam recalled, but explained that not all Palestinians could stand by: some openly joined the revolution and others supported the regime. While Salam's father did not want any of his children engaged in the revolution, and was afraid his sons would be forced to enlist in the army, her uncle was very active and ended up caught by the regime forces. 'I do not know his fate. Nobody does,' Salam noted wistfully. As her uncle and his connection to opposition groups was well-known, Salam's father feared the regime or other groups might seek revenge on his family, particularly her brothers. Hence, a plan was made for each of the four kids: the girls would have arranged marriages and the boys would escape to Europe. The parents, on the other hand, stayed in the camp as long as they could, but eventually also had to leave as the situation worsened: 'They are now in Lebanon, and my brothers are trying to get them to Denmark.' Only Salam's grandparents continue to live in al-Aideen camp, her uncles, cousins, neighbours, friends and other relatives all left.

No one else from her family, friends or relatives moved to Jordan; Salam was the only one. 'My parents' first choice was to come to Jordan, but it was not possible, you know how things are,' Salam said, referring to restrictions that make it impossible for Palestinian refugees from Syria to enter Jordan. However, Salam felt unlucky to move to Jordan, as she was separated from both her family and previous life as a woman: 'In Syria, I was happier. I was active in the camp. My family had faith in me. I was never told not to mingle with people or who I should not speak to. I was working and contributing to my family's income. I had many friends. We partied a lot. Camps in Syria are different than here.' What the camp in Syria represented for Salam has been challenged by her experience in the camp in Jordan; thus, she felt no sense of belonging to the new place.

Salam's idea of connection with the camp is an individual – not collective – one, and this idea clearly appeared in her recalling of life in the camp in Syria and comparison to life in the camp in Jordan, where her husband and in-laws restrict her: movement, mobility and interactions with others in the camp. The feeling of living in a Palestinian community has been denied to her, and thus her connection with the camp as a Palestinian space does not exist. In Salam's narrative, the camp in Syria was a space of appearance, where her presence as a Palestinian was enmeshed with her freedom to work, move freely, engage in activism and mingle with friends. Living in a Palestinian camp in Jordan, in comparison, generated a sense of disappearance from what she used to *do* and *be* in Syria.

Clearly, to identify with the camp, as a Palestinian space to which one can belong, is only possible, when this space allows individuals' presence within the collective. This presence was described by my research participants in terms of: hopes, norms, activism, achievements and the chance to have self-diligence over their actions. Palestinian refugees' existence in the camps is not only determined by their belonging to geo-political space: Palestine, but also by how the camp represents them as individuals and in turn creates a space for their existence to appear. Hence, refugees' relationship with the camp intersects with their personal experiences, positionality and ability to interact freely with others.

Immediately after Salam became Jordanian, she went to Homs to visit her grandparents in al-Aideen camp. When she arrived, she could not recognize her past life. 'Everything has changed. Syrians displaced from the surrounding areas were occupying the houses of Palestinians who'd left the camp. I could not relate to the place. I had to return to Jordan earlier than planned, there was nothing for me to do there.' Whilst, as Salam described, the camp was not destroyed and remained relatively intact, unlike other Palestinian camps in Syria, it has been transformed by significant demographic changes, the scars of war, as there is now a large presence of displaced Syrians. Especially significant for Salam was the disappearance of all her family, friends, shops she used to frequent and her workplace; basically, no trace of her life remains in the camp. It seemed particularly painful for Salam that the place to which she had belonged will never be the same, as she stated: 'I will never return to live in that place again.' Salam was seeking out her past life in Syria, the active life, the one that was recognized, but she could no longer find it there and cannot recreate it in Jordan.

Throughout our interview, Salam spoke of home as rooted in Palestine, but this sense of home is incomplete without her own, primary, first-hand experience of belonging to a place, not just the belonging of her parents or grandparents. Her life in al-Aideen Camp connected her to her parents and grandparents' past and a future she previously envisioned. She is a third-generation Palestinian refugee; while she has no doubt about return to Palestine, she has lost the connected-place, al-Aideen camp, her own place.

Salam's arranged marriage was the only way she could escape death and enter Jordan, but she was not keen on the marriage: 'I never met my husband before. My mother knew the family and she was the one who made the marriage arrangements. They did not force me but there was no other option, my parents were desperate to find solution for each one of us.' In her married life in Jordan, the restrictions on her movement, lack of control over her life and her inability to be part of the community with which she shares the space, detached her from it and what it represents at the collective level. There was no distinction between private and public realms in Salam's narrative, they were enmeshed. The freedom she enjoyed in Syria at her parents' home allowed her to exist as a Palestinian woman through activism, while the immobility, restrictions on her movement and the new way of being in her husband's house forced her into the shadows. Salam is now a legal resident and, through her husband, a Jordanian citizen, but she still has no sense of place/belonging to either the camp she lives in or the nationality she holds.

There were also other layers of Salam's feeling of difference and lack of belonging to the camp expressed during our discussions, including her in-laws' poor status and difficult living conditions in the camp. She was not content with her quality of life, which was quite different from the life with her parents in Syria. Furthermore, as someone who had previously worked and contributed to the family income, she felt unhappy that she had been unable to do the same in Jordan. While her husband did not mind her getting a job, she explained:

> There were limited jobs I could do without a nationality number in the first three years of marriage, before I got Jordanian nationality, but those jobs were deemed inappropriate by my husband and his family, like working at a hairdresser or in a shop. I tried jobs they approved of, like nurseries and schools, but all required a nationality number.

After giving birth to two kids, working became even more of a challenge and, hence, Salam is not thinking of looking for a job again until her kids reach school-age, even though she now holds Jordanian nationality. Her ability to contribute financially has been obstructed by both her limited options of work – i.e. those deemed appropriate – and state-imposed restrictions on refugees' right to work; both gender norms and state policies and practices entwined to limit her options and, thus, affect her belonging to the camp in Jordan. Salam could not separate her own experience, as a Palestinian raised in a Palestinian camp in Syria, from her gender experience in an environment 'completely different' from the one in Jordan, as she consistently described. The links between Palestinianism, gender, and socio-economic conditions in her feelings of both being and belonging to the camp in Syria and detachment from the camp in Jordan were greatly dependent on whether her new life in the camp permits her presence or forces her into an absent – presence.

Unlike Um Walid, Salam lives in the country legally, but she is still less visible in the camp than Um Walid. Salam's legal status was only made possible through an arranged marriage and, while her family did not force her to accept the marriage, it was Hobson's choice. As a woman there was no choice. In her case, consent was absent due to a lack of options. Um Walid, on the other hand, was the decision-maker for her own actions, which also made her able to challenge her status of illegality through performing an invisible life in the camp. Both have strong and shared connections to Palestine in a collective sense as well as a feeling of distinctiveness as Palestinian refugees from Syria; a feeling informed by their own experiences and active presence in the camp in Syria. What made their sense of belonging to the camp in Jordan different, however, was the im-possibility with which they continue to engage with the camp as a Palestinian space. Despite her legal status, Salam could not perform Palestinianism, which for her meant to be active, have freedom of mobility and contribute to her community. Her legality did not permit her visible presence or allow her to enjoy rights such as work. Her legal status is like 'ink on paper', as her lived experience resembles a status of illegality. Um Walid's status of illegality, on the other hand, did not prevent her from finding ways to continue to perform her duties and engage in activism in the camp. Whilst restrictions on her movement outside the camp, her son's deportation, the difficult living conditions and her forced disappearance outside the camp have greatly affected her, she seemed more content with her life than Salam.

Self-diligence, autonomy and self-governance, over one's own action and the ability to perform an active life, make a new beginning, and achieve something rather than being forced into choices are essential in defining refugees' relationship with the camp as a Palestinian space. Although both Salam and Um Walid were forced to leave their camps in Syria, Salam's arranged marriage is a life-long direction, with no end in sight, whilst Um Walid can still envision a return to Yarmouk. Furthermore, appearance and disappearance, visibility and invisibility do not merely reflect a status of legality or illegality, or a distinction between the private/public realms, but also a representation of women as actors who are positioned differently depending on their ability to appear – *where, when and to whom*. The capacity to act, to be, or be acted upon as in the case of Um Walid and Salam, created different conditions and perspectives between the two in terms of how they perceived the camp, as either a space of appearance or disappearance. It clearly impacted on how they expressed feelings of being, belonging or to the lack of belonging. Such conditions for appearance/disappearance are shaped by the interplay of gender and social relationships as well as existing forms of solidarity networks – or lack thereof – and state policies and practices.

Nonetheless, Salam also shared an account similar to that of Um Walid with regard to her strong sense of belonging to a shared history with Palestinians in the camp and the importance of preserving her status as a Palestinian refugee from Syria. Maintaining a connection with Palestinianism and their visibility as Palestinian refugee women from Syria is a form of action, resistance and appearance that challenges the forced disappearance imposed by the State of Jordan on Palestinian refugees from Syria. For both Salam and Um Walid, the categorization of the self as a Palestinian refugee from Syria, although under differing conditions, is an act of resistance, preserving the relevance of their grandparents first displacement, their distinctive life in Syria, the experience of re-displacement and their current conditions in Jordan. The political meanings each gave to their displacement experiences were reflected through the Palestinian condition, as this condition is embodied in both of their lived experiences of the everyday, displacement, self-invented ways of reflecting their positions from power, and their ways of challenging and refusal to be defined by its conditions.

Conclusion

Mahmoud Darwish, in one of his poems, states: 'Identity is what we bequeath and not what we inherit. What we invent and not what we remember.' The inventive act of self-creation and renewal, alongside the identification of the self as related to our own remaking rather than merely inherited, was noticeably articulated by Palestinian women from Syria. Although linked to a past, they have transformed their identity and that which has past into their own presence. They explained their personal stories as fundamentally connected to their existence as Palestinians, who are all painted by the forces that try to erase and obstruct their existence and articulated their general relationship with Palestine as something that all Palestinians share. However, each one's response to the Palestinian condition has also allowed for a level of personal diligence, explained in terms of the various actions and choices they make to keep strong ties with both their Palestinian case and distinctive experience. Indeed, the gender norms and arrangements that shaped their displacement and relocation experiences could not be explained outside the Palestinian condition. The links between the choices they had to make, their gender and Palestinian selves were inseparable. As stated at the start of the chapter, it was not easy for me to understand how the new displacement experience has affected women's narrative of home, belonging to the camp as a space for Palestinian community and the relationship with the collective Palestinian memory. However, in articulating their ideas, the line women used to narrate their stories is first understood and connected to the Palestinian condition. Their reference to the Palestinian condition was more than an attempt to explain the relevance of Palestine to their current reality. It was about their existence and experience as Palestinian beings constructed by the framework of history, politics, subjugation, displacement and war that created their condition. Hence, the Nakba – which, in this narrative, is a sequence, nonlinear, liminal and multi-directional – is their present, not the past they inherited.

In women's narratives, this designation of the self as distinct established their particular relationship with multiple places and experiences of dispossession, but did not necessarily manifest in the dual, fluid or hybrid way that the identities of 'African American' or 'Caribbean British' have, as discussed by scholars such as Gilroy (1993) and Hall and Gay (1996). Instead, in the words of Malkki, this designation is 'a refusal to be categorized, a refusal to be fixed within one and only one nation or categorical identity, one and only historical trajectory' (1995, p. 4). Indeed, Malkki further posits that 'in universalizing particular displaced people into "refugees" – in abstracting their predicaments from specific political, historical, cultural contexts – humanitarian practices tend to silence refugees' (1996, p. 378). This analysis is of a particular relevance to the Palestinian case, as configuring one Palestinian refugee figure who belongs to a nation like other nations not only misrepresents Palestinian refugees but also negates the particularities of the Palestinian case, the various consequences of displacement for each group, the impacts of the different state systems on different Palestinian groups and the connections these systems have with the global order.

Palestinian refugees from Syria have exclusively experienced something new, a new displacement. While this exclusive experience has not changed their collective sense and connection to Palestine, as they understand the new experience in relation to the past, it has generated a plurality of perceptions around being and belonging to the camp as a Palestinian space. When women were able to appear, to be present, to act, they are able to turn their forced disappearance into appearance. When women could not appear as actors because of gender arrangements and other social and political conditions, their social and communal ties with the camp as a Palestinian space were weakened. Here, the camp can only be a space of being and belonging when it is seen as a space that allows individual appearance.

Sayigh (2007), in her analysis of Palestinian refugee identity making in Lebanon, argues that the long duration of displacement increases Palestinians' connection with Palestine, positing that there is a sense of shared identification. Furthermore, other positions 'deepen colorings of "self-identification" through different locations, class positions, politics and ideologies. This poses the likelihood of a growing gap between a shared "Palestinianness" and differing class, regional, political or individual interests' (Sayigh, 2007). In the case of

Palestinian refugees from Syria, as discussed throughout this chapter, this gap has been felt more in women's accounts of their mobility and ability to act, to be visible and be present, shaped by their il-legal statuses and gender norms and practices. The ability to act does not mean to do things but instead 'to take initiative, to begin …, to set something into motion', which also means to lead and have power over one's own acts (Arendt, 2019, p. 175). The ability to act, in the words of Arendt (2019, p. 208), is 'the greatest that man[woman] can achieve is his [her] own appearance and actualisation'. Correspondingly, the in/ability to act and disclosures of the self in the act created multiple relationships with the camp and Palestinian community in Jordan. In this respect, the in/ability to act and in/visibility determined the extent and degree to which the new displacement impacted 'who women are'; and, as such, its impact on their agency over their own choices differed.

5

Masculinist manoeuvring: Doing gender or righting wrongs

In this chapter, I look at the ways in which masculinist manoeuvrings occur in the context of the displacement of Palestinian refugees from Syria to Jordan. Masculinist manoeuvrings are defined as both the management of masculinity, in cases of men's legal vulnerability, and the ways in which men and women try to restore normative gendered traits and roles when they are challenged in practice. In this, I look at how women understand the support they provide to their husbands' reclaiming of masculinity as an integral part of reclaiming their Palestinian identity; identity not in the narrow nationalist sense, but a national belonging closely connected to the quest for justice.

This chapter analyses the narratives of Palestinian refugee women and Syrian refugee women married to Palestinian refugee men of entering the country, experiences at entry points, border guard practices and the lived realities of 'illegal' refugee-ness strictly applied to Palestinian refugee men from Syria. Such analysis aids in understanding the conditions under which gender norms can be reconstructed, displayed and differently played off during displacement, and thus how gender relations and roles challenged within families during conflict and displacement can be re-managed and manipulated through acts of masculinist manoeuvring. As discussed throughout the chapter, these manoeuvrings are refugees' ways to restore past gender relationships and power dynamics, as these norms are defined within and connected to structural inequalities and injustice. Here, the focus is not on the role women play in restoring masculinity during war and displacement, but instead how masculinity intersects with questions of belonging, rights, justice, immigration policies, and the kind of history and politics present in refugee women's articulation of those notions.

Indeed, this chapter tries to capture the conditions under which masculinist manoeuvring choices are made and, hence, challenge the unidirectional and linear processes through which masculinity is often examined, particularly in relation to refugee men trying to restore their position. Thus, this chapter looks at masculinity as a mutual process involving both men's and women's interaction in a relational sense; a sense that ties masculinity to nationalism, resistance and justice.

Masculinity, nationalism and displacement

The study of masculinity emerged, over the last few decades, to first investigate men's gender practices in modern Western history, embodying a social theory of gender that aimed to understand gender inequalities through tracing men's lives in specific contexts and processes of change. The field has grown since its inception, diversifying to include and explore – among other things – relationships between masculinity, citizenship, militarism and nationalist projects (Ridd and Callaway, 1987; Anthias and Yuval-Davis, 1989; Enloe, 1990; Kawar, 1993; Yuval-Davis, 1993; Massad, 1995; HASSO, 1998; Nagel, 1998; Nilsson, 2018). For example, Nagel (1998) examined the connection between masculinity and nationalism, concluding that 'women appear to have very different goals and agendas for the "nation"':

> Given this difference in men's and women's connection and conception of the nation and the state, it is not surprising that there is a 'gender gap' dividing men and women on so many political issues. Thus, the intimate link between masculinity and nationalism, like all hegemonic structures, shapes not only the feelings and thinking of men, it has left its stamp on the hearts and minds of women as well.

> (Nagel, 1998, p. 261)

In addition, Cynthia Enloe noted that 'nationalism has typically sprung from masculinized memory, masculinized humiliation and masculinized hope' (Enloe, 1990, p. 45). This, for Enloe, is because men are the main actors in war and conflict; men defending their nation, their freedom, their honour, their homeland, and their women (Enloe, 1990, p. 45).

Both Enloe and Nagel presume and develop their arguments in a context where men are in charge and lead the narrative of the national struggle, a context of gender hierarchy and male domination. If at all existent, women's role is seen as secondary, merely a substitute for men. In contexts where women are seen as taking the lead, these situations are discussed in relation to the manipulation of gender norms during conflict, where nationalists take advantage of women's status and the perception of women as less dangerous. In such contexts, women can thus perform men's militant roles temporarily or actively engage in recruitment and support services for militia groups (Sayigh and Petteet, 1987; Enloe, 1990; Kawar, 1993; Yuval-Davis, 1993; Nagel, 1998; Petteet, 1998). In his essay 'Conceiving Masculine: Gender and Palestinian Nationalism' (1995), Massad argues in the same vein, concluding:

> Palestinian women may have more say in Palestinian politics in the near future, but given their discursive construction in nationalist thought, they will be able to do so not as Palestinian women struggling for Palestinian women's rights, but as Palestinian women struggling for discursively constituted Palestinian rights, where Palestinian is always already conceived in the masculine.
>
> (Massad, 1995, p. 483)

In the above-mentioned studies, women's role in processes of masculine construction is largely absent. Whilst agency has been a crucial issue in studies of masculinity and nationalism, analysis primarily stems from the idea of a relatively stable gender hierarchy and order. Indeed, as Kandiyoti (1994, p. 212) argued, 'behind the facade of male privilege lie ambiguities which may give rise to defensive masculinist discourse and genuine desire and contestation for change', but what happens to masculinity in a context where women are in a less marginalized position than men? How do women perceive their position in the new changing context? Is the change in women's position necessarily a change in gender norms, roles and relationships, or is there a need to situate both men's and women's choices in relation to the politics under which masculinity is challenged? If gender is situated within a 'multidimensional structure of relationships', as Connell suggests (2005, p. 1801), and 'operates at every level of human experience, from economic arrangements, culture, and the state to interpersonal relationships and individual emotions', then it is imperative to look not only at perceptions and roles, but also at the historical and political arrangements under which these roles and perceptions are preferred and the intersectional nature of political, economic, displacement and gender within these arrangements. Thus, the importance of studying masculinity and femininity during displacement is not only in articulating these notions in relation to each other, but also in defining both in relation to existing political projects, such as those of states, nationalist projects, and international humanitarian responses and agendas.

This chapter challenges the idea that notions of masculinity and femininity are merely assumptions about gender roles and norms. Articulation of these notions, as the narrative of Palestinian refugee women shows, overlaps with assumptions of the self and others, as the self is defined with respect to other belief systems – in the context of this research, the idea of Palestinianism as it relates not only to the national struggle, but also to the notion of justice. Hence, the narrative of Palestinian refugee women, and Syrian women married to Palestinian men, challenges the narrow conceptualization of nationalism defined in terms of the relationship to self and others and the role of gender in the politics of identity. Women's voices, often, articulate their nationalist sense in the quest for justice and rights.

Deniz Kandiyoti (2013, 2019, 2020) coined the term 'masculinist restoration' to examine GBV practices in the Arab region in the aftermath of the Arab revolutions of 2011. She argues the necessity to break with past analysis and identify 'a phase when patriarchy is no longer secure and requires higher levels of coercion and the deployment of more varied ideological state apparatuses to ensure its reproduction' (2019, p. 37). In this vein, Kandiyoti examines new patterns of GBV practices; practices that can no longer be explained with reference to the assumptions of patriarchy, but instead 'point to its threatened demise at a point in time when notions of male dominance and female subordination are no longer securely hegemonic' (2019, p. 37). In the case of Palestinian refugees from Syria, masculinity, as both women and men's narratives reveal, appears threatened by the state's discriminatory policies and international and human rights organizations' negligence of the pleas of Palestinian refugees from Syria. Palestinian refugees do not see this threat outside the threat to their Palestinianism and, hence, articulate it as both a danger to national identity and to the downfall of justice and rights. Thus, in the invisible reality determined by their illegality in the country, patriarchy can no longer be understood as the main force preserving and protecting male privilege and interests.

The state's contradictory practices expose its political agenda; an agenda that denies Palestinian refugees from Syria the right to enter and live legally in the country, as discussed in a greater detail in Chapters 1 and 2. Palestinian refugees see such practices as aiming to destabilize and threaten their sense of Palestinianism, and hence any change to gender roles, status and privileges are carefully, relationally calculated according to injustice based on their Palestinianism. In this context, not only are changes to gender roles and norms rejected, but tactics are also developed to manage the new reality without risking any significant change to gender beliefs until they normalize. This management is 'masculinist manoeuvring'. Masculinist restoration, as explained by Kandiyoti, requires higher intervention at the level of state apparatuses, while masculinist manoeuvring involves an individual's self [in]voluntary commitment and thus occurs at the individual and family levels.

Here, I argue that for masculinist restoration to succeed, especially after conflict, war, or revolutions, a previous and connected phase is required in which individuals manage and manipulate changes to masculinity, without which masculinist restoration cannot be fully realized by states and their apparatuses; it is a necessary phase in the process of restoration. There is a wide body of literature examining the ways in which women are pushed back to traditional gender roles after liberation and revolution, whether in the case of national liberations – e.g. Algeria – or in contemporary literature on the 2011 Arab revolutions. Existing scholarship examines the post-revolution processes that led either to the restoration of old regimes or to conflict and displacement; literature largely focused on the revolution's outcomes rather than the preconditions, contradictory and connected prejudices that produced its aftermath (Dabashi, 2012; Bayat, 2015/17; Abu-Lughod and El-Mahdi, 2011; Al-Ali, 2012; Kandyioti, 2011, 2012, 2013, 2019; Johansson-Nogués, 2013).

Feminist literature on conflict, post-armed conflict and displacement exposes the processes by which the structural inequalities that marginalize, exclude or render women invisible (e.g. Cockburn, 1998; Giles and Hyndman, 2004; Nilsson, 2018). The study of masculinity within forced migration studies moved beyond treating men as a heterogeneous group, advocating instead for the multiplicity of masculinities among refugee men, acknowledging the intersectionality of race, ethnicity, sexual orientation, class and refugee status in the examination of men's experiences of negotiating or reclaiming their masculinity. Nonetheless, the study of masculinity, particularly within the context of displacement, continues to pose some key questions: is masculinity to be considered only in relation to the changing nature of men's traditional roles, perceptions, behaviours and interests? Is it crucial to reflect on the differences in the ways in which men and women situate their relationship to gender notions – e.g. masculinity – or better to understand the reciprocated reasons and interests of situatedness in both of their gendered positions?

Within literature examining masculinities in the Syrian refugee 'crisis', the focus continues to be mainly on men's experiences and the impacts of displacement on men's masculinity, be it with respect to men's changing roles (especially the inability to support their families financially), the transformation of fatherhood, the labour market, poverty, jobs, the fragility of refugee-ness, or men's emotions and vulnerabilities (Suerbaum, 2018, 2020; Monroe, 2020; Huizinga and van Hoven, 2021; Çarpar and Göktuna Yaylaci, 2021). Such studies primarily focus on men's perception and experiences in situations where both they and women are residing legally and have recognized refugee status. By bringing the case of Palestinian refugees from Syria, who both share the Syrian experience of displacement and experience an additional layer of discrimination, I show how displacement differently impacts and shapes gender notions based on the politics defining who qualifies for refugee-ness. I also extend my analysis of masculinity to women's experiences in order to introduce fresh perspectives on a different context, where, relative to men, women are less marginalized due to their social status as women. Through this analysis, I offer a new epistemology via an in-depth examination of how the management of masculinity – which is entangled with questions of power and structural inequality, taking the form of masculinist manoeuvrings – form and shape women's choices in their survival of displacement and countering the state's political prejudices.

This analysis also feeds into discussions of agency and choices, as these choices and the ability to act are neither decided upon freely nor forcibly; rather, with imperative reasoning and calculated rational. Next, I argue that seemingly contradictory state practices and laws that may allow women to enjoy certain privileges because they are women are also challenged and rejected by women when such privileges are coupled with a misrecognition of their Palestinian refugee status in Jordan. This context – where men lose their jobs, are unable to move freely due to fear of deportation or detention and cannot be involved in political activism simply because they are Palestinian – has generated defiance to the two-sided axes of injustice they face: masculinity and nationality. In such a situation, refugee men and women try to mutually manage their gender beliefs, as women, regardless of their acceptance or rejection of these norms prior to the conflict, take an active role in protecting and defending masculinity in order to counter state prejudices and as an integral part of their struggle for status and recognition.

Masculinist manoeuvring and political identity and belonging

In my interviews with Palestinian refugees in Jordan, it was not easy to ask about gender issues, as their difficult conditions, traumatic stories and feelings of despair made me hesitant. In addition, it was not always possible to hold interviews privately, as houses were small and sometimes it was cold; the whole family had to stay where it was warm. However, even when it was difficult to pose the question directly, the gender issues were apparent in stories of their journeys, entrance to the country, Jordan's entry regulations and customs practices, and the ways in which refugees attempt to counter the gender representation of these practices and regulations. These research conditions also sometimes required just listening to the interactions and discussions between men and women themselves, and other times necessitated follow-up conversations with women privately.

Being present whilst men and women recalled experiences of displacement, tried to make sense of why they were not allowed into the country, and managed their daily lives helped my understanding of how men and women develop mutually dependent survival interests. However, conversations around such shared survival interests in the context of living illegally and keeping a low-profile life mainly pertained to protecting men from deportation or detention. The skewing of this dialogue was first due to men's increased risk of deportation or detention because they are Palestinian, and secondly because men dominated these conversations. According to Palestinian refugees, the primary target of Jordan's harsh measures is their national belonging to Palestine, manifesting in discriminatory practices against men, as men present a greater threat to Jordan's national identity. Thus, Palestinian refugees developed their counter tactics within the same belief systems dominating Jordanian policy: protecting their national identity and masculinity.

This was very clear in my discussion with Ameera, a Palestinian refugee from Syria whose husband is also a Palestinian refugee from Syria. Ameera discussed how her position as a woman, who is less at risk of identity-checks and hence being caught and deported, gives her some power over her husband, but still she chooses to empower him by reminding him of the man he was before the start of the conflict in Syria:

> When I look at my husband and see how sad he is, my heart melts. I don't care if he is mad at me sometimes, he needs to channel his anger somewhere. I understand his position, any man who could no longer provide for his family would be angry. I always remind him of who he was when we were in Syria. This always brings a smile to his face.

In the first visit to Ameera's house, she did not share much about their past life in Syria or how they managed to enter Jordan, but the second time she was more open, revealing that her husband was a member of one of the Palestinian factions in the Yarmouk camp. Before moving to Syria, the husband had been a freedom fighter in Beirut and participated in defending the camps during Israel's invasion in 1982: 'He was so young at the time, but still he played a major role in the protection of Palestinians in Lebanese camps. Everybody knew him and appreciated his courage.' Ameera's aiding of her husband's reclaiming of masculinity is determined by her appreciation of his role in the Palestinian struggle; a role he could no longer play. In addition to her empathy for his inability to perform masculine roles related to financial provision, both are reasons why Ameera endeavoured to find ways to restore her husband's masculinist traits.

Thuryyah explained another aspect of women's role in masculinist manoeuvring, stating 'the man is the pillar of the house. If a man loses authority, confidence, and pride, the family loses its meaningful purpose.' When women are left out of all forms of protection, they may hold on to the forms they are familiar with, i.e. masculinity and what it represents is a familiar form of living and protection. The challenges posed to masculinity by displacement are hence, as articulated clearly by Thuryyah, a form of loss added to the losses of home, identity, and belongings. It was clear from women's narratives that unfamiliarity with new surroundings, with people, and with the new place should not lead to detachment from social norms and relationships. These are the things refugee populations claim authority over, and in some sense help them believe they still exist as independent human beings with some say over their lives. Thuryyah added:

> War has changed us a lot, the way we eat, what we eat and wear, who we speak to, where we go, what we dream about, and even our hopes for a peaceful future for our kids. But it will not change who we are and it should not change the respect we have for our elders and our men.

Authority and control over gender norms seemed very significant to the men and women I interviewed, and any challenge to these norms appeared to meet greater resistance. Thuryyah is a well-educated Palestinian woman. From observing her relationship with her husband and children, it was clear she is not a submissive woman. On the contrary, she corrected her husband several times whilst he was speaking, asked him to boil water for the tea, and works as a private teacher. Even though the tuition fees are meagre for her work, she still is the breadwinner of the family. During my stay at her home, however, I observed her asking her son to go buy something and asking her husband to give the son money. Knowing that her husband did not work, only she did, when he left I took the opportunity to ask how they managed family expenses and financial decisions. She explained: 'When we were in Syria, it did not matter who paid or if the children asked me or their father for money. Here, it's different. I try to make him feel good by letting him manage the financial affairs. I give him almost all of what I earn and let him decide.' Wanting to understand, I followed-up as to her reasons why, and she responded:

> He is a good man, a loving husband and father, I don't think he'd mind if I made these decisions, but I am afraid if things continue in the same way, he will be changed. He is already becoming sadder and sadder. We lost everything, but he lost the most: his freedom, his name, and his identity.

He sees no future for him in this country, his hands are tied. Imagine being transformed in the blink of an eye from someone who had everything to nothing.

Thuryyah's decision to empower her husband through performing gender normative roles – like giving him control over financial decisions – is a measured choice with several meanings. First, the fear of the husband changing from good to bad, which stems from a common cultural perception of unemployed men who cannot provide for their families as less masculine. For instance, a traditional Palestinian proverb states, 'the man is only faulted by his pocket', indicating that, as long as he provides financially, all a man's faults can be overlooked; if he is not providing, this is only his fault. This understanding of men also justifies acts of violence against women, as well as men's changed behaviour when they are unable to provide for their families. As such is the case for Thuryyah's husband, there is an expected impact on his behaviour. By giving him control over the finances, Thuryyah is trying to avoid this result. Such normative perceptions are society's method of keeping both men and women in check, justifying gendered roles and relationships, giving legitimacy to and reaffirming the value of masculine identity.

Thuryyah's statement also shows how men's loss of masculine traits due to conflict and displacement appears to be mourned by both men and women. However, in some studies addressing men's changing role due to war, conflict and displacement, as well as the impact of such on masculinity, women's roles in and views of restoring and protecting masculinity are largely absent. In an interesting article on masculine nostalgia among men in Palestine, MacKenzie and Foster (2017) discuss the occupation's impact on men's ability to fulfil their gender identities, pointing to men's yearning for peace in connection with their yearning for the return to patriarchal gender roles. In my research on Palestinian refugees from Syria, I found the same to be true with regard to men's hopes for the future, whether such involved a return to Syria, resettlement in a third country, or obtaining legal residence in Jordan; all these choices were conceived in relation to their return to their complete manhood. Indeed, men's longing to return to their perception of normal is another form of masculinist manoeuvring. Through conveying their loss as greater than women's, men keep women feeling for them, keep women emotionally attached to their feelings in order to take advantage of the situation. In this sense, while there is really no loss to their gender role, there is a new method of manipulation that evolves during such times. For men to be sad, in despair, or miserable conveys an uncertain future for women. Still, masculinist manoeuvrings would not succeed without women playing an active role, such as Thuryyah and the others discussed in this chapter. This active choice needs to be understood and analysed within the context of and in relation to factors placing these women in a position to assist men's regaining of authority and reclaiming their gender identity.

Thus, the issue here is not the role women play in restoring masculinity during war and displacement, but instead how women's interpretation of the challenges they face intersect with their understanding of belonging, rights, immigration policies, and the kind of history and politics present in refugees' articulation of those notions. Thuryyah's statement that her husband is 'losing the most' is a very good example of how women interpret these experiences. Thuryyah, her husband and their four children entered Jordan with fake Syrian identity cards. While the entire family lost their name and Palestinian identity, Thuryyah felt this was a greater loss for her husband than for herself or her children. As a woman, traditionally and legally, she does not bear the responsibility of passing-on her family name or nationality; this is a man's right and an important aspect of male authority. For a man to lose his name and nationality is to lose his nationhood, his belonging to a certain group, without the choice or ability to join another. If a man loses this right, the same is automatically applied to his wife and children. As I did not want to wrongly interpret Thuryyah's statement, I asked her directly: 'Why do you think, in losing his name and identity, your husband lost more than you?" Thuryyah took a moment to think and then replied, 'if he could say he was Palestinian and reveal his real name, there would be no problem in the first place. I know Palestinian women married to Syrians who managed to correct their situation after entering the country illegally.' In this sense, Thuryyah's husband bears more responsibility than her to preserve the national identity.

The connection made between the political, legal and personal losses in Palestinian refugees' narratives all translated into gendered losses, with men's losses felt as somehow of greater significance. For a man, the inability to reveal his Palestinian refugee identity created a feeling of masculinist defeat perceived not only in relation to men, but also as a political defeat felt at the collective level of belonging to Palestine for both men and women; a matter at the heart of the Palestinian struggle. This was also the case for Ameera and her husband, as his loss of both his role in the resistance and his identity led to him losing his role in the camp as a political leader. These losses are explained with respect to masculinity as relational to nationalism and resistance in their multiple forms, be it direct affiliation with political activities or the role of preserving the Palestinian struggle through the protection of the Palestinian refugee status.

Nonetheless, the expressions women used to convey their messages of and reasons for protecting masculinity and Palestinian national identity go beyond questions of nationalism and identity politics. Indeed, such expressions were mainly tied to the misrecognition of their Palestinian refugee status. In her discussion of recognition and ethics, Nancy Fraser (2001) proposes to treat recognition 'as a question of social status'. In the status model developed, she posits:

> [W]hat requires recognition is not group-specific identity but rather the status of group members as full partners in social interaction. Misrecognition, accordingly, does not mean the depreciation and deformation of group identity. Rather, it means social subordination in the sense of being prevented from participating as a peer in social life.

To amend the injustice resulting from misrecognition requires a politics aimed at overcoming subordination (Fraser, 2001, p. 89). For instance, when Jordanian policies denote Palestinian refugees from Syria as inferior to Jordanians and other Palestinian and Syrian refugees by excluding them from humanitarian response and protection, rendering them invisible, then this situation, according to Frazer's analysis, represents a case of misrecognition and status subordination. The attempt to reclaim recognition should be aimed 'not at valorising group identity, but rather at overcoming subordination' (Fraser, 2001, p. 89). Masculinist manoeuvrings could be conceptualized as 'claims for recognition' that seek to challenge the subordinate status assigned to Palestinian refugees from Syria. As women explained, masculinist manoeuvrings are women's attempts at countering Jordan's policies and their effects on Palestinian refugee men from Syria's capacity to perform their traditional gender roles of work, freedom of mobility and political activities. These manoeuvrings are acts of resistance against prejudice and the denial of a recognized refugee status.

Agency – as discussed by Gökalp (2010) in the context of Kurdish women displaced in Turkish cities – cannot be defined merely as 'liberating or emancipating', but rather should be 'conceptualized in terms of the "politics of survival"' (Gökalp, 2010, p. 564). In her analysis of Kurdish women in Turkey, Gökalp posits that the politicization of identity among displaced Kurdish women has grown out of a 'politics of survival' developed to make sense of their experiences and find hope for the future (Gökalp, 2010, p. 564). Therefore, understanding the ways in which women make their decision either to embrace or resist gendered norms, such as masculinity, should be situated within the politics of the state, its apparatuses and the support, or lack thereof, of humanitarian and women's NGOs. Women's ability to act and make decisions should not be seen only through the lens of resistance to patriarchy or gender hierarchies, but also with respect to how women define and respond to politics aimed at marginalizing them. In this situation, women set out priorities that resist and defy the marginalization of Palestinians from Syria. Based on the understanding that men pose a greater danger than women to society and hence need to be checked, deported or detained, men are the first target of Jordan's policies; and women use the same gender normative framework to counter and challenge the state's anti-Palestinian gender politics.

Masculinist manoeuvring, rights and justice

In my interview with Mohammed (discussed in further detail in Chapter 2) when asked how his family had entered the country, he answered:

> My wife is Syrian. She had her ID on her and talked to the officers and told them that my passport and the children's ID cards had been burned when our house was bombed. That was actually true; the only wrong piece of information was that I was Syrian. Samar was heavily pregnant and they felt for her. We were lucky, I guess.

Samar, who had a plain and tired face, smiled at Mohammed's response and so I asked her what she remembered. 'I do not know, so many things, but the funniest thing was when Mohammed acted like an idiot. I think the border officers thought you [referring to her husband] were mentally disabled, or something like this,' she replied. I asked why they would think that, 'Because he was silent, standing behind me and holding our kids,' Samar responded. 'You were our one and only hope of passing through, I was so desperate,' Mohammed added calmly, but he did not seem to like Samar's comment. Now in Jordan, Mohammed does not want to remember the masculine roles he had to relinquish for them to pass. Mohammed knew it was not luck that got his family into the country.

At the moment of Mohammed and Samar's interaction with the border officers, gender beliefs were displayed, expressed and played off differently. Mohammed knew the officers' mentality and thus agreed to his wife speaking on his behalf – he let her take the lead in the conversation – while he remained passive, entirely contradictory to how he would act under 'normal' circumstances. Therefore, gender norms did not matter at all; indeed, through this act Mohammed took advantage of such gender norms in order to pass. The officers, who are often of Bedouin tribal origins, understood that a 'good' man would not let his wife speak on his behalf unless he had a serious problem. In this sense, they felt for Samar. While being pregnant may have also garnered the officers' sympathy, the main reason they got through was Samar's position as a woman with a man who seemed 'unstable', merely because he kept quiet and stood behind her. If the opposite had been true – i.e. a woman standing behind her husband in silence – this would not have been exceptional or problematic to the officers, but rather the norm. Not revealing his masculine traits by not taking control in the conversation with the border officers worked to Mohammed's advantage. For the border officers, maybe Mohammed did not appear as a danger, perhaps a man who could not represent himself and his family did not seem to pose any risk, and hence his identity was not checked based purely on the assumption of how a man ought to behave.

In the beginning of our interview, Mohammed did not like discussing the details of how they managed to enter the country. Later, however, he opened up and narrated the story to show how he mocked and tricked the system. As Mohammed said, 'when life is at stake, everything needs to be manoeuvred and carefully planned'. Gender norms are clearly at the heart of such manoeuvres in these situations, thus Mohammed took pride in doing something he would have normally considered shameful for a man. For Mohammed, he was 'correcting the wrong-doing of the government decision to ban Palestinians from entering Jordan'. However, prior to Samar mentioning how they got into the country, Mohammed did not speak of his experience of deportation. To correct his image, he immediately told of how he had himself smuggled back into the country after being deported: 'If I had the slightest fear of being caught, I would not be here today. The journey from Syria to Jordan was too risky and I had to take that risk to protect my family. Imagine if I had not returned, what would have happened to Samar and my kids.'

In this situation, a masculinity manoeuvre is not something planned for one moment, such as Mohammed's experience at the border, but a continuous practice used by men to restore the masculine order within the household in situations where women are in a position of privilege. By revealing his illegal entry, and the courage it took, Mohammed was attempting to reinstate his position as a man. Samar nodded in agreement when Mohammed said, 'Imagine if I had not returned, what would have happened to Samar and my kids.' Her confirmation of his statement was also approval of his masculine manoeuvring practice. Samar is a Syrian refugee who can legally live in Jordan; she is in a more privileged position than Mohammed. She is a registered asylum seeker with the UNHCR, can move freely around the country, can take the kids to kindergarten, and manages issues with the UNHCR and other agencies working in the camp. However, Samar was not happy with this freedom and privilege: 'I used to be spoiled. Never took care of issues outside the house. Mohammed's work was very good; there was no need for me to work. We were happy in Syria. I hope one day things will be normal again.' Not only has Samar not taken advantage of the situation, she also contributes to Mohammed's attempt to restore his masculine-self.

However, this does not indicate that women do not want rights or to be empowered. Rather, when rights are gained not based on women's priorities and choices, but instead come as a result of discrimination against their husbands and male family members, women may side with men and take an active role in the 'masculinist restoration' process. Mohammed's position as a Palestinian refugee man, and Samar's position as a Syrian refugee woman with privileges of residency, work and mobility, challenges male domination over women. Still, both Mohammed and Samar's articulation of the situation with reference to Mohammed's courage and significance in protecting the family – even though he could not leave the house and the family relies entirely on Samar – clearly points to the fact that for masculinist restoration to take place in the aftermath of war or crisis, a phase of masculinist manoeuvre is required, whether within households, at border check points, in interactions with service providers, etc.

Almost all five of the Syrian women married to Palestinian men that I interviewed in Jordan shared Samar's experience. The sense of injustice against their husbands, who were mainly exposed to discrimination due to their Palestinian-ness, made it difficult for these women to enjoy or conceive of rights outside the political. The question of rights here is significant, and women expressed this in terms of 'what it is right and what is wrong', not in terms of a universal view of rights; a point I engage with in a more detail when addressing cases of Jordanian women married to Palestinian refugee men in Chapter 4. Hence, in these situations, aiding their husbands' reclaiming of masculinity is the 'right thing to do'.

Both Mohammed and Samar's positions and roles in the manoeuvring/reclaiming of masculinity challenge account on the transformation of gender roles and norms and the perceived 'crisis' of masculinity in war and conflict. Both their positions confirm that women's perceptions cannot be understood in relation to the changing nature of gender roles, but rather point to conditions, policies, rights, privileges, and the ways in which unconventional gender roles are increased and performed at the expense of husbands and male relatives.

Similar to Palestinian refugee women from Syria, Syrian refugee women married to Palestinian refugee men also define their acts and roles vis-à-vis their understanding of the politics shaping their daily lives. Their account of masculinity is closely connected to questions of justice in legal, political and socio-economic conditions. Thus, masculinist manoeuvring is a choice shaped by their experience of war and displacement both as Syrians and as Syrian women married to Palestinians. Their politicization, hence, is a consequence of their complex relationship with the Syrian state, Jordanian state, Palestinian national struggle, and humanitarian organizations that recognize their right to humanitarian assistance but deny it to their husbands and children. The national struggle for Syrian women is not based on their national affiliation with Palestine, but it is based on their understanding of justice. For such Syrian refugee women, the demands of justice for their Palestinian men surpass claims of gender rights.

Conclusion: the political is very personal

Although the role of the state and its apparatuses appears not to be directly linked to the management of masculinity within the households of Palestinian refugees from Syria, its discriminatory policies, threat to men's role and denial of their rights have shaped women's choice to take an active role in masculinist manoeuvrings. The differing treatment between Syrians and Palestinian refugees from Syria made it impossible for Palestinians to articulate anything other than their Palestinian-ness; the injustice is an injustice for Palestine. Since it is this identity aspect under attack by Jordan's entry regulations, deportations and other discriminatory practices, it is therefore important for this identity aspect to be defended. Whilst their stories, daily activities, and roles made it clear that gender positions are never determined or fixed, the value of gender notions – such as that of masculinity – interacted with belonging, context, politics, and the ways in which women articulated that context with respect to the larger question of Palestine. Power gains or losses during displacement, however, are mutual losses for both men and women when identified as an attack on the Palestinian identity and right to collective struggle. Hence, the role of masculinist manoeuvring is a deliberate choice for women. Against all attempts to push either their own or their husbands' Palestinian-ness away, leaving them with an illegal vulnerability, women reclaim their agency through challenging inequalities and demanding justice. The priorities here are clear: national belonging coupled with their understanding of the attack on men's role as an attack on the Palestinian struggle, women thus see the survival of masculinity as a necessary condition of the survival of the struggle for Palestine and part of their quest for justice.

Consequently, any conceptualization of women's agency and capacity to act should not overlook their understanding of their rights and roles within a framework of justice shaped by their interaction with states and national and international politics. In fact, Palestinian and Syrian refugee women expressed similar feelings, alongside a rebuke of the wrongs committed against Palestinian refugee men from Syria because they are Palestinian and because they are men. The violation of men's rights based on nationality determines women and children's rights and access to education, health, decent work and freedom of mobility. Hence, the political is very personal for these women and necessitates a response at the private level; their support for their husbands' reclaiming of masculinity is their way to right the state's wrongdoings.

6

Multi-layered misrecognition, claims for justice and GBV

> I wish I did not come to Jordan; my nationality grants me nothing. Coming to Jordan was my first choice as I thought, as a Jordanian woman, I would be able to live normally in the country with my husband and kids. I am in a situation now where I cannot go back to Syria, death is awaiting us there if we return, since destruction is everywhere. Where we used to live in Aleppo nothing is left, it's a ghost city. I cannot return to Palestine, I cannot live in Jordan with my husband and children, and we cannot apply for asylum to resettle in another country. What are we supposed to do?

Ibtihal's above statement summarizes the dilemma of Palestinian women with Jordanian nationality married to Palestinian refugee men from Syria. Jordan is the first and obvious choice for these women and their families. As women, however, they cannot pass their nationality to their children and husbands, as men can. Furthermore, they also cannot apply for the *mazaya* (privileges) system established in 2014, which helps children of Jordanian women married to non-Jordanian men access health, education and other residency privileges. As Jordanian women, they also cannot apply for asylum under the UNHCR, as they hold Jordanian citizenship. Still, since 2013, Jordan has retained a no-entry policy for Palestinians, so their husbands and children cannot enter the country; if they do manage to enter, they cannot apply to the UNHCR for asylum, since Palestinians are excluded from the UNHCR mandate (see Chapter 2 for discussion on Palestinian's exclusion from the UNHCR mandate).

In this chapter, I discuss GBV practices evident in the narratives of Palestinian/Jordanian women married to Palestinian refugee men from Syria. I raise the case of Palestinian refugee women with Jordanian nationality to address a link between questions of Palestinian dispossession, multiple displacements, misrecognition of Palestinian-ness in the Syrian 'crisis' and state gender politics, which all systematically lead to exposing Palestinian refugee women with Jordanian nationality to multiple forms of GBV. In the preceding chapter, I discussed how Palestinian refugee women from Syria respond to attempts to subordinate Palestinian refugee men by adopting a form of masculinist manoeuvring aimed at resisting the state's prejudiced practices and policies against such men. In my interviews, this response was not articulated in relation to gender roles, as these norms are disconnected from politics, but rather by closely linking the personal and political as informed by structures of power, systems of inequalities, and questions of justice and rights. Claims for political and gender identity are entangled with the right of recognition; in Fraser's words, these are 'claims for justice'. In this chapter, I further develop this idea of connecting recognition to justice by exploring another group of women amongst Palestinian refugees from Syria: Jordanian Palestinian women married to Palestinian refugee men from Syria.

Recognizing the specificity of these women's experiences, as Joan Scott explains, is an 'examination of the workings of the ideological system itself, its categories of representation, its premises about what these categories mean and how they operate, and of its notions of subjects, origin, and cause' (1991, p. 778). The case of Palestinian/Jordanian women displaced from Syria demonstrates that not only is refugee-ness denied based on categorizing Palestinian refugees from Syria as distinct from other refugees, but this situation has also created subcategories whose experiences require addressing both directly and in relation to the history and politics of the main group, as well as the ideologies surrounding its existence. Discussing such experiences is not, however, an argument for hierarchies of vulnerability, whether they are more or less vulnerable than other categories of women, but rather 'an examination of knowledge-making and living at the same time' (1991, p. 778).

In assessing Jordan's practices, regulations and entry policies in relation to Jordanian/Palestinian refugee women from Syria, alongside the effects of these practices on women's lived experience of displacement, I employ Fraser's model of 'recognition and redistribution'. In doing so, I argue there are two types of classification requiring connection. First, the classification of Palestinian refugees from Syria as a distinct and unwelcome group of the Syrian refugee 'crisis'. If categories exist to classify people and determine entitlements accordingly, as Stuart Hall (Grossberg, 1986) insists, then classifying Palestinian refugees from Syria in this way has concrete material effects. As their exclusion from protection and asylum is based on their Palestinianism, the implications of displacement on both gender and refugee status must address and link classification, recognition and effects. The second type of classification is the gender category, as Jordan's legal system and social/cultural practices class women as a subordinate group, with material effects on their rights within the family and vis-à-vis the nationality law. This means there are two closely linked classification types that must be recognized in order to redress injustices related to Jordanian/Palestinian refugee women from Syria: women's equal rights with Jordanian men and Palestinian refugee status on equal footing with other refugees. The redistribution aspect of Fraser's model both reflects what women expressed, discussed in detail below, and proposes a new way of looking at rights: not in an abstract sense, but through redressing gender injustice, as such requires structural and societal transformation, which first must tackle the question of classifications that enable misrecognition and injustice, manifesting in discriminatory and GBV policies and practices.

In order to understand the particularity of Jordanian/Palestinian refugee women's experiences in relation to discriminatory state practices and societal GBV, an understanding of how misrecognition of both gender and politics and the maldistribution of power at the political, legal and socio-economic levels formed the unity of their situation. Therefore, this chapter connects analysis of GBV to questions of misrecognition and injustice, two analytical frameworks often delinked in addressing gender issues of the displacement experience.

Linking misrecognition, maldistribution of power and gender injustice

The Jordanian/Palestinian refugee from Syria subcategory reflects both the complexity of marriage and family relationships between Palestinian refugees living in Jordan and Syria, and the different refugee status and rights these countries assign to them (the situation of Jordan is discussed in detail in

Chapter 2). All Jordanian/Palestinian refugee women interviewed were living in Palestinian camps in Jordan prior to their marriage, and thus considered themselves both Jordanian and Palestinian refugees. These women had moved to Syria after marrying their cousins, who were Palestinian refugees in Syria. Such marriages are a way to keep family ties between Palestinians' relatives alive, as many are scattered over two or more countries. For instance, before Ibtihal began narrating her story of displacement, she made sure I was aware of where it started:

> Before experiencing war in Syria, I had never known what my family had been through when forced to leave their home and belongings twice, first in 1948 and second in 1967. I grew up listening to their story of displacement but never thought I would have the same fate. We are from Safed, a city in the Galilee in the north of Palestine. My mother used to tell us stories about Safed, about the Nakba, and about the many refugee camps she and her family moved to before settling in Husun Camp, it seemed an endless journey. I did not live much with my family in the camp in Jordan. A year before *twjihi* (the last year of high school), I got engaged to my cousin at the age of 17. My uncle lived in Aleppo in Syria, so I left my school, my life in the camp, my friends and moved to Aleppo. That was not easy, to say the least, but I understood my father's reason: he wanted to maintain a connection with his family in Syria through my marriage. Life was not stress-free at my uncle's house; my mother-in-law was particularly harsh on me. I was young and we had many disagreements. I lived with my uncle's family for 16 years, I gave birth to my four children, two girls and two boys, while I was living in one room of my uncle's house. I would be lying if I said I had a happy life in Aleppo, but at least it was a safe life, it was our life even if it was not perfect. My husband's job was good, and we had what we needed. I had dreamt of leaving Syria and coming back to Jordan, or taking my children and travelling anywhere else, especially after my husband got married for a second time and brought me a *doruh* (fellow wife in a polygamous marriage, referred to as *doruh*/from the noun *darar*, a form of harm). The new wife was a Syrian from Aleppo, her name is Samah. Taking another wife was like adding salt to the wound, I was already unhappy but could cope. With his marriage, things become unbearable.

Undoubtedly, Ibtihal lived a challenging life prior to the conflict in Syria, as a young woman travelling to a new city, new country, new family. Her narration revealed that even after conflict, displacement and what she and her family had been through, she could not talk about her current situation without recalling past memories of her family's displacement from Palestine, the injustice of marrying her off at only seventeen and dropping out of school, and the tough life she had with her in-laws and her husband's second wife. It was startling listening to women, like Ibtihal, make sense of their situation. Their ability to historicize their own experience and connect multiple systems of discrimination was particularly remarkable. Recalling Hall's definition of articulation, discussed in Chapter 2, it is important to emphasize that women, when expressing their thoughts, are also trying to understand, put into perspective, and offer their own analysis of connected events.

As Hall explained, an articulation is 'the connection that can make a unity of two different elements, under certain conditions', in Ibtihal's narration, she connected two important elements: her family's multiple displacements and her father's subsequent attempt to reunite the scattered clan through her marriage; and her own life as shaped by these conditions, i.e. living in a Palestinian camp in Jordan or Aleppo, being exposed to early and forced marriage, dropping out of school, living in an extended family house and her husband's second marriage. This was not just her way of expressing her thoughts; rather, as a Palestinian refugee with Jordanian nationality married to a Palestinian from Syria, she had to tell her complete story. The starting point for Ibtihal was her family's displacement to Jordan and her uncle's to Syria. This needed to be acknowledged before she could recall the war and conflict in Syria and her own displacement as a Jordanian Palestinian woman with limited rights. When I asked Ibtihal how she felt when she had to leave school, she answered: 'I was very good at school, not in the top 10, but I was good and I could have completed my education. But, as you know, we were poor, big family of 10, my parents and eight siblings, and my father was very happy about reconnecting with his family in Syria.' Ibtihal summed up the unity of her historical, economic, political and personal conditions in an answer to one question.

Fraser proposes a framework of analysis for the justice of social practice; a framework that makes examining Hall's conceptualization of articulation – as a form of unity – possible in practical terms. Fraser posits that justice should 'put recognition at its centre' (1998, p. 1), as such is crucial to understanding the axes of injustice that Palestinian refugee women with Jordanian nationality married to Palestinian refugee men face when treated as refugees in their country of nationality. Their demand for justice includes social and political recognition, as both Jordanian women and Palestinian refugees, and hence a redistribution of power at the social, economic and political levels. Fraser's contention is that arguments of redistribution or recognition are alone insufficient; to understand and redress gender injustice requires attention to both, as gender is a 'two-sided category' encompassing both the economic and political face of redistribution and the cultural face that brings it within the realm of recognition (1998, p. 2). Conversely, redressing gender injustice requires transformation of the structures and status order of society.

For Fraser, misrecognition stems from distinctive, institutionally constructed characteristics assigned to individuals and groups (1998, p. 3). Thus, the denial of justice is a consequence of political, economic and cultural arrangements that result in the unequal participation of certain groups in society. Furthermore, recognition of self-realization claims, especially those linked to self-consciousness, might also lead to another form of victim blaming. This perspective, for Fraser, feeds into universalistic views of justice instead of considering the distinctiveness of certain groups; hence, analysis of these distinctions should depend on forms of misrecognition and 'what the misrecognised people need in order to be able to participate as peers in social life' (1998, p. 5).

The distinctiveness of Jordanian/Palestinian refugee women lies in the fact that they are Palestinian refugees with Jordanian nationality married to Palestinian refugee men from Syria. The key aspect, and perhaps what makes Fraser's analysis relevant to this research, is precisely this point of distinctiveness among groups within the same context. This is central, as it is incorrect to assume that all people in one context share the same needs; we must acknowledge the multiple forms of misrecognition and their connection to the distribution of power. Furthermore, it is important to see various needs as well as shifting needs: 'which people need which kind(s) of recognition in which context depends on the nature of the obstacles they face with regard to participatory parity' (1998, p. 6). The big task for theory is to adopt 'an approach that accommodates differentiation, divergence, and interaction at all levels', without reducing one to another (1998, p. 7). Thus, Fraser proposes what she terms 'perspectival dualism' as an analytical framework, which, instead of collapsing redistribution and recognition as one in the same, analyses how they impinge on one another 'in ways that may give rise to unintended effects' (1998, p. 8). This framework allows us to assess the justice of any social practice and conceptualize the practical obstacles that could emerge in the political struggle for redistribution and recognition (1998, pp. 8–10).

As the next analysis shows, Palestinian refugee/Jordanian women's rights narrative is expressed in terms of what they feel is right and wrong, i.e. the entitlements of Jordanian citizenship for women is not equal to men, as women cannot pass Jordanian nationality to their children, and also does not allow them to enter the country and flee war like other refugees; these, according to my interviewees, are 'wrongdoings'. For these women, however, righting such wrongdoings would require more than just gaining equal rights with men, as their claims for justice address both the historical and political foundations of structural discrimination in terms of both their gender and Palestinianism classification, reflecting the distribution of power within legal, cultural and social structures.

Justice and recognition vs. rights claims

Khitam is Jordanian and married to her cousin, Ismael, a Palestinian refugee from Syria. Prior to the conflict, they had lived in Dera'a Camp for fifteen years. However, when they decided to escape and go to Jordan after the camp came under heavy bombardment, they never imagined they would be refused entry. Only Khitam was allowed to enter, while her husband and five children were taken to the Cyber City Detention Centre. In the beginning, Khitam refused to leave her family and stayed in the detention centre with them: 'It was not right for me to live freely in the country while my husband and kids were detained.' As such, Khitam was made to feel that the exercise of her citizenship rights would be at the expense of her children and husband.

In Khitam's account, she could not enjoy her citizenship rights unless she abandoned her husband and children, and these are not rights if they do such injustice: 'our rights should not go against justice for our families'. Khitam and other Jordanian women married to Palestinian refugee men could not define their rights outside their familial responsibilities to their children and husbands; thus, the rights such women have in this situation are 'useless'. Khitam decided to leave detention in order to help secure her family's release from Cyber City. When I met her, she had been out for around three months using everything at her disposal to get her family out of detention. Since then, she has felt 'a sense of guilt that is killing me, being free while my kids are not. My citizenship rights are like chains around my neck. You want the best for your kids and family. Am I supposed to be happy to be Jordanian? I am certainly not.' Through Khitam, I also learnt she was not the only Jordanian woman detained in Cyber City:

> There were three other Jordanian women. One was very old; she was with her old husband. Their sons and daughters had gone to Lebanon after several failed attempts to enter Jordan. The old lady, Zakeeh, whose husband I managed to speak to over the phone, thought that because she was a Jordanian, the government might let them in, but that did not happen. They tried *wasta* (connection) and everything else, but it did not work. This is not right; it should not be right.

As Cockburn (2004) argued, 'gender power relations in many societies result in discrimination against women by law and custom'. Feminist literature has addressed the connection between questions of national identity, gender, and family laws in Jordan and the Arab region (Charrad, 2001, 2011; Massad, 2001), especially with regard to laws that govern the guardianship over women provision of the Jordanian Personal Status Law (JPSL) (Jabiri, 2016). Guardianship, which designates women with the status of legal minor, not only forms the basis of women's legal and social subordination but also plays a key role in the construction and reproduction of a gender hierarchy system in Jordan. Based on this system, women's rights to education, travel and choice of marriage are overseen by men, with a patrilineal principle designating children of Jordanian women as foreigners (Jabiri, 2016). The 1928 Jordanian Nationality Law stated: 'The wife of a foreigner is a foreigner.' Though amended in 1961 and 1963, this law has denationalized hundreds of women, depriving them of their Jordanian nationality. Indeed, it was not until 1987 that women married to foreigners were able to retain their nationality (Massad, 2001). However, this award of Jordanian nationality has been promulgated to naturalize a model of the 'extended male-centred patrilineage' governing kinship relations (Charrad, 2001, p. 5). Thus, when Jordanian women marry non-Jordanian men, the children's blood descent is assumed to belong to the paternal line only (Joseph, 2000).

In 2014, the government of Jordan issued the *nizam el-mazaya* (privileges system). Under the *mazaya* system, children of Jordanian women married to non-Jordanians can access privileges such as free public education and health care, jobs, residence permits, driver's licenses and permission. However, such *mazaya*, while limited in scope and yet to materialize in practice due to numerous obstacles, are denied to women married to Palestinian refugees from Syria. For example, Ibtihal detailed how her family entered Jordan and the time it took to get her children out of the Cyber City Detention Centre as follows:

> We tried three times to enter Jordan, but we failed to do so. Each time, it took us around seven days on the road from Syria to Jordan. After these failed attempts, we decided to buy fake Syrian identity cards. Myself and my husband's second wife entered legally as we were both allowed in. My husband and kids entered with fake identity cards. We rented an apartment near my family in the Palestinian camp. A year later, *el-mukhabarat* came to our house and took my husband. He was accused of forgery and put in prison, and then deported back to Syria. My four children were sent to the Cyber City. My two girls only stayed there for a few days, as I applied for a reunion for them and they were granted a visitation right for a week. [After that] They did not return to the Cyber City; nobody asked us to take them back and we did not. My two boys stayed for two years. In the Cyber City, it was very difficult, they lived with four other young men in one room. I applied for reunion but was also given visitation rights, in the beginning for few hours a week. Then, visitation rights were extended to one day a week. It took two years to get them out of the Cyber City.

However, although Ibtihal's kids are now out of detention, they still do not enjoy the *mazaya* given to children of Jordanian women married to foreigners. As Ibtihal explained:

> My daughter could not register to sit the *twjihi* exams and had to drop out of school as a result. She was brilliant in school. I had hoped, through education, for her to have a better future than mine, but we could not register her for

the exams. So, my family and I arranged her marriage to one of my relatives from my mother's side. She was not happy and nor was I, but my family felt it was for the best. After all, she was marrying her cousin not a stranger.

Ibtihal clearly felt that her daughter's fate duplicated her own: '*hasrah fi qalbi anaha ma darast ashan ma eindaha raqm julu*' (It is an anguish in my heart that she did not study and did not have a seat number for the exam). In order for Ibtihal's daughter to get a seat number, she needed to have either a Jordanian national identity number, recognized UNHCR refugee status, or a passport from another country. Travel documents issued by Syria and Lebanon are not valid. As Ibtihal implored, 'I did my best to get her a seat number, but all I got was one answer: "Palestinian travel-document holders are not eligible".'

Ibtihal believed her daughter's ability to obtain Jordanian citizenship through marriage, unlike her sons, was an advantage: 'In a year or so, my daughter will be Jordanian. I wish I could arrange the same for my boys, but marrying a Jordanian woman would not help them get any rights.' However, while men's reserved right to pass nationality to spouses and children worked in Ibtihal's daughter's favour in terms of obtaining Jordanian nationality, it also exposed her to multiple forms of discrimination and violence. Palestinian refugee men from Syria, on the other hand, are denied the opportunity to obtain Jordanian citizenship even if married to Jordanian women. As both the family and nationality laws make women dependent on and followers of men, if a woman marries a foreigner she becomes a foreigner herself.

Khitam's statement, 'My rights are chains around my neck,' clearly reflects that the intent of rights representing certain group privileges is to create distinctions, exclusion and differentiations. Conversely, these rights are elements of exclusion themselves, as they are not enjoyed or exercised based on humanity; instead, they are ascribed based on patriotic affiliations and conditions, and hence should not be celebrated by their holders as long as they are not enjoyed by all, regardless of race, gender, ethnicity and so forth. Hannah Arendt posited that 'The "human" in human rights was a mockery' (1951, p. 300), as those most in need of human rights – refugees, stateless people, those deprived of citizenship – are the least able to exercise them. As she explained, 'The right to have rights: primordial human right is the right to political community' (1951, p. 302). In the case of Palestinian women with Jordanian citizenship married to Palestinian refugee men, the Jordanian nationality rights granted are both gendered and political. Not only do these laws not protect everyone equally, they also contribute to the continuity of discrimination and GBV practices. While the conditions under which Ibtihal and her daughter were forced into marriage differed, the legal system that treats women as 'minors', allows the early marriage of girls, prioritizes family ties over women's choices, complicates family relationships during displacement, upholds discriminatory practices and policies against refugees, and economic hardships all interacted to contribute to both being denied opportunities, deprived of better life choices and exposed to GBV. This is what I examine in detail next.

Manifolded misrecognition, injustice and GBV

Ro'a is nineteen years old, a Palestinian refugee from Syria, and married to another Palestinian refugee from Syria. Ro'a's mother, a Jordanian woman married to a Palestinian refugee man from Syria, lived in Yarmouk Camp and died when Ro'a was six years old. Ro'a's father died in 2013, but his Syrian wife managed to get out of Syria by fabricating her sons' identity cards. After her stepmother fled, Ro'a was left with relatives and neighbours in Yarmouk Camp. Her father had been a politician, engaged in resistance and had many friends willing to help her. They tried sending her to live with her maternal grandparents in Jordan, but she was denied entry. So instead, with the help of her father's friends, Ro'a moved to Lebanon to live with her paternal grandparents, where she lived for four years. Due to the fight in the camp, attempts to get to Jordan, and arrangements for Lebanon, she had missed a few years of school and felt it was too late to catch up. However, the fact that she was not enrolled was heart-breaking for Ro'a: 'My father had great plans for me. He used to tell me "no matter what, you will finish your university education." That was before the war. Things changed a lot after his death.' By losing her father, Ro'a felt she had lost her only source of protection, and her experience at her grandparents' house in Lebanon confirmed this. She did, indeed, not feel safe there:

My grandmother was an angry woman, she screamed all the time but that was fine, I did not mind it. But, my grandfather sexually harassed me, although he never touched me. The first time I noticed his indecency was when I was taking a bath. The bathroom had no door, just a curtain, and he opened the curtain while I was bathing. After that, I became afraid to go into the bathroom unless my grandmother was sitting in the living room, to make sure he would not open the curtain again. My baths were very quick after that; I used to wash my body whilst wearing my bra and underwear. He also looked strangely at my private parts, things like this always made me uncomfortable. My grandmother even caught him sneaking into my bed one night while I was asleep. I only woke up when I heard her asking him what he was doing. He said he was just trying to cover me.

While Ro'a did try to speak to her grandmother after this incident, she was silenced, as her grandmother denied the whole thing. At this point, Ro'a called a very close friend of her father in Syria, uncle Salim, who had repeatedly told her to call if she ever needed anything, and told him she was unhappy and not treated well at her grandparents' house. Salim had a son who had managed to enter Jordan, and Salim asked if she would agree to marry him; Ro'a accepted without hesitation. The only problem was how to get Ro'a into Jordan, as there is no direct smuggling route from Lebanon to Jordan. As the road was too dangerous for her to travel to Jordan through Syria, they decided to find an alternative. Salim's son, Ali, proposed a scheme: a fake marriage between Ro'a and Ali's Jordanian friend, who would divorce her when they arrived in Jordan so that she could then marry Ali. After negotiation and discussions, Salim, Ro'a and her grandparents agreed to this plan and arrangements for the marriage and travel were made. Two months later, Ro'a arrived in Jordan and moved in with her maternal grandparents. However, Ali's Jordanian friend, who had, until this point, fully cooperated throughout the process, changed his mind and refused to divorce Ro'a. 'I am not sure what happened to him, but I think it was about money,' Ro'a explained. Indeed, the friend wanted to take advantage of the situation, and an amount of money was agreed and received before he divorced Ro'a. Six months later, Ro'a and Ali married.

When I met Ro'a, she was just nineteen-year-old and had been in Jordan for three years, meaning she married at the age of sixteen. However, her marriage was never officially registered since both she and Ali are illegal in the country. Still, Ro'a did not fully recognize the precarity of her situation until she had a son, as they could not get a birth certificate issued for him. At one point, her son fell, broke his leg, was in severe pain and there was nothing she could do to help him. She ended up having to knock on the doors of all her neighbours to find a boy of her son's age to impersonate so they could go to the public hospital. As Ro'a described, 'that was the most painful experience I had ever been through'. Ro'a has also had to face these challenges on her own, as Ali is detained at the Gardens Camp and only allowed out once a week (the Gardens Camp was established to accommodate Palestinian refugees from Syria formerly detained in the Cyber City).

In addition to living illegally, Ro'a had also fabricated a marriage and been involved in an illegitimate relationship, as a marriage is not recognized in Jordan unless it is registered (Article 36 of the JPSL) and it is a criminal offence not to register. In the eyes of the law, she has committed three offences. When I asked if she was afraid of being arrested, this was her response:

> *Khaliha ala allah* (leave it to God), I have not seen a good day since I left Syria. I do not know what the future holds for us, *enshallah khair* (hopefully something good). My current situation, I live alone except for one day a week when Ali is allowed to leave the camp. Ali asked a lawyer, who told us that if the authorities discover our undocumented marriage, we would have to serve a sentence of three months and pay around 3000 JOD.
>
> (around $4500 USD)

Even though Ro'a's mother was Jordanian, she still had to go through a painful and dangerous journey to enter Jordan and is currently an illegal resident in the country, and hence has to hide. Having relatives in the Palestinian camp helps her to hide there without attracting the attention of authorities. I listened to Ro'a's interview several times, with one question in my mind: how could she make sense of going through all this and her current reality? Her status as a refugee child is misrecognized because she is the daughter of a Jordanian woman and Palestinian refugee man from Syria. Although both her parents are deceased, her misrecognition stems from both her mother's gender status and her father's Palestinian-ness. The material effects of this manifolded misrecognition have been severe for Ro'a, as she experienced multiple forms of GBV: forced to drop out of school, sexual violence, exposed to dangerous smuggling, married at an early age, and living in constant fear of detention and deportation.

The literature on the subject broadly and vaguely refers to GBV and cases like that of Ro'a in terms of those with irregular or undercommented refugee status, e.g. 'Women with irregular status are increasingly vulnerable to sexual and gender-based violence as they cannot rely on the local authorities for protection' (Freedman, Kivilcim, and Baklacıoğlu, 2019, p. 2). However, such an outlook fails to acknowledge and connect GBV practices to the politics making these women more vulnerable, and does not inform our knowledge of the conditions under which those with irregular status have become increasingly marginalized within the Syrian refugee crisis. Furthermore, this perception also does not contextualize, politicize or historicize the experiences of such women. For instance, if Ro'a had been able to flee Syria with her stepmother – who is currently somewhere in Europe – or reunite with her maternal grandparents in Jordan, her first choices, she might have been spared at least some of the GBV practices she experienced.

While we will never know exactly what Ro'a's two preferred options might have involved, certainly the particularity of her experience – as the daughter of a Jordanian Palestinian woman and Palestinian refugee man from Syria – made her journey to safety much harder than her Syrian counterparts. Moreover, Ro'a's safety from war and destruction was only made possible through being subject to multiple forms of GBV. However, this does not mean that representation of issues related to GBV in the context of Syrian refugees is more adequately addressed by the literature. Indeed, the broad and vague representation of cases like Ro'a has also affected analytical accounts of GBV with regard to Syrian refugee women, as GBV practices are largely addressed in isolation from other structural issues. Generally speaking, most literature on the matter looks at GBV against Syrian refugee women in Jordan only through the lens of physical violence, emotional violence, factors that contribute and perpetuate intimate partner violence, and the effects of such violence on women (Al-Natour, Al-Ostaz and Morris, 2019; Daoud, 2021; Gausman *et al.*, 2021). Another noticeable tendency in research on Syrian refugee women in Jordan, especially related to child marriage, is the particular focus on and linking of GBV to health (e.g. El Arab and Sagbakken, 2019; Al-Ostaz and Morris, 2019). This is the type of representation Syrian refugee women receive in the literature and studies about them. Although more visible than other groups, still this representation is not adequate, as it continues to reflect male violence rather than the structural components of connected forms of oppression. In the case of Palestinian refugees from Syria, this is embodied in the links between settler colonialism, patriarchy, militarization and nationalism.

Recognition and justice in decolonizing analysis of GBV – the way forward

I asked Ibtihal if I could also speak to her daughter, as she lived only a few blocks from Ibtihal's house, but Ibtihal replied: 'her husband would not allow her to speak to you. She rarely visits us. Unless he is with her, she does not come to visit us. She is young and he feels he needs to protect her.' Ro'a expressed almost the exact same sentiment in terms of visiting her grandparents or leaving the house for shopping, but added: 'You know, there is no one to protect me but Ali. He thinks I should always be within his sight, just in case.' I asked how that was possible when Ali spent six days a week in the Gardens Camp, and she replied: '*Walah* (by the name of god), sometimes I spend days with no food until he comes to do the shopping. You may not believe it, but this is how my life is now. What if I got caught when Ali was in the camp? Who would help me and my kid? It's better like this.'

Women's mobility inside Palestinian camps is not a matter of concern for women, as they visit family, neighbours and friends in the camps spontaneously and, in most cases, freely. These visits are part of women's daily interactions with each other and their families, providing them with a feeling of protection, as they can disclose and share marriage problems and partner abuse with each other, brothers and fathers if an intervention is needed. State protection measures, such as reporting abuse to police or providing shelters for battered women, although limited, are unavailable to Palestinian refugee women in the camps; hence, kinship relations and daily interactions are women's only means of protection when subjected to GBV. However, for Palestinian refugee women from Syria, these means are also unavailable. They are excluded from both formal and informal means of protection, other than their husbands, who clearly take advantage by limiting their movement and access to social networks.

Feminist literature on GBV in war and conflict has addressed a wide range of gender and sexual violence as well as introduced new methodological and conceptual underpinnings for such forms (Cockburn, 2004; Giles and Hyndman, 2004; Korac, 2006, 2018; Gökalp, 2010; Al-Ali and Pratt, 2011; Wirtz *et al.*, 2014, 2018; Jabiri, 2017; Al-Ali, 2018; Schulz, 2018). This literature represents not only a growing interest within feminist theory to address gender forms, perpetrators and actors, but also a new conceptualization of GBV that moves beyond the male-centric framework attributing GBV to culture and violent men rather than structural issues. Liz Kelly (1987), for instance, first discussed violence against women as a continuum, and her work has been particularly significant to feminist theorization of GBV. Reflecting on her own work, Kelly argued that although 1970s feminist research linked various forms of violence against women, the absence of the concept of a continuum left out issues of social status in relation to class and migration. This literature, including her own work, thus contributed to drawing generalizations about women's common experiences of GBV (Kelly, 2019). Therefore, Kelly turned her attention to the need for 'rather than levelling the severity of violence or equalizing forms and effects, the continuum underlines how domination and appropriation of women's bodies by men is a structuring link' (Kelly, 2019, p. 1).

Cockburn (2004) broadened the understanding of the GBV continuum in war and conflict by linking household and battlefield violence to gender power 'seen to shape the dynamics of every site of human interaction, from the household to the international arena'. Al-Ali (2018) addressed ISIS's sexual violence against women in Iraq, particularly Yazidi women, contributing to the discussion through adopting an analysis of sexual violence that looks at both 'macrostructural configurations of power pertaining to imperialism, neoliberalism and globalization on the one hand, and localized expressions of patriarchy, religious interpretations and practices and cultural norms on the other hand'. Making such links contributes to understanding GBV in terms of the unequal gender power relations that lead to gender inequalities in the economic, social, and political spheres, be it nationally or globally. The case of

Yazidi women also presents other forms of categorization, such as sectarianism and ethnicity.

The above discussion of feminist contributions to the study of GBV, especially during war and conflict, links patriarchy, authoritarianism and militarized gender regimes, which Vergès (2022) contends 'offers a theoretical and practical opportunity: that of making this violence the very terrain on which to challenge patriarchal capitalism'. Furthermore, Vergès also argues against a feminist analysis that fights only for gender equality (Vergès, 2021, p. 34):

> A decolonial feminism cannot conceivably separate 'violence against women' or against 'minorities' from a global state of violence: the children who commit suicide in refugee camps, the police and military's massive recourse to rape in armed conflict, systemic racism, the exile of millions of people due to the multiplication of war zones and to economic and climatic conditions that have rendered zones of living uninhabitable, femicide, and the relentless increase in precarity. Can we imagine addressing only part of this violence without considering the rest?
>
> (Vergès, 2022)

To decolonize feminist analysis of GBV, Vergès poses a number of questions that feminist inquiry must ask in order to free itself of accounts that render some women's experiences in the Global South invisible. First, Vergès asks 'Who are these women that the patriarchal State considers worthy of protection?' In the case of Palestinian refugee women from Syria with Jordanian nationality, due to their marriage to foreign men and their affiliation with men with Syrian/Palestinian travel documents, these women have been found unworthy of state protection. Thus, Palestinian refugee women with Jordanian nationality experience three times the discrimination other Jordanian women experience: as women, as women married to foreigners, and as women married to Palestinian men from Syria.

The Palestinian refugee women I interviewed clearly articulated the links between the two cases of dispossession, from Palestine and then Syria, in addressing the distinctiveness of their position by showing the continuity of the dispossession of the 1948 Nakba to their displacement from Syria. In making the case for their distinctiveness, they were making claims of recognition and justice; recognition of Palestinianism as a valid ground for refugee-ness. In this sense, these women's call for justice, in Angela Davis's words, 'involves so much more than gender equality. And it involves so much more than gender' (Cited in Ahmed and Irani, 2020). In this case, the GBV narrative connects GBV to the dispossession of the settler colonial project in Palestine, militarism in Syria, and nationalism and the gender regime in Jordan. It also responds to Vergès's call to decolonize feminism by connecting violence against women to 'the fight against policies of dispossession, colonization, extractivism, and the systematic destruction of the living' (Vergès, 2021, p. 32).

Second, Vergès queries 'How to explain the State's differentiation of children who have the right to a protected childhood and those who do not?' Ro'a and Ibtihal's daughter's childhoods – as female child refugees, daughters of refugee women and Palestinian men from Syria – were rendered insignificant through their lack of access to the country, experience in detention, and exposure to great danger. In looking at the state's role in reproducing and enabling GBV, such was clear in the case of Ibtihal's daughter and Ro'a, as their only avenue to access the country depended on other forms of repression. The limited opportunity to escape war and family violence has only increased due to security, borders, entry measures, and discriminatory family and nationality laws and practices.

To address cases of GBV without falling into the trap of Western representation, which gives more value to ready-made accounts and analysis of male violence stemming from culture, feminists should insist on creating new 'methods of thought and action that urge us to think things together that appear to be separate, and to de-segregate things that appear to naturally belong together' (Angela Davis cited in Ahmed and Irani, 2020). From the narrative of Palestinian refugee women from Syria, their voices clearly know how to narrate, connect, and represent their stories as a cohesive whole rather than one event separate from the history and politics that arranged its making. Thus, redressing gender injustice starts with an analysis of the structures and status order that organize society based on gendered and political classifications; classifications that create subgroups within one group, ultimately leading to misrecognitions that manifest as injustices against these groups. In the case of Jordanian Palestinian refugee women, and their Palestinian daughters, their experience of displacement is embroiled between settler colonialism, militarism, nationalism and gender regimes that create multiple forms of misrecognition, which in turn translates into GBV practices and discriminatory policies and laws. The only way for GBV to end is for oppressive systems to end, through destabilizing the connections tying these systems together. Freedom from GBV is not possible without justice and recognition, as the absence of latter continues to legitimize the former.

Conclusion: Epistemic violence, intersectionality and decoloniality of feminist knowledge

I participated as a member of the Jordanian NGO women's delegation at the sixty-sixth CEDAW Session in February 2017. In our statement, the delegation highlighted the situation of Palestinian refugees in Jordan, particularly those detained in the Cyber City Detention Centre. On the first day of discussion, CEDAW committee members were very sympathetic with the Jordanian state's position. One member even defended the state, arguing: 'Jordan has a lot to deal with right now.' Indeed, although not as outspoken, most members insinuated that it was not the time to raise the issue of Palestinians refugee women from Syria, as Jordan was dealing with a much bigger issue and already hosted hundreds of thousands of refugees, including Palestinians. When pushed to acknowledge the severity of the conditions experienced by Palestinian refugee women displaced from Syria, a member indicated that the committee had been asked to 'be nice to Jordan's delegation'. This comment led our delegation to issue a statement at the lunch to which both the committee and we were invited. There, the delegation of women's NGOs threatened to go public with a statement accusing CEDAW committee members of sympathizing with a government that uses refugees as a bargaining chip and allows its discriminatory gender policies to escape scrutiny.

Indeed, what was particularly frustrating for the delegation was that nearly a year earlier, a coalition had arranged to deliver a statement at the annual conference of the Commission on the Status of Women (CSW) in New York. This statement was to urge the commission to pay attention to the situation of Palestinian refugee women from Syria in both Jordan and Lebanon, but the date of delivering the statement to the General Assembly was delayed until after the coalition had already left New York. Furthermore, the coalition's efforts to mobilize feminists through the special caucuses that often take place during the CSW did not work, as the CSW NGO management board decided that the caucuses should be used to train NGOs in proposal writing and funding strategies. Although the coalition protested the board's degrading decision and made a public statement – a statement I delivered at the NGO daily morning briefing – they left the conference feeling that their issues had been ignored and their voices marginalized at a women's conference. After this experience, our CEDAW delegation was determined not to leave Geneva with the same disappointment. Thus, we applied considerable pressure to the CEDAW committee members, and they, in turn, highlighted two issues of concern, which were also included in the committee's concluding observations on Jordan:

> (a) The policy of non-admission of Palestinian refugees fleeing the conflict in the Syrian Arab Republic, which was adopted in January 2013, as well as the reported forcible return to the Syrian Arab Republic of a number of Palestinian refugees, including women and girls;

> (b) Cases of Palestinian mothers fleeing the Syrian Arab Republic being prevented from entering the State party, while their Syrian husbands and children were allowed to do so (CEDAW Committee, 2017).

Expectedly, the government delegation denied any discriminatory practices against Palestinians and, instead, justified Jordan's treatment by reiterating their support for the Palestinian right of return and emphasizing that Jordan should not bear the sole burden of hosting Palestinian refugees. The question of aid mentioned by Ensour and the state delegation to CEDAW is also relevant to the treatment Palestinian refugees from Syria experience. With recent cuts to UNRWA funding (UNRWA, 2021), the organization will no longer be able to perform its role and cover the costs of education, health and relief services for Palestinian refugees already living in Jordan; thus, any additional Palestinians would be an added 'burden' on the Jordanian state.

By the end of 2017, Jordan had closed the Cyber City completely and moved its Palestinian refugee inhabitants to King Abdullah Park Camp in North Jordan. Although Palestinians' living conditions were somewhat improved in the new camp, restrictions on their movement, mobility, and access to education and health facilities remained unchanged. However, while the closure of the Cyber City is considered a success for women's NGO advocacy in Jordan, the fact that they were unable to gain the support of other feminist organizations has meant they still face the consequences of standing alone against the government in an international arena.

As demonstrated throughout this book, the politics of concealing the Palestinian refugee experience within analyses of gendered processes of humanitarianism in the broader context of it is termed the 'Syrian refugee crisis' has weakened the possibility of transnational, intersectional feminist theorizing and solidarity work. The lack of attention to and articulation of the particularity of Palestinian women displaced from Syria to Jordan is a lost opportunity for feminists to decolonize a dominant mode of knowledge. Rather, they opt to avoid connecting the geopolitical ideologies that shape gender relations or challenging the politicized and territorialized nature of gender norms that continue to be a dominant form of producing gendered subjects in the context of the Middle East's nation-states.

This final chapter is concerned with the question: what do inclusive feminist politics and intersectional analysis mean in the study of gender processes in the context of Palestine? Chandra Mohanty proposes that feminists should be 'attentive to the politics of activist feminist communities in different sites in the global South and North as they imagine and create cross-border feminist solidarities anchored in struggles on the ground' (Mohanty, 2013, p. 987). To do so, feminism must pay attention to different forms of power, variations within these forms, and the multiple, interconnected forms of gender, colonial and neoliberal bigotries. Mohanty's analysis suggests a commitment to the radical feminist politics of 'the contextual as both local and structural and to the collectivity that is being defined out of existence by privatization projects' (Mohanty, 2013, p. 987). This also requires a recommitment to revolutionary knowledges and the complex politics of antiracist, anti-imperialist feminisms (Mohanty, 2013, p. 987). An inclusive feminist politics, hence, means a serious attempt to decolonize and analyse multiple systems of oppression, their past and present relations, and the material, actual and political implications of power domination on the lived realities of women caught at the intersections of these powers. In this book, I proposed that to understand the current reality of Palestinian refugee women from Syria in Jordan, an examination of the magnitude of the 1948 Nakba in world politics – its connection to settler colonialism, militarism, nationalism, gender regimes, and global asylum and refugee governance – is necessary to see the ways in which relations between these systems continue to create new modes of categorizing and processes of othering.

This book examined the case of Palestinian refugee women from Syria in Jordan in relation to Jordan's 2013 strict no-entry policy, humanitarian organizations' denial of services and protection, and the absence of Palestinian refugee women from refugee and GBV reporting processes, women's empowerment programming and feminist literature on the 'Syrian refugee crisis'. I analysed feminist geopolitics, approaches to intersectionality, and the ways in which such literature fails to capture the subjective nature of the definition and treatment of refugee women when their refugee-ness represents a continuous, multi-layered struggle for liberation and remains connected to a settler colonial past. Indeed, such literature presents the Palestinian case as 'politically complex' and Palestinian refugees as a differentiated category. As such, I argued the need to revisit intersectionality and feminist geopolitical frameworks altogether, as these approaches neither defy categorization nor respond to cases like that of Palestinian refugee women, who exist within larger displacements and refugee movements. This absence and otherness in feminist literature is pointedly critiqued by Mohanty (2013) in terms of:

> None of these 'post' frameworks is useful in making sense of the landscape of violence, oppression, and incarceration that constitutes everyday life for Palestinians in the 1948 territories and in the occupied West Bank. An analysis of the gendered, racialized, capitalist colonial project of the Israeli state, ably supported by US economic and military aid, must remain at the heart of any Palestinian feminist struggle, and at the center of emancipatory knowledges and the theorizing of feminist solidarity.
>
> (Mohanty, 2013, p. 968)

Mohanty's critiques specifically mentioned Palestinians in 1948 and in the West Bank, my analysis of feminist geopolitical frameworks pertaining to refugee women showed an entanglement of feminist literature with the colonial and neoliberal logic and institutional arrangements in the governance of refugees in Jordan. As I discussed in Chapter 2, this is manifested in both the absence of representation in feminist literature and limited transnational solidarity spaces available to Palestinian refugee women from Syria; those available within the UN are governed by the neoliberal professionalization of women's NGOs and governance of capacity-building and empowerment projects. The experience of the women's delegation at the CSW and CEDAW above-mentioned exemplifies that while transnational links and connections may be available to local women's groups, the issues deemed acceptable are conditional, limited, and do not consider local priorities unless defined within the same neoliberal rationale of privatization, market-based issues and skills. Lack of feminist attention to the struggle of women's groups on the ground, as well as the absence of research on the particularity of Palestinian refugee women, creates gaps in both solidarity actions and knowledge production, particularly knowledge that could counter the state's narrative of linking gender to religion and culture. Throughout this book, I showed how, by countering the state's narrative of gender and women's rights, Palestinian women's narratives of crossing borders could be used to open a discussion around issues long-deemed taboo.

In *Decolonizing Feminism: Transnational Feminism and Globalization* (2017), edited by Margaret A McLaren, the main goal is to offer visionary feminist analysis and the tools to decolonize hegemonic feminisms. This important book is organized around themes related to decolonizing both epistemologies and methodologies, rethinking questions of rights and citizenship, reconceptualizing migration and refugees, and thinking of new visions and methods for feminist solidarity. While contributing authors largely take Mohanty's vision of feminist inclusive politics as a departure point, this inclusivity still fails to both acknowledge settler colonialism in Palestine and connect it to global forces and hegemonic powers. This clearly is displayed in Kelly Oliver's chapter, 'The Special Plight of Women Refugees', which aims to disrupt and problematize questions of national borders, state sovereignty, and humanitarian and asylum practices. The 'Refugees Today' section shows data and statistics on refugees from across the world; data primarily gleaned from UNHCR global reports. While UNHCR practice is challenged and the data includes major conflict and displacement contexts, the author fails to make any reference to Palestinian refugee women and thus does not problematize the epistemological grounding of the data and figures (Oliver, 2017). Indeed, in Chapter 2 I discussed the figure of 5.7 million Palestinian refugees cited in UNHCR reports, noting how the UNHCR both acknowledges the existence of Palestinian refugees and simultaneously disregards their plight and excludes them from protection by placing them in a differentiated category: UNRWA refugees. By taking no notice of the number, Oliver favours the UNHCR's reasoning and accepts the othering and categorization of different refugees based on the politics of humanitarianism that emerged out of the 1948 Nakba juncture-point, as discussed in Chapter 2.

In the same book, Gaile Pohlhaus critiques this kind of selective knowledge, which she terms 'epistemic gathering', in her chapter 'Knowing Without Borders', which seeks to expose solidarity inherently determined by feminist privileges of knowing and run 'the serious risks of enacting epistemic violence' (2017, p. 37). Pohlhaus poses a number of questions she believes feminists must engage with in order to avoid the harm of epistemic violence, not only in terms of who knows what and whose knowledge is counted, but, more importantly, in terms of 'with whom am I knowing', 'at whose expense might this knowing be made', 'how does my knowing make possible or undermine the practice of solidarity with others' (Pohlhaus Jr, 2017, p. 51). Pohlhaus questions self-knowledge in an attempt to alleviate the harmful epistemic effects of feminist knowledge on women and achieve feminist solidarity without borders (Pohlhaus Jr, 2017, p. 38).

Oliver's discussion of current refugees from Syria, similar to literature discussed in various chapters throughout this book (Yasmine and Moughalian, 2016; Cherri et al., 2017; Nasser-Eddin, 2017; Canefe, 2018; Al-Natour, Al-Ostaz and Morris, 2019; Freedman, Kivilcim, Baklacıoğlu, 2019; Gissi, 2019), brings attention to 'Syrian women refugees' as one group of refugee women. Rather than destabilizing such a category by acknowledging diversity and using inclusive terminology – such as 'refugee women from Syria', a category that incorporates the specific experiences of Palestinian refugee women and others, such as those displaced to Syria from Iraq in 2003 and then re-displaced from Syria to other countries – this kind of categorization accepts the state's forms of classification. In doing this, the literature related to refugee women and gender processes continues to reflect the conceptual dilemmas in feminist analysis identified by Alcoff (2017) in terms of three main problems: a generalized understanding of how identities form and a negation of the specific significance of the geopolitical and historical factors involved in such formation; a universalist approach to gender formation; and acceptance of the state's account of identity construction without acknowledging the multiple causes that contribute to this dominant construction. This also corresponds with Dhamoon's critique of what she calls feminists' 'three specific anxieties': how to deal with the state, as a site of liberation or oppression; navigating power differentials that connect multiple forms of power; and 'the simultaneity of being a member of an oppressed group and being structurally implicated in Othering' (Dhamoon, 2015, p. 21).

Analysis of feminists' implication in othering is essential to decolonizing feminism. As suggested by Toni Morrison, the first step to such decolonization is to look at how othering works. In her book *The Origin of Others* (2017), Morrison proposed looking at the origin of othering as a process that naturalized racism, by either brute force or romance. Turning to historical meanings of the 'other', she explained how racism paved the way for identity politics in US past and present history and the mass incarceration seen today. Morrison asked: how does one become a racist or sexist? And answered: 'since no one is born a racist and there is no fetal pre-disposition to sexism, one learns Othering not by lecture but by example' (Morrison, 2017, p. 6). Example, as explained by Morrison, are the historically repeated acts that desensitize people to atrocities committed against certain groups; making these atrocities appear normal. Throughout this book, I showed how the naturalization of Palestinian refugees as a displaced population means treating them as a differentiated category, translating to reality as the normalization of suffering. To understand this, I proposed looking at the ways in which the 1948 Palestinian Nakba is not treated as the de-nationalization of Palestinians. Instead, Palestinians are addressed as a displaced population, 'UNRWA refugees', undocumented refugees and the Palestine question represented as a complex issue. This is one of the ways in which the Nakba juncture-point as an othering process clearly manifests in feminist literature.

Looking at epistemic violence as a technique of settler colonialism is not applicable only to the case of Palestinian refugee women from Syria within analysis of refugees from Syria, but extends to all accounts and literature that aim to decolonize through building connections, encouraging contextual analysis, and considering geopolitics and historical factors to challenge hegemonic feminisms; in some cases, whilst still excluding others, like Palestine. Accordingly, Mohanty's concern – voiced in her first 'feminist publication' in 1984 – regarding the colonial appropriation of women's experiences in feminist and left writings is still valid, even for those who challenge and aim to decolonize hegemonic feminisms. Still, in a book that very seriously takes decolonization as its core, we find contradictions between the theorization and the application of theories on women's lives.

Anti-Palestinianism, as conceptualized in this book, is an attempt made in light of the calls of Mohanty (1984, 2003, 2013) and Spivak (1988) to expose epistemic violence, its effects on women refugees, and its implications on feminist writings and agendas. For Mohanty, exposing the 'power-knowledge nexus' has a threefold objective: uncovering the effects of feminist knowledge on women; encouraging feminists to know more, as a feminist responsibility; and building connections that generate feminist solidarity without borders (Mohanty, 2003). Anti-Palestinianism, as discussed, is the denial of the 1948 Nakba juncture-point in history, the naturalization of Palestinian displacement, and the legitimation of practices of settler colonial epistemic violence. The non-questioning of settler colonial techniques, the silencing and denial of Palestinian accounts, and the lack of acknowledgement of the varied, wide-ranging and continuous harm inflicted on Palestinians is what constitutes anti-Palestinianism. In this, I departed from racial, ethnic and apartheid accounts (Yuval Davis, 1993; Pappe, 1994; Nagel, 1998; Abu El-Haj, 2010; Santos, 2013) often examined as a framework for analysing the Palestine question. The naturalization of Palestinian refugee women's suffering, the denial of services and asylum, and erasure of their narrative from literature is not grounded in their race or ethnicity, but in their historical and geopolitical affiliation to Palestine. This affiliation to land, geography and the politics of dispossession is what informed the displacement experiences of Palestinian refugee women from Syria in Jordan.

The racial explanation of the question of Palestine resembles Alcoff's application of Weber's description of ethnic beliefs as 'artificial origin' to challenge the fixed and universal nature given to race and gender, which is an obfuscation of the story's origin (Alcoff, 2017, p. 28). Ethnic and racial discussions around group beliefs of identity construction do not apply to Palestinianism as discussed and defined in this book, as this form of identification is not constructed around differences in religion, class, ethnicity or colour, nor around an imagined belief. Instead, Palestinianism that emerged in women's narrative relates to a shared memory of uprooting and dispossession, an actual, extended experience of displacement and women's association with a just cause and common struggle for liberation. The racial explanation to the Palestine question is commonly addressed, whether directly or indirectly, with antisemitism in Europe. This is a superficial link; one that must be disconnected from analyses of the settler colonial project in Palestine. Whilst the two forms of injustice – anti-Palestinianism and antisemitism in Europe – *can* coincide in their connection to eurocentrism and colonialism. Associating antisemitism and the suffering of Jews in Europe to the Palestine question contributes only to obfuscating the straightforward answer; thus, any direct connection is fundamental to the epistemic violence perpetrated against Palestinian.

Additionally, Palestinianism is also distinct from Palestinian nationalism as a political, state-building project, which, similar to other forms of nationalism, can negatively affect self-identification in a narrow sense and in relation to other imagined and constructed identities and political projects (Massad, 1993, 1995). Anti-Palestinianism is the antithesis of what Palestinianism represents, hence articulating it in relation to either race or ethnicity represents a false, fabricated origin that covers up and denies the 1948 Nakba juncture-point, when settler colonial logic and ideology prevailed over people's rights over their land and freedom from oppression. This is not to negate what is a rather complicated intersection of the categories of ethnicity, race, colour, religion, class and sect within the Palestinian case; instead, the intention here is to first acknowledge the dominant form of power's significance in relation to anti-Palestinianism as settler colonial epistemic violence that leads to Palestinians' differentiation. While the epistemological effect of anti-Palestinianism implicates all Palestinians, the harm inflicted based on this epistemology is also differential and fundamentally connected to Palestinians' location, refugee status, class, race, ethnicity, etc. Analysis of inequalities within, not only between, the categories, as McCall (2005) proposed for inter-categorical analysis of neglected groups or issues, is indeed essential. However, analysis within and between categories cannot be the first enquiry in cases where a unitary dominant category of differentiation exists.

Crenshaw (1991) looks at the particularities of groups at points of intersection, proposing two types of intersectionality: structural intersectionality, the intersection of unequal social groups; and political intersectionality, the intersection of political agendas and projects (Crenshaw, 1991). In feminist literature, the focus on the latter weakens analysis of structural intersectionality. However, Walby *et al.* critiqued Crenshaw's focus on two actors, white women and black men: 'in this focus on the agency of these two disadvantaged groups her analysis curiously loses sight of the actions of the powerful and the racist structures' (Walby, Armstrong and Strid, 2012, p. 226). The authors argued against the unitary category analysis, proposing instead to look at the set of social relations of inequality: 'the focus is on the set of social relations of inequality rather than on a unitary concept of a "strand" or "category", then it is easier to identify the significance of the actions of the powerful as well as of the disadvantaged' (Walby, Armstrong and Strid, 2012, p. 230). While relations between different forms of inequality are important, a focus on this also runs the risk of treating all forms equally, losing sight of the problem's origin, and assuming a stable relation between forms of domination. Dominant categories help in looking at root-causes, origins of othering, and processes of differentiation without essentially disconnecting the structural from the political, representational and institutional forms of domination.

Thus, it is necessary to look at the order of categorization using historical analysis; in my research, this is crucial to centring the articulation of refugee women's narratives relationally with the settler colonial project in Palestine as the first dominant form of power. It also connects women's articulation of multiple, changing, current and past forms of domination. While the order of categorization may change according to context, it still helps to identify the 'action of the powerful' and the dominant form of episteme that both links the techniques of one dominant force of power and exposes how this force's episteme travels across time and place through techniques of epistemic violence. This also extends to other forms of domination not necessarily directly linked or enacted for the same purpose. As shown throughout this book, in the case of Jordan's nationalism, humanitarian organization practices, global refugee governance, and gender power relations within households, the use of settler colonial techniques of epistemic violence has not always been directly connected to the settler colonial project in Palestine, but nonetheless corresponds with the erasure of Palestinian drive, be it at the epistemological or material level; a core purpose of Zionism and settler colonialism in Palestine.

Each chapter of this book analysed one force of domination as well as linked relationships with that force to structural epistemic violence via analysis of categories of differentiation, but without neglecting the harmful effects on and the actions and agency of the group itself. Accordingly, this book's order and organization of chapters is intended to first centre the narrative of Palestinian women in a way that reflects their view of the basis, foundation and origin of discriminatory practices against them. While gender was one of multiple categories they identified, it was not the first or the dominant. Rather, the women pointed to what they termed the 'Palestinian condition' as the most essential and dominant way of living imposed on Palestinian refugees since the 1948 Nakba, revealing that the settler colonial project in Palestine is the first dominant power of their narrative. To understand the Palestinian condition, I did not dig into women's stories of their parents and grandparents' displacement in 1948, however. Instead, I investigated the relationship between the settler colonial project in Palestine and Jordan's nationalism and policies towards Palestinians, following a line of historical events that led to the 2013 no-entry policy, which was the second dominant power outlined by women. Jordan's nationalism, as both a competing nation and a co-operating project, shares an interest with the Zionist colonial enterprise that largely springs from the deep, cumulative and continued thirst for legitimacy that both entities demand from Palestinians. Jordan's nationalism cannot be given the same weight as settler colonialism nor can it be disregarded; both projects require historical tethering to understand their practices in relation to one another.

The examination of humanitarian practice in the response to refugees from Syria in Jordan showed how the 1948 juncture-point underlines humanitarianism's current acts of exclusion. The two elements of epistemic violence analysed in relation to humanitarian practice, as a third dominant force of power, in Jordan: silencing and inflicting harm. Palestinian refugee women from Syria's voices are silenced through the creation of the 'UNRWA refugee' category and use of 'displaced population' language in reporting mechanisms. The harm inflicted on Palestinian refugee women discussed in terms of actual, material and epistemological harm. The exclusion of Palestinian women from services available to Syrian and Jordanian women has exposed them to various forms of structural and gender-based violence (GBV), both linked to the denial of Palestinians' existence in the response to refugees from Syria. Chapter 2 links gender and UN and international agencies' humanitarian approaches that – by adopting a feminist universality-based analysis of GBV within the Syrian refugee crisis – define gender and GBV in terms of cultural and social norms. As such, these approaches actively aid in perpetuating structural violence against women and the settler colonial epistemic violence of anti-Palestinianism.

Identity formation – in terms of how Palestinian refugee women from Syria spoke of themselves as a distinct group, but still connected to the collective – discussed to understand the effects of what women termed 'the Palestinian condition' in explaining the continuity of the Nakba, Jordan's no-entry policy, and humanitarianism's acts of exclusion. Since this new displacement is exclusive to Palestinian refugees from Syria, a plurality of perceptions around belonging, camp life and refugee-ness have mushroomed. The designation of the self as distinct establishes their relationship with multiple places and experiences of dispossession linked to anti-Palestinianism as an ideological force. This is extremely important to challenging analytical universality in relation to both women's experience as a group and the Palestinian refugee figure. Indeed, configuring only one particular experience of Palestinian refugee women negates the particularities of the Palestinian case, the consequences of displacement for each group, different states' impacts on different Palestinian groups, and the connections these systems have to the global order that emerged from the 1948 Nakba juncture-point.

Chapters 4 and 5, primarily related to GBV and household relationships, did not focus solely Palestinian refugee women as a homogeneous group, it rather looked at sub-categorizations and the specificity of subgroups within the larger whole and in relation to the broader question of Palestine. For example, in studying Palestinian refugee women from Syria with Jordanian nationality, one such sub-group, I examined Jordan's practices, regulations, entry policies, and gender laws, practices, and effects on women's lived experience of displacement, showing how this subgroup experiences three more discrimination than other Jordanian women: as women, as women married to foreigners, and as displaced women married to Palestinian refugee men from Syria. Women with Gazan refugee status displaced from Syria is another subcategory that required special attention. However, the case of both Gazans and those with Jordanian nationality could not be examined without first looking at Jordan's history of categorizing Palestinians. Thus, an analysis of the multiple processes of misrecognition followed in order to understand how women's gender-based misrecognition is connected to the politics of categorization that led to the misdistribution of power at the political, legal and socio-economic levels, forming the unity of this subgroups' situation.

I have argued (Jabiri, 2016) elsewhere the significance of Jordan's gendered politics, which, through the concept of guardianship, dictates what is and is not suitable for women. Interestingly, however, how Jordan treats Palestinian women contradicts its own politics, only further confirming that gendered norms can be differently played off in the making of state geopolitics. Jordan's state and institutions have defended the concept of guardianship – which is a provision of the JPSL and puts women's choices of education, travel, and marriage in the hands of male relatives – as inherently part of authentic Jordanian culture, but the state's enactment of this concept in relation to Palestinian and Jordanian women is very contradictory. For instance, based on the 2013 no-entry policy for Palestinian refugees, Jordanian women married to Palestinian refugee men from Syria can only enter the country alone, not with their husbands and children. As a consequence, such women choose either to return to Syria or stay with their families in detention centres; their Jordanian citizenship does not include full citizenship rights, so women become refugees in their own country. This practice is derived from the norm that governed the Jordanian nationality law until 1987, that 'wives of foreigners are foreigners'.

Despite changes to the law, this practice reflects an understanding of women as followers of their husbands.

Then, we have Palestinian refugee women from Syria married to Syrian refugee men. These women are, conversely, not considered their husbands' followers. Indeed, while their Syrian husbands are allowed to enter the country, these women are deported back to Syria, forced to take a very dangerous journey on their own. In this case, women are treated as equal to Palestinian men: their legal position as their husband's 'dependent' (under his guardianship) is not a reason to grant entry. Here, a Palestinian travel document becomes more important than the gender roles the Jordanian state 'normally' advocates as part of its authentic Islamic culture. Such contradictory and discriminatory state practices – not only between men and women, but between women based on their own and their husbands' nationality – clearly show that the gender norms governing state policies are not culturally constructed; rather, such norms are politically determined.

Intersectionality, a successful feminist project that explains difference in terms of the intersection of processes of differentiation, is still incomplete insofar as it does not engage with the multiple meanings of experience as connected to the dominant episteme. In line with Stuart Hall, who greatly influenced my analysis in this book, I do not think experience can be addressed without acknowledging the significance of the dominant episteme in analysing relations between different forces of power. Anti-Palestinianism, as a dominant episteme of settler colonialism, is central to the understanding of the different treatment Palestinian refugee women from Syria have experienced, which is profoundly related to them being Palestinians before being women or refugees.

For Hall, the constitution of domination in ideology can be analysed through what he termed 'ideological effects', defined as 'the relative power and distribution of different regimes of truth in the social formation at any one time – which have certain effects for the maintenance of power in the social order' (Grossberg, 1986, p. 49). Hall tries to explain the intersection of ideologies and their effects through articulation, which is his way of explaining how an analysis of different regimes of truth in the formation of social order are 'not simply plural – they define an ideological field of force' (Grossberg, 1986, p. 48). Hall also pays attention to subordinated regimes of truth that offer some rationality for subordinated subjects, even though not necessarily part of the dominant episteme. Following this logic, militarism, nationalism and global refugee governance regimes are seen as dominant forces legitimizing settler colonialism's epistemic violence of anti-Palestinianism, which is the dominant episteme. The dominant episteme may also intersect with subordinated regimes of power like gender, religion, sectarianism, ethnicity and other social categories in various ways.

Conversely, if gender, like other social formation, is fluid and unfixed, then it is not a dominant form; it is a subordinate regime of power. Hence, its undoing cannot be first in the order of things to be undone. Hall explains articulation as a 'lorry where the front (cab) and back (trailer) can, but need not necessarily, be connected to one another. The two parts are connected to each other, but through specific linkage, that can be broken' (Grossberg, 1986, p. 52). To undo gender, we must break the linkage connecting the social formation of gender to the dominant episteme associated with dominant forces of power. To understand the linkage between the two parts, it is important to ask: 'under what circumstances can a connection be forged or made?' (Grossberg, 1986, p. 53). This means the business of undoing gender must entail an understanding of the conditions under which gender relations, norms, and practices are embraced and become essential to identity formation.

Addressing the linkage between the dominant episteme and group social formation using articulation as a method means thinking of the dependent and non-dependent connections between different practices – 'between ideology and social forces, and between different elements within ideology, and between different social groups composing a social movement' (Grossberg, 1986, p. 53). Hall offers an explanation for religion through the ways in which humans make sense of their world via what he calls 'lines of tendential force'. Non-understanding of relations between these forces leads to generalizations and essentialism, as we detach religion from its environment and historical embeddedness. In this sense, religion is not 'free-floating', Hall stresses, it exists in a particular formation and is directly fixed to a particular time or place in relation to a number of different forces: 'Its meaning – political and ideological – comes precisely from its position within formation', which is why the expression and practice of religion are different from one place to another. 'If you want to move religion, to rearticulate in another way, you are going to come across all grooves that have articulated it already,' Hall surmises (Grossberg, 1986, p. 54).

Gender, similar to religion and race, is a 'signifier [that] floats in a sea of relational differences' (Hall, 2021). To understand women's articulation of gender norms, we need to first understand the environment and historical embeddedness that relates to the dominant episteme. For example, in order to understand why some women reinforced gender norms rather than take the relative freedom of a situation that saw their husbands under threat of deportation and them become the breadwinners, it is first necessary to understand how women appropriate gender norms vis-à-vis the Palestinian condition, Jordan's nationalism, their husbands' unjust treatment and how this treatment is understood as a threat to masculinity. Masculinist manoeuvrings, detailed in Chapter 4, are conceptualized as 'claims for recognition and justice' that seek to challenge the subordinate status assigned to Palestinian refugees from Syria. As women explained, such masculinist manoeuvrings are women's attempts to counter Jordan's policies and their effects on Palestinian refugee men from Syria's capacity to perform their traditional gender roles: work, freedom of mobility and political activities. These manoeuvrings are women's acts of resistance against prejudice and the denial of a recognized refugee status.

Gender norms here are, like religion in Hall's example, not free-floating; women have developed masculinist manoeuvrings in relation to a number of different forces, with direct and indirect linkages between dominant and subordinate. In studying these manoeuvrings, the most important element is how the articulation of gender norms and relations has been linked to women's articulation of the Palestinian condition. As this practice was shared by women with relative freedom, albeit at the expense of their husbands' freedom, they did not think of themselves as reinforcing gender norms, but instead as correcting wrongdoings committed against their husbands because they are Palestinian, refugee and men. In light of their experience, strongly entangled with the forces of the dominant episteme, these women articulated their understanding of 'right' and 'wrong'. The Palestinian condition here is the front cab of the lorry, the fixed part that links to the various trailers, each of which serves varying purposes depending on what they are carrying and for whatever reason.

The book aimed to centre anti-Palestinianism as the dominant episteme of relations of power. It is the fixed element in relation to Palestinian refugee women's lived experience of displacement that links other floating categories of identity differentiation of gender, ethnicity, refugee-ness and nationality. Therefore, giving similar or equal weight to dominant force relations that created the conditions and contingencies of the epistemic violence of anti-Palestinianism runs the risk of legitimizing and reproducing the techniques of settler colonialism and the state's structural violence against Palestinian women. Unfortunately, such can be found in feminist literature, where either gender ideologies and settler colonialism are treated as equal forces and epistemes in the context of Palestine, or settler colonialism is neglected entirely in studies of the gendered geopolitics of forced migration and refugees.

References

Abdo, N. (2005) 'Israel, diaspora, and the routes of national belonging', *Journal of Palestine Studies*, 35(1), pp. 112–13. Available at: https://doi.org/10.1525/jps.2005.35.1.112.

Abu El-Haj, N. (2010) 'Racial palestinianization and the Janus-faced nature of the Israeli state', *Patterns of Prejudice*, 44(1), pp. 27–41. Available at: https://doi.org/10.1080/00313220903507610.

Abu-Lughod, L. and ElMahdi, R. (2011) 'In press beyond the "woman question" in the Egyptian revolution: A conversation between Lila Abu-Lughod and Rabab El Mahdi', *Feminist Studies* (News and Views).

Abu Moghli, M., Bitarie, N. and Gabiam, N. (2015) *Palestinian refugees from Syria: Stranded on the margins of law 1*. Al Shabaka: The Palestinian Policy Network.

Achilli, L. (2014) 'Disengagement from politics: Nationalism, political identity, and the everyday in a Palestinian refugee camp in Jordan', *Critique of Anthropology*, 34(2), pp. 234–57.

Achilli, L. (2015) *Syrian refugees in Jordan: A reality check*. Migration Policy Centre, Policy Briefs, 2015/02 – https://hdl.handle.net/1814/34904

Adelman, H. (2001) 'From refugees to forced migration: The UNHCR and human security', *The International Migration Review*, 35(1), pp. 7–32.

Agier, M. (2002) 'Between war and city: Towards an urban anthropology of refugee camps', *Ethnography*, 3(3), pp. 317–41.

Ahmed, A. and Irani, L. (2020) 'Feminism as a design methodology', *Interactions*, pp. 42–5. Available at: https://doi.org/10.1145/3426366.

Akram, S.M. (2002) 'Palestinian refugees and their legal status: Rights, politics, and implications for a just solution', *Journal of Palestine Studies*, 31(3), pp. 36–51. Available at: https://doi.org/10.1525/jps.2002.31.3.36.

Al Adem, S. *et al.* (2018) 'International and local NGO supply chain collaboration: An investigation of the Syrian refugee crises in Jordan', *Journal of Humanitarian Logistics and Supply Chain Management* [Preprint].

Al-Ali, I. (eds.) (2018) 'Palestinians of Syria: Life under restrictions', *Palestine Return Centre*. Available at: http://bit.ly/2A5jxsk

Al-Ali, N. (2012) 'Gendering the Arab Spring', *Middle East Journal of Culture and Communication* (5), pp. 26–32.

Al-Ali, N. (2018) 'Sexual violence in Iraq: Challenges for transnational feminist politics', *European Journal of Women's Studies*, 25(1), pp. 10–27. Available at: https://doi.org/10.1177/1350506816633723.

Al-Ali, N. and Pratt, N. (2011) 'Conspiracy of near silence: Violence against Iraqi women', *Middle East Report*, 41(258), pp. 34–48.

Alcoff, L.M. (2017) 'Decolonizing feminist philosophy', *Decolonizing feminism: Transnational feminism and globalization*, edited by Margaret A. McLaren. London: Rowman & Littlefield International, pp. 21–36.

Al-Hardan, A. (2012) 'The right of return movement in Syria: Building a culture of return, mobilizing memories for the return', *Journal of Palestine Studies*, 41(2), pp. 62–79.

Al-Hardan, A. (2016) 'The Palestinian refugee community in Syria', in *Palestinians in Syria*. New York: Columbia University Press (Nakba Memories of Shattered Communities), pp. 50–71. Available at: http://www.jstor.org/stable/10.7312/al-h17636.7 (Accessed: 16 May 2022).

Alhayek, K. (2016) 'ICTs, agency, and gender in Syrian activists' work among Syrian refugees in Jordan', *Gender, Technology and Development*, 20(3), pp. 333–51.

Al-Natour, A., Al-Ostaz, S.M. and Morris, E.J. (2019) 'Marital violence during war conflict: The lived experience of Syrian refugee women', *Journal of Transcultural Nursing*, 30(1), pp. 32–8. Available at: https://doi.org/10.1177/1043659618783842.

Alameddine, M., Fouad, M., Fouad, K., Diaconu, Z., Jamal, G., Lough, S. and Witter, A. (2019) 'Ager, Resilience capacities of health systems: Accommodating the needs of Palestinian refugees from Syria', *Social Science & Medicine*, 220, https://doi.org/10.1016/j.socscimed.2018.10.018.

Anthias, F. and Yuval-Davis, N. (1989) 'Introduction', in *Woman-nation-state*, edited by N. Yuval-Davis, F. Anthias, and J. Campling. London: Palgrave Macmillan UK, pp. 1–15. Available at: https://doi.org/10.1007/978-1-349-19865-8_1.

Arendt and Baehr, P. (2000) *The portable Hannah Arendt*. London: Penguin Classics.

Arendt, H. (1951) *Origins of totalitarianism*. 18th edn. New York: Harcourt, Brace and Co.

Arendt, H. (2019) *The human condition*. 2nd edn. Chicago: University of Chicago Press.

Ayoob, M. (2004) 'Third world perspectives on humanitarian intervention and international administration', *Global Governance*, 10(1), pp. 99–118.

Barakat, H.I. (1973) 'The Palestinian refugees: An uprooted community seeking repatriation', *The International Migration Review*, 7(2), pp. 147–61. Available at: https://doi.org/10.2307/3002425.

Barnett, M. (2005) 'Humanitarianism transformed', *Perspectives on Politics*, 3(4), pp. 723–40.

Barnett, M. (2009) 'Evolution without progress? humanitarianism in a world of hurt', *International Organization*, 63(4), pp. 621–63.

Bayat, A. (2015) 'Revolution and despair', *Mada Masr*, 25 January. Available at: http://www.madamasr.com/opinion/revolutionand-despair

Baylouny, A.M. (2020) 'Enter the Syrians', in *When blame backfires*. Cornell University Press (Syrian Refugees and Citizen Grievances in Jordan and Lebanon), pp. 36–64. Available at: http://www.jstor.org/stable/10.7591/j.ctvv417k4.8 (Accessed: 24 June 2022).

Beardsley, K. and Schmidt, H. (2012) 'Following the flag or following the charter? Examining the determinants of UN involvement in international crises, 1945-2002', *International Studies Quarterly*, 56(1), pp. 33–49.

Beaujouan, J. and Rasheed, A. (2019) *Syrian crisis, Syrian refugees: Voices from Jordan and Lebanon*. Mobility and Politics, Cham: Palgrave Macmillan. https://link.springer.com/book/10.1007/978-3-030-35016-1

Besiou, M. and Van Wassenhove, L.N. (2020) 'Humanitarian operations: A world of opportunity for relevant and impactful research', *Manufacturing & Service Operations Management*, 22(1), pp. 135–45.

Bjørkhaug, I. (2020) 'Revisiting the refugee–host relationship in Nakivale Refugee Settlement: A dialogue with the Oxford Refugee Studies Centre', *Journal on Migration and Human Security*, 8(3), pp. 266–81.

Brand, L. (1988) 'Nasir's Egypt and the reemergence of the Palestinian national movement', *Journal of Palestine Studies*, 17(2), pp. 29–45. Available at: https://doi.org/10.2307/2536862.

Brown, N. (1970) 'Palestinian nationalism and the Jordanian state', *The World Today*, 26(9), pp. 370–8.

Buckler, S. (2011) 'Theorising political action', in *Hannah Arendt and political theory*. Edinburgh University Press (Challenging the Tradition), pp. 82–103. Available at: http://www.jstor.org/stable/10.3366/j.ctt1r263k.7 (Accessed: 11 April 2022).

Bunch, C. (2008) 'Strike at Samu: Jordan, Israel, the United States, and the origins of the Six-Day War', *Diplomatic History*, 32(1), pp. 55–76.

Butler, J. (2016) *Frames of war: When is life grievable?* London and New York: Verso Books.

Canefe, N. (2018) 'Invisible lives: Gender, dispossession, and precarity amongst Syrian refugee women in the Middle East', *Refuge: Canada's Journal on Refugees/ Refuge: Revue canadienne sur les réfugiés*, 34(1), pp. 39–49.

Çarpar, M.C. and Göktuna Yaylaci, F. (2021) 'Forced migration as a crisis in masculinity: A sociological approach to refugee men's remasculinization strategies in Turkey', *Journal of Refugee Studies*, 34(4), pp. 3846–70. Available at: https://doi.org/10.1093/jrs/feaa138.

CEDAW Committee (2017) 'CEDAW concluding observation to Jordan', UN Treaty Body Database. Available at: https://tbinternet.ohchr.org/_layouts/15/TreatyBodyExternal/Download.aspx?symbolno=CEDAW%2fC%2fJOR%2fCO%2f6&Lang=en (Accessed: 17 August 2018).

Charles, L. and Denman, K. (2013) 'Syrian and Palestinian Syrian refugees in Lebanon: The plight of women and children', *Journal of International Women's Studies*, 14(5), Article 7. Available at: https://vc.bridgew.edu/jiws/vol14/iss5/7

Charrad, M.M. (2001) *States and women's rights: The making of postcolonial Tunisia, Algeria, and Morocco*. California: University of California Press.

Charrad, M.M. (2011) 'Gender in the middle east: Islam, state, agency', *Annual Review of Sociology*, 37(1), pp. 417–37. Available at: https://doi.org/10.1146/annurev.soc.012809.102554.

Cherri, Z. *et al.* (2017) 'Early marriage and barriers to contraception among Syrian refugee women in Lebanon: A qualitative study', *International Journal of Environmental Research and Public Health*, 14(8), p. 836.

Cockburn, C. (1998) *The space between us: Negotiating gender and national identities in conflict*. London: Zed Books.

Cockburn, C. (2004) 'Sites of violence: Gender and conflict zones', in *Sites of Violence: Gender and Conflict Zones* edited by W. Giles and J. Hyndman. California: University of California Press, pp. 24–44. Available at: https://doi.org/10.1525/9780520937055-004.

Cohen, I. (2013) *Syrian refugees and the challenge to Jordan*. Institute for National Security Studies. Available at: http://www.jstor.org/stable/resrep08752 (Accessed: 24 June 2022).

Connell, R.W. (2005) 'Change among the gatekeepers: Men, masculinities, and gender equality in the global arena', *Signs: Journal of Women in Culture and Society*, 30(3), pp. 1801–25. Available at: https://doi.org/10.1086/427525.

Crenshaw, K. (1991) 'Mapping the margins: Intersectionality, identity politics, and violence against women of color', *Stanford Law Review*, 43(6), pp. 1241–99. Available at: https://doi.org/10.2307/1229039.

Culbertson, S. *et al.* (2016) 'An overview of coordination in Jordan and Lebanon', in *Rethinking coordination of services to refugees in urban areas*. RAND Corporation (Managing the Crisis in Jordan and Lebanon), pp. 27–58. Available at: http://www.jstor.org/stable/10.7249/j.ctt1c2crxs.10 (Accessed: 10 January 2023).

Dabashi, H. (2012) *The Arab Spring: The end of postcolonialism*. London: Zed Books.

Daoud, N. (2021) "'I will stay with him through thick and thin": Factors influencing the incidence and persistence of intimate partner violence against Syrian refugee women in Jordan', *Journal of Immigrant & Refugee Studies* 19(2), pp. 170–83.

DeJong, J. *et al.* (2017) 'Young lives disrupted: Gender and well-being among adolescent Syrian refugees in Lebanon', *Conflict and Health*, 11(1), pp. 25–34.

Department of Statistics (2019) 'Jordan population and family health survey 2017–18'. Department of Statistics. Available at: http://www.dos.gov.jo/dos_home_e/main/linked-html/DHS2017_en.pdf.

Dhamoon, R. (2015) 'A feminist approach to decolonizing anti-racism: Rethinking transnationalism, intersectionality, and settler colonialism', *Feral Feminisms*, 4(1), pp. 20–37.

Dumper, M. (2009) 'Future prospects for the Palestinian refugees', *Refugee Survey Quarterly*, 28(2–3), pp. 561–87.

El Arab, R. and Sagbakken, M. (2019) 'Child marriage of female Syrian refugees in Jordan and Lebanon: A literature review', *Global Health Action*, 12(1), p. 1585709. Available at: https://doi.org/10.1080/16549716.2019.1585709.

El-Abed, O. (2009) 'The Palestinians in Egypt: Identity, basic rights and host state policies', *Refugee Survey Quarterly*, 28(2/3), pp. 531–49.

Enders, D. (2008) 'No roads out, no roads home: Palestinian refugees in Iraq', *The Virginia Quarterly Review*, 84(3), pp. 192–207.

Enloe, C.H., 1938– (1990) *Bananas, beaches & bases : Making feminist sense of international politics/Cynthia Enloe.* Berkeley: University of California Press.

Erakat, N. (2014) 'Palestinian refugees and the Syrian uprising: Filling the protection gap during secondary forced displacement', *International Journal of Refugee Law*, 26(4), pp. 581–621.

Farah, R. (2020) 'Expat, local, and refugee: "Studying up" the global division of labor and mobility in the humanitarian industry in Jordan', *Migration and Society*, 3(1), pp. 130–44.

Feldman, I. (2012) 'The humanitarian condition: Palestinian refugees and the politics of living', *Humanity: An International Journal of Human Rights, Humanitarianism, and Development*, 3(2), pp. 155–72. Available at: https://doi.org/10.1093/jrs/fes004.

Ferris, E. and Kirisci, K. (2016) *The consequences of chaos: Syria's humanitarian crisis and the failure to protect.* Washington DC: Brooking Institution Press.

Fiddian-Qasmiyeh, E. (2015) 'Refugees helping refugees: How a Palestinian camp in Lebanon is welcoming Syrians', *The Conversation*, 4.

Fiddian-Qasmiyeh, E. (2016a) 'On the threshold of statelessness: Palestinian narratives of loss and erasure', *Ethnic and Racial Studies*, 39(2), pp. 301–21.

Fiddian-Qasmiyeh, E. (2016b) 'Refugee-refugee relations in contexts of overlapping displacement', *International Journal of Urban and Regional Research* [Preprint].

Fiddian-Qasmiyeh, E. (2016c) 'Refugees hosting refugees', *Forced Migration Review* (53), p. 25.

Fiddian-Qasmiyeh, E. (2020) 'Shifting the gaze', in *Refuge in a moving world,* edited by E. Fiddian-Qasmiyeh. London: UCL Press (Tracing refugee and migrant journeys across disciplines), pp. 402–14. Available at: http://www.jstor.org/stable/j. ctv13xprtw.33 (Accessed: 15 April 2022).

Fraser, N. (1998) 'Social justice in the age of identity politics: Redistribution, recognition, participation', *Wissenschaftszentrum Berlin für Sozialforschung (WZB), Berlin,* FS I(WZB Discussion Paper), pp. 98–108.

Fraser, N. (2001) 'Recognition without ethics?', *Theory, Culture & Society,* 18(2–3), pp. 21–42. Available at: https://doi.org/10.1177/02632760122051760.

Freedman, J. (2016) 'Sexual and gender-based violence against refugee women: A hidden aspect of the refugee "crisis"', *Reproductive Health Matters,* 24(47), pp. 18–26. Available at: https://doi.org/10.1016/j.rhm.2016.05.003.

Freedman, Kivilcim, Baklacıoğlu, J., and Zeynep, Nurcan Özgür (2019) *A gendered approach to the Syrian refugee crisis.* 1st edn. Routledge. Available at: https://doi. org/10.4324/9781315529653.

Freier, L. F. (2022). The power of categorization: reflections on UNHCR's category of `Venezuelans displaced abroad'. In C. Pao, & M. Zubok (Eds.), Measuring Migration Conference 2022 Proceedings (pp. 51–54). (Migration Series; No. 42). Transnational Press London Ltd

Frost, L. (2022) *Report on citizenship law: Jordan.* Florence: European University Institute.

Gabiam, N. (2012) 'When "humanitarianism" becomes "development": The politics of international aid in Syria's Palestinian refugee camps', *American Anthropologist,* 114(1), pp. 95–107.

Gabiam, N. and Fiddian-Qasmiyeh, E. (2016) 'Palestinians and the Arab uprisings: Political activism and narratives of home, homeland, and home-camp', *Journal of Ethnic and Migration Studies,* 43(5), pp. 731–48.

Gausman, J. *et al.* (2021) 'Understanding attitudes and norms related to sexual and gender-based violence among youth in Jordan: An egocentric social network study protocol', *BMJ Open,* 11(12), p. e047615. Available at: https://doi.org/10.1136/ bmjopen-2020-047615.

Giles, W. and Hyndman, J. (eds.) (2004) *Sites of violence: Gender and conflict zones.* Berkeley: University of California Press.

Gilroy, P. (1993) *The black Atlantic: Modernity and double consciousness.* London: Verso.

Gissi, A. (2019) '"What does the term refugee mean to you?"': Perspectives from Syrian refugee women in Lebanon', *Journal of Refugee Studies*, 32(4), pp. 539–61.

Gökalp, D. (2010) 'A gendered analysis of violence, justice and citizenship: Kurdish women facing war and displacement in Turkey', *Special Issue – Women's Agency: Silences and Voices*, 33(6), pp. 561–9. Available at: https://doi.org/10.1016/j.wsif.2010.09.005.

Gramsci, A., 1891–1937 (1971) *Selections from the prison notebooks of Antonio Gramsci*. [1st edn]. New York : International Publishers, [1971] [©1971]. Available at: https://search.library.wisc.edu/catalog/999473246802121.

Gregory, D. (1995) 'Imaginative geographies', *Progress in Human Geography*, 19(4), pp. 447–85. Available at: https://doi.org/10.1177/030913259501900402.

Grossberg (1986) 'On postmodernism and articulation: An interview with Stuart Hall', *Journal of Communication Inquiry*, 10(2), pp. 45–60.

Hall, S. (1990) 'Cultural identity and diaspora', *1990*, pp. 222–37.

Hall, S. (2021) *Selected writings on race and difference*. Durham & New York: Duke University Press.

Hall, S. and Gay, P. du (1996) *Questions of cultural identity*. London: Sage.

Hanafi, S. (2020) 'Normativity of migration studies ethics and epistemic community', in *Migration and Islamic ethics,* edited by R. Jureidini and S.F. Hassan. Leiden, Netherlands: Brill (Issues of Residence, Naturalization and Citizenship), pp. 110–35. Available at: http://www.jstor.org/stable/10.1163/j.ctv2gjx01g.11 (Accessed: 1 January 2023).

HANSARD 1803–2005 (1950) 'Jordan and Israel (government decision)', in *Commons Sitting*, Commons sittings and Westminster Hall sittings. Available at: https://api.parliament.uk/historic-hansard/commons/1950/apr/27/jordan-and-israel-government-decision#column_1137.

Hasso, F.S. (1998) 'THE "WOMEN'S FRONT": Nationalism, feminism, and modernity in Palestine', *Gender & Society*, 12(4), pp. 441–65. Available at: https://doi.org/10.1177/089124398012004005.

van Hear, N. (1995) 'The impact of the involuntary mass "Return" to Jordan in the wake of the Gulf crisis', *The International Migration Review*, 29(2), pp. 352–74. Available at: https://doi.org/10.2307/2546785.

Hollis, R. (2000) 'Still waiting', *The World Today*, 56(6), pp. 20–2.

Holt, M. (2016) 'A crisis of identity: Palestinian women, memory and dissent', *The Future of Palestinian Identity*, p. 1.

Huizinga, R.P. and van Hoven, B. (2021) 'Hegemonic masculinities after forced migration: Exploring relational performances of Syrian refugee men in The

Netherlands', *Gender, Place & Culture*, 28(8), pp. 1151–73. Available at: https://doi.org/10.1080/0966369X.2020.1784102.

Human Rights Watch (2006) 'Nowhere to flee: The perilous situation of Palestinians in Iraq', *Human Rights Watch*, 18(No. 4(E)). Available at: https://www.hrw.org/reports/iraq0706web.pdf.

Hyndman, J. (2000) *Managing Displacement: Refugees and the Politics of Humanitarianism*. Minneapolis: University of Minnesota Press.

Hyndman, J. (2019) 'Unsettling feminist geopolitics: Forging feminist political geographies of violence and displacement', *Gender, Place & Culture*, 26(1), pp. 3–29.

Hyndman, J. and Giles, W. (2017) 'It's so cold here, we feel this coldness": Refugee resettlement after long-term exile"', *Jennifer Hyndman and Wenona Giles, Living on the Edge: Refugees in Extended Exile*. Routledge [Preprint].

IOM (2018) 'Institutional framework for addressing gender-based violence in crises'. Available at: https://www.iom.int/resources/institutional-framework-addressing-gender-based-violence-crises (Accessed: 18 May 2022).

Jabiri, A. (2016) *Gendered politics and law in Jordan: Guardianship over women*. London & New York: Palgrave Macmillan.

Jabiri, A. (2017) 'Gendered politics of alienation and power restoration: Arab revolutions and women's sentiments of loss and despair', *Feminist Review*, 117(1), pp. 113–30. https://doi.org/10.1057/s41305-017-0085-4.

Jacques-da-silva, F. (1966) 'The world refugees and the United Nations', *Pakistan Horizon*, 19(4), pp. 330–8.

JAD, I. (2007) 'Rereading the British mandate in Palestine: Gender and the urban–rural divide in education', *International Journal of Middle East Studies*. edn,. 39(3), pp. 338–42. Available at: https://doi.org/10.1017/S002074380707047X.

Jeffries, J.M.N. (2017) *Palestine: The reality: The inside story of the Balfour declaration 1917–1938*. Bloxham and Northampton: Olive Branch Press & Skyscraper.

Johansson-Nogués, E. (2013) 'Gendering the Arab Spring? rights and (in)security of Tunisian, Egyptian and Libyan women', *Security Dialogue*, Special issue on the new Middle East: A critical appraisal, 44(5–6), pp. 393–409.

Joseph, S. (2000) *Gender and citizenship in the Middle East*. New York: Syracuse University Press .

JPC News (2013) 'Palestinian refugees from Syria stuck in Jordan', *2013*, 21 May. Available at:http://www.jbcnews.net/article/13361اللاجئون-الفلسطينيون-من-سوريا-عالقون-في-الأردن.

Kádár, J. (2019) 'The Jordanian nationalism', *Études sur la Région Méditerranéenne*, 28, pp. 91–100.

Kandiyoti, D. (1994) *The paradoxes of masculinity: Some thoughts on segregated societies, from dislocating masculinity: Comparative ethnographies* (Cornwall, A. and Lindisfarne, N. eds.). UK: Routledge.

Kandiyoti, D. (2011) 'Promise and peril: Women and the "Arab spring"', *Open Democracy*. Available at: https://www.opendemocracy.net/5050/deniz-kandiyoti/promise-and-peril-women-and-'arab-spring' (Accessed: 16 April 2021).

Kandyioti, D. (2012) 'Disquiet and despair: The gender sub-texts of the "Arab spring"', *Open Democracy*. Available at: https://www.opendemocracy.net/5050/deniz-kandiyoti/disquiet-and-despair-gender-sub-texts-of-arab-spring (Accessed: 20 April 2021).

Kandiyoti, D. (2013) ' 'Fear and fury: Women and post-revolutionary violence'. *Open Democracy*. Available at: https://www.opendemocracy.net/en/5050/fear-and-fury-women-and-post-revolutionary-violence/#.

Kandiyoti, D. (2019) 'Mainstreaming men and masculinities: Technical fix or political struggle?', *Masculinities – A Journal of Culture and Society*, 12(Autumn), pp. 30–41.

Kandiyoti, D. (2020) 'The pitfalls of secularism in Turkey: An interview with Deniz Kandiyoti', *Feminist Dissent*, pp. 135–54. Available at: https://doi.org/10.31273/fd.n5.2020.762.

Kattaa, M. and Byrne, M. (2018) 'Quality of work for Syrian refugees in Jordan', *Forced Migration Review* [Preprint] (58).

Kawar, A. (1993) 'National mobilization, war conditions, and gender consciousness', *Arab Studies Quarterly*, 15(2), pp. 53–67.

Kazziha, W. (1979) 'The political evolution of Transjordan', *Middle Eastern Studies*, 15(2), pp. 239–57.

Kelly, Liz (1987) 'The continuum of sexual violence', in *Women, violence and social control*, edited by Jalna Hanmer and Mary Maynard. London: Palgrave Macmillan UK, pp. 46–60. https://doi.org/10.1007/978-1-349-18592-4_4.

Kelly, L. (2019) 'The continuum of sexual violence', *Cahiers du Genre*, 66(1), pp. 17–36.

Khalidi, R.I. (1992) 'Observations on the right of return', *Journal of Palestine Studies*, 21(2), pp. 29–40.

King Hussein Disengagement Statement (1988) 'Jordan: Statement concerning disengagement from the West Bank and Palestinian self-determination', *International Legal Materials*, 27(6), pp. 1637–45.

Korac, M. (2006) 'Gender, conflict and peace-building: Lessons from the conflict in the former Yugoslavia', *Women's Studies International Forum*, 29(5), pp. 510–20.

Korac, M. (2018) 'Feminists against sexual violence in war: The question of perpetrators and victims revisited', *Social Sciences*, 7(10). Available at: https://doi.org/10.3390/socsci7100182.

Krause, U. (2022) 'The powerful (Vagueness of) numbers?: (Non) Knowledge production about refugee accommodation quantifications in UNHCR's Global Trends Reports', *Migration and Society*, 5(1), pp. 141–51.

Kurd, D.E. (2014) 'The Jordanian military: A key regional ally', *The US Army War College Quarterly: Parameters*, 44(3), p. 7.

Labelle, M.J.M. (2020) 'On the decolonial beginnings of Edward Said', *Modern Intellectual History*, pp. 1–25.

Lautze, S. and Raven Roberts, A. (2006) 'Violence and complex humanitarian emergencies: Implications for livelihoods models', *Disasters*, 30(4), pp. 383–401.

Le Troquer, Y. and Al-oudat, R.H. (1999) 'From Kuwait to Jordan: The Palestinians' third exodus', *Journal of Palestine Studies*, 28(3), pp. 37–51. Available at: https://doi.org/10.2307/2538306.

Lenner, K. and Turner, L. (2018) 'Learning from the Jordan compact', *Forced Migration Review*, 57, pp. 48–51.

Levitt, P. and Schiller, N.G. (2004) 'Conceptualizing simultaneity: A transnational social field perspective on society 1', *International Migration Review*, 38(3), pp. 1002–39.

Lindholm, H. (2020) 'Emotional identity and pragmatic citizenship: Being Palestinian in Sweden', *Diaspora Studies*, 13(2), pp. 133–51.

Loddo, S.A. (2017) 'Palestinian perceptions of home and belonging in Britain: Negotiating between rootedness and mobility', *Identities*, 24(3), pp. 275–94.

Loescher, G. (2001) 'The UNHCR and world politics: State interests vs. institutional autonomy', *The International Migration Review*, 35(1), pp. 33–56.

Lokot, M. (2018) 'Syrian refugees: Thinking beyond gender stereotypes', *Forced Migration Review*, 57, pp. 33–5.

Lugones, M. (2016) 'The coloniality of gender', in *The Palgrave handbook of gender and development*, edited by W. Harcourt. London: Palgrave Macmillan, pp. 13–33. https://doi.org/10.1007/978-1-137-38273-3_2.

MacKenzie, M. and Foster, A. (2017) 'Masculinity nostalgia: How war and occupation inspire a yearning for gender order', *Security Dialogue*, 48(3), pp. 206–23. Available at: https://doi.org/10.1177/0967010617696238.

Malkki, L. (1996) 'Speechless emissaries: Refugees, humanitarianism, and dehistoricization', *Cultural Anthropology*, 11(3), pp. 377–404. https://doi.org/10.1525/can.1996.11.3.02a00050.

Malkki, L.H. (1995) *Purity and exile: Violence, memory, and national cosmology among Hutu refugees in Tanzania*. Chicago: University of Chicago Press.

Malkki, L.H. (2005) 'Speechless emissaries: Refugees, humanitarianism, and dehistoricization', in *Siting Culture*. Oxford, UK: Routledge, pp. 233–64.

Mallison, W.T. and Mallison, S.V. (1980) 'The right of return', *Journal of Palestine Studies*, 9, pp. 125–36.

Marlowe, J. and Elliott, S. (2014) 'Global trends and refugee settlement in New Zealand', *Kotuitui: New Zealand Journal of Social Sciences Online*, 9(2), pp. 43–9.

Martin, S.F. *et al.* (2019) 'International responsibility-sharing for refugees', *Geopolitics, History, and International Relations*, 11(1), pp. 59–91.

Masalha, N. (2003) *The politics of denial*. London, UK: Pluto Press. Available at: https://doi.org/10.2307/j.ctt18dztmq.

Massad, J. (1993) 'Palestinians and the limits of racialized discourse', *Social Text* (34), pp. 94–114. Available at: https://doi.org/10.2307/466356.

Massad, J. (1995) 'Conceiving the masculine: Gender and Palestinian nationalism', *Middle East Journal*, 49(3), pp. 467–83.

Massad, J. (2001) *Colonial effects: The making of national identity in Jordan*. New York: Columbia University Press.

Mays, R.E., Racadio, R. and Gugerty, M.K. (2012) 'Competing constraints: The operational mismatch between business logistics and humanitarian effectiveness', in *2012 IEEE Global Humanitarian Technology Conference*, IEEE, pp. 132–7.

McCall, L. (2005) 'The complexity of intersectionality', *Signs,* 30(3), pp. 1771–800. https://doi.org/10.1086/426800.

Miller, R. (2010) *Britain, Palestine and Empire: The Mandate Years*. 1st edn. Ashgate Farnham and Surrey: Routledge. https://doi.org/10.4324/9781315570006.

Mills, K. (2005) 'Neo-humanitarianism: The role of international humanitarian norms and organizations in contemporary conflict', *Global Governance*, 11(2), pp. 161–83.

Moghli, M.A., Bitarie, N. and Gabiam, N. (2015) 'Palestinian refugees from Syria: Stranded on the margins of law', *Al Shabaka* [Preprint]. Available at: al-shabaka policy brief.

Mohanty, C.T. (1984) 'Under western eyes: Feminist scholarship and colonial discourses', *Boundary 2*, 12(13), pp. 333–58. https://doi.org/10.2307/302821.

Mohanty, C.T. (2003) '"Under western eyes" revisited: Feminist solidarity through anticapitalist struggles', *Signs*, 28(2), pp. 499–535. Available at: https://doi.org/10.1086/342914.

Mohanty, C.T. (2013) 'Transnational feminist crossings: On neoliberalism and radical critique', *Signs*, 38(4), pp. 967–91.

Monroe, Kristin V. (2020) 'Masculinity, migration, and forced conscription in the Syrian war', *Cultural Anthropology*, 35(2), pp. 264–89. Available at: https://doi.org/10.14506/ca35.2.08.

Morrison, L. (2014) 'The vulnerability of Palestinian refugees from Syria', *Forced Migration Review*, vol. 47, Refugee Studies Centre, University of Oxford, pp. 41–2.

Morrison, T. (2017) *The origin of others*. Cambridge, USA: Harvard University Press.

Nagel, J. (1998) 'Masculinity and nationalism: Gender and sexuality in the making of nations', *Ethnic and Racial Studies*, 21(2), pp. 242–69. Available at: https://doi.org/10.1080/014198798330007.

Nasser-Eddin, N. (2017) 'Gender performativity in diaspora: Syrian refugee women in the UK', in *A gendered approach to the Syrian refugee crisis*, edited by Jane Freedman, Zeynep Kivilcim, Nurcan Özgür Baklacıoğlu. London: Routledge, pp. 142–54.

Nilsson, M. (2018) 'Kurdish women in the Kurdish–Turkish conflict – perceptions, experiences, and strategies', *Middle Eastern Studies*, 54(4), pp. 638–51. Available at: https://doi.org/10.1080/00263206.2018.1443916.

Oliver, K. (2017) 'The special plight of women refugees', in *Decolonizing feminism: Transnational feminism and globalization*, edited by Margaret A. McLaren. London: Rowman & Littlefield International, pp. 177–200.

Palestine Return Centre (2016) 'Palestinians of Syria between displacement and disappearance'. Published Date: 22 November 2016. Available at: http://bit.ly/2Cboi4H.

Palestine Return Centre (2018) 'Palestinians of Syria. Life under restrictions' Annual Field Report Prepared by Action Group for Palestinian Refugees from Syria (AGP), available on the link: Palestinian Return Centre - London (prc.org.uk) (Accessed: 20 May 2021).

Palestine Return Centre (2019) 'Palestinians of Syria (PRS) – Destruction and Reconstruction' Annual Field Report Prepared by Action Group for Palestinian Refugees from Syria (AGPS), available on the link: SyriaReport2019.pdf (prc.org.uk) (Accessed: 22 May 2021).

Palattiyil, G. *et al.* (2022) 'Global trends in forced migration: Policy, practice and research imperatives for social work', *International Social Work*, 65(6), pp. 1111–29.

Pappe, I. (1994) *The making of the Arab-Israeli conflict, 1947–1951*. London, UK: IB Tauris.

Pérez, M.V. (2011) 'Human rights and the rightless: The case of Gaza refugees in Jordan', *The International Journal of Human Rights*, 15(7), pp. 1031–54. Available at: https://doi.org/10.1080/13642987.2010.482911.

Peteet, J. (1992) *Gender in crisis: Women and the Palestinian resistance movement*. New York: Columbia University Press. Available at: https://books.google.co.uk/books?id=wopfWwEV6EAC.

Peteet, J. (1998) 'Post-partition Palestinian identities and the moral community', *Social Analysis: The International Journal of Social and Cultural Practice*, 42(1), pp. 63–87.

Pohlhaus Jr, G. (2017) 'Knowing without borders and the work of epistemic gathering', in *Decolonizing feminism: Transnational feminism and globalization*, edited by Margaret A. McLaren. London: Rowman & Littlefield International, pp. 37–54.

Quijano, A. (2000) 'Coloniality of power and Eurocentrism in Latin America', *International Sociology*, 15(2), pp. 215–32.

Ramadan, A. (2013) 'Spatialising the Refugee Camp', *Transactions of the Institute of British Geographers,* 38. 10.1111/j.1475-5661.2012.00509.x.

Ridd, R. and Callaway, H. (1987) *Women and political conflict: Portraits of struggle in times of crisis*. New York: New York University Press, 1987.

Robins, P. (1989) 'Shedding half a kingdom: Jordan's dismantling of Ties with the West Bank', *Bulletin (British Society for Middle Eastern Studies)*, 16(2), pp. 162–75.

Rollins, T. (2020) 'Talking about water pipes: The fraught reconstruction of Syria's Yarmouk camp', *The Middle East Institute*. Available at: https://www.mei.edu/publications/talking-about-water-pipes-fraught-reconstruction-syrias-yarmouk-camp (Accessed: 15 June 2020).

Sabaghi, D. (2015) 'Born and bred without rights: Gaza Strip refugees in Jordan', *Reliefweb*. Available at: https://reliefweb.int/report/jordan/born-bred-without-rights-gaza-strip-refugees-jordan (Accessed: 30 May 2021).

Said, E. (1979) *The question of Palestine*. New York: Vintage Book.

Said, E. (1981) *The question of Palestine*. New York: Vintage Books.

Said, E. (1993) *Culture and imperialism*. New York: Knopf: Distributed by Random House.

Sakran, F.C. (1948) *Palestine dilemma: Arab rights versus Zionist aspirations*. Washington, DC: Public Affairs Press.

Santos, M. (2013) 'Relations of ruling in the colonial present: An intersectional view of the Israeli imaginary', *The Canadian Journal of Sociology/Cahiers canadiens de sociologie*, 38(4), pp. 509–32.

Sayigh, R. (1977) 'The Palestinian identity among camp residents', *Journal of Palestine Studies*, 6(3), pp. 3–22. Available at: https://doi.org/10.2307/2535577.

Sayigh, R. (2007) 'Product and producer of Palestinian history: Stereotypes of "Self" in camp women's life stories', *Journal of Middle East Women's Studies*, 3(1), pp. 86–105. Available at: https://doi.org/10.2979/mew.2007.3.1.86.

Sayigh, R. (2013) 'The price of statelessness: Palestinian refugees from Syria', Retrieved May, 15, p. 2013. al-shabaka policy brief.

Sayigh, R. and Petteet, J. (1987) 'Between two fires: Palestinian women in Lebanon', in *Women and political conflict: Portraits of struggle in times of crisis,* edited by R. Ridd and H. Callaway. New York, NY: New York University Press.

Sayigh, Y. (1989) 'Struggle within, struggle without: The transformation of PLO politics since 1982', *International Affairs (Royal Institute of International Affairs 1944–),* 65(2), pp. 247–71. Available at: https://doi.org/10.2307/2622071.

Sayigh, Y.A. (1988) 'The Intifada and the balance of power in the region', *The International Spectator,* 23(4), pp. 203–14. Available at: https://doi.org/10.1080/03932728808456656.

Schiocchet, L. (2019) 'Palestinian refugees in Brazil between nations and humanitarian tutelage', *MAYDAN,* 6 June. Available at: https://themaydan.com/2019/06/palestinian-refugees-in-brazil-between-nations-and-humanitarian-tutelage/ (Accessed: 6 June 2021).

Schulz, P. (2018) 'Displacement from gendered personhood: Sexual violence and masculinities in northern Uganda', *International Affairs,* 94(5), pp. 1101–19. Available at: https://doi.org/10.1093/ia/iiy146.

Scott, J.W. (1991) 'The evidence of experience', *Critical Inquiry,* 17(4), pp. 773–97.

Sevastov, K.V. (2021) 'Convergence of socio-humanitarian knowledge: Postmodern discourse', in *Process management and scientific developments: Materials of the International Conference. Birmingham,* pp. 121–6.

Shalhoub-Kevorkian, N. and Ihmoud, S. (2014) 'Exiled at home: Writing return and the Palestinian home', *Biography,* 37(2015), pp. 377–97.

Shanneik, Y. (2021) 'Displacement, humanitarian interventions and gender rights in the Middle East: Syrian refugees in Jordan as a case study', *Journal of Ethnic and Migration Studies,* 47(15), pp. 3329–44. Available at: https://doi.org/10.1080/1369183X.2021.1926944.

Shatz, A. (2021) 'Palestinianism', *London Review of Books,* 43(9).

Siklawi, R. (2019) 'The Palestinian refugee camps in Lebanon post 1990: Dilemmas of survival and return to Palestine', *Arab Studies Quarterly,* 41(1), pp. 78–94. Available at: https://doi.org/10.13169/arabstudquar.41.1.0078.

Singh, S. (2015) 'Black September: A turning point in the Palestinian national movement', *International Journal of Applied Social Science,* 2(5/6), pp. 135–45.

Sliwinski, A. (2020) 'Neutrality', in *Humanitarianism: Keywords,* edited by A. De Lauri. Brill, pp. 149–51. Available at: http://www.jstor.org/stable/10.1163/j.ctv2gjwwnw.74 (Accessed: 1 January 2023).

Soh, C., You, Y. and Yu, Y. (2016) 'Once resolved, stay resolved? The refuse policy of Jordan toward Palestinian refugees', *Journal of International and Area Studies,* 23(1), pp. 1–16.

Spivak, G.C. (1988) 'Can the subaltern speak?' in *Marxism and the interpretation of culture*, edited by C. Nelson and L. Grossberg. Urbana/Chicago: University of Illinois Press.

Spivak, G.C. (2015) 'Can the subaltern speak?', in *Colonial discourse and post-colonial theory*, edited by P. Williams and L. Chrisman. Oxford, UK: Routledge, pp. 66–111.

Strong *et al.* (2015) 'Health status and health needs of older refugees from Syria in Lebanon', *Conflict and Health*, 9(12). DOI 10.1186/s13031-014-0029-y

Suerbaum, M. (2018) 'Becoming and "Unbecoming" refugees: Making sense of masculinity and refugeeness among Syrian refugee men in Egypt', *Men and Masculinities*, 21(3), pp. 363–82. Available at: https://doi.org/10.1177/109718 4X17748170.

Suerbaum, M. (2020) *Masculinities and displacement in the Middle East: Syrian refugees in Egypt*. 1st edn. London: I.B. Tauris. Available at: https://doi.org/10.5040/9781838604073.

Tal, L. (1995) 'Britain and the Jordan crisis of 1958', *Middle Eastern Studies*, 31(1), pp. 39–57.

Tappis, H. *et al.* (2021) 'Neonatal mortality burden and trends in UNHCR refugee camps, 2006–2017: A retrospective analysis', *BMC Public Health*, 21(1), pp. 1–9.

Tareh, M.S. (2020) 'On the violence of self-determination: The Palestinian refugee as the ontological other', *Arab Studies Quarterly*, 42(3), pp. 181–225. Available at: https://doi.org/10.13169/arabstudquar.42.3.0181.

Ticktin, M. (2014) 'Transnational humanitarianism', *Annual Review of Anthropology*, 43, pp. 273–89.

Tobin, S.A. (2016) 'NGO governance and Syrian refugee "Subjects" in Jordan', *Middle East Report* 278 (Spring 2016), pp. 4–9.

Trends, U.G. (2020) 'Figures at a glance', *UNHCR*, 18 June, p. 2021.

Tsourapas, G. (2019) 'The Syrian refugee crisis and foreign policy decision-making in Jordan, Lebanon, and Turkey', *Journal of Global Security Studies*, 4(4), pp. 464–81.

UNFPA (2019) 'Evaluation of the UNFPA response to the Syria crisis'. New York: UNFPA Evaluation Office.

UNFPA (2021a) 'Expanding the evidence base on cash, protection, GBV and health in humanitarian settings'. John Hopkins Centre & UNFPA. Available at: https://jordan.unfpa.org/sites/default/files/pub-pdf/en_jhu_jordan_cash_in_gbv_case_management_report_final.pdf.

UNFPA (2021b) 'ORDAN GBV IMS task force: Annual report'. Available at: https://jordan.unfpa.org/sites/default/files/pub-pdf/gbvims_2021_report_ en.pdf.

UNHCR (2007) 'Iraq: Brazilian resettlement breakthrough for Palestinians in desert camp', 3 July. Available at: https://www.unhcr.org/uk/news/ briefing/2007/7/468a3e3d4/iraq-brazilian-resettlement-breakthrough-palestinians-desert-camp.html (Accessed: 19 May 2021).

UNHCR (2021) 'Global compact on refugees indicator report'. https://www. unhcr.org/global-compact-refugees-indicator-report/wp-content/uploads/ sites/143/2021/11/2021_GCR-Indicator-Report_spread_web.pdf

United Nations, G.A. (1948) 'United Nations General Assembly Resolution 194 (III) of 11 December 1948'. Available at: https://www.un.org/Depts/dpa/qpal/docs/A_ RES_194.htm.

United Nations, G.A. (1950) 'United Nations Conciliation Commission for Palestine', in *General Progress Report Covering the period from 11 December 1949 to 23 October 1950*. New York: United Nations.

UNRWA (2021) 'Syria: 10 years of multiple hardships for Palestine refugees', *UNRWA*, 15 March. Available at: https://www.unrwa.org/newsroom/press-releases/syria-10-years-multiple-hardships-palestine-refugees.

UNRWA (2022a) 'Jordan: Context and operational developments'. Available at: https://www.unrwa.org/sites/default/files/content/resources/syria_lebanon_and_ jordan_emergency_appeal_progress_report_2022.pdf.

UNRWA (2022b) 'Where we work: Palestinian refugees in Syria': Available at: Where We Work | UNRWA (Accessed: 19 Jan 2022).

Vergès, F. and Translated by Ashley J. Bohrer (2021) *A decolonial feminism*. London, UK: Pluto Press.

Vergès, F. and Translated by Melissa Thackway (2022) *A feminist theory of violence: A decolonial perspective*. London, UK: Pluto Press.

Walby, S., Armstrong, J. and Strid, S. (2012) 'Intersectionality: Multiple inequalities in social theory', *Sociology*, 46(2), pp. 224–40. Available at: https://doi. org/10.1177/0038038511416164.

Wengert, G. and Alfaro, M. (2006) 'Can Palestinian refugees in Iraq find protection?', *Forced Migration Review*, 26, pp. 19–21.

White, G.D. (2013) 'Conflict in Syria compounds vulnerability of Palestine refugees', *Forced Migration Review*, 44(September), p. 79.

Wilson, M.C. (1987) 'King Abdullah and Palestine', *Bulletin (British Society for Middle Eastern Studies)*, 14(1), pp. 37–41.

Wirtz, A.L. *et al.* (2014) 'Gender-based violence in conflict and displacement: Qualitative findings from displaced women in Colombia', *Conflict and Health*, 8(1), p. 10. Available at: https://doi.org/10.1186/1752-1505-8-10.

Wirtz, A.L. *et al.* (2018) 'Lifetime prevalence, correlates and health consequences of gender-based violence victimisation and perpetration among men and women in Somalia', *BMJ Global Health*, 3(4), p. e000773. Available at: https://doi.org/10.1136/bmjgh-2018-000773.

Yasmine, R. and Moughalian, C. (2016) 'Systemic violence against Syrian refugee women and the myth of effective intrapersonal interventions', *Reproductive Health Matters*, 24(47), pp. 27–35.

Yuval Davis, N. (1993) 'Gender and nation', *Ethnic and Racial Studies*, 16(4), pp. 621–32. Available at: https://doi.org/10.1080/01419870.1993.9993800.

Zaatari, Z. *et al.* (2014) *Unpacking gender: The humanitarian response to the Syrian refugee crisis in Jordan*. New York: Women's Refugee Commission.

Index

www.ingramcontent.com/pod-product-compliance
Lightning Source LLC
Chambersburg PA
CBHW062028270326
41929CB00014B/2354